Transcending Member States

Babatunde Fagbayibo

Transcending Member States

Political and Legal Dynamics of Building Continental Supranationalism in Africa

Springer

Babatunde Fagbayibo
Public, Constitutional and International law, College of Law
University of South Africa
Pretoria, South Africa

ISBN 978-3-031-12450-1 ISBN 978-3-031-12451-8 (eBook)
https://doi.org/10.1007/978-3-031-12451-8

This Springer imprint is published by the registered company Springer Nature Switzerland AG
The registered company address is: Gewerbestrasse 11, 6330 Cham, Switzerland

For my father, Samuel Olabode Fagbayibo (1948–2010), whose library shaped my curiosity for African affairs. In memoriam.

Acknowledgment

This book is a result of my ideational engagements with the subject of continental integration in Africa in the past 15 years. In journal articles, book chapters, and opinion pieces, I have over the years explored the politico-legal dynamics of clothing the African Union (AU) with assertive powers to make binding norms, and ultimately achieve transformative continental integration in Africa. Two of such works have played an important role in shaping the discursive direction of this book. The first is my doctoral thesis, "A politico-legal framework for integration in Africa: Exploring the attainability of a supranational African Union", which was submitted for the fulfilment of my doctoral degree in law at the University of Pretoria in 2010. The second is a book chapter titled "*Can Africa ever achieve continental sovereignty in the shifting West-to-East strategic landscape? The geopolitics of integration and autonomy*" in Kornegay Jnr. F & Mthembu P (eds), *Africa and the world: Navigating shifting geopolitics*. Mapungubwe Institute for Strategic Reflection (MISTRA), Johannesburg (2020). This book builds on this book chapter in Chaps. 2 and 5. I would like to extend my appreciation to MISTRA for granting the permission to re-use the work in this book.

I would like to express sincere gratitude to Ueli Staeger and Udoka Ndidiamaka Owie for providing comments on individual chapters of the book. Special thanks also go to Michele Olivier, Frans Viljoen, and André Thomashausen for their invaluable mentorship over the years. I am grateful to my employer, the University of South Africa (UNISA), for providing the enabling environment to advance and enrich my research capacity. I am thankful to close friends and mentees who I have not named but have provided the much-needed support and understanding. Finally, I am indebted to all my family for their unwavering support: my late father, who I have dedicated this book to; my mother; siblings; and uncles and aunts.

It is my hope that this work will make a significant contribution to scholarly and policy-making arenas of achieving meaningful and sustainable regional integration and development in Africa.

Contents

1 Introduction 1
1.1 Background 1
1.2 A Diverse Continent 3
1.3 Commingling of Law and Politics 5
1.4 Structure of the Book 8
References 9

2 The Idea of Continental Supranationalism 11
2.1 Introduction 11
2.2 The Concept of Supranationalism 11
2.3 Pan-Africanism: The Philosophical Underpinning of Unity 18
2.4 Continental Supranationalism in Africa 23
2.4.1 Pace 24
2.4.2 Nature 27
2.4.3 Context 30
2.5 Conclusion 32
References 33

3 The African Union 37
3.1 Introduction 37
3.2 The Establishment of the AU 38
3.3 The AU Constitutive Act 40
3.4 How Supranational Is the AU? 46
3.4.1 Intention 48
3.4.2 Action 52
3.4.3 Outcomes 58
3.5 Conclusion 59
References 63

4 Understanding the Interplay of Law and Politics in the Matrix of Continental Supranationalism 69
4.1 Introduction 69
4.2 Imitation: Copying and Pasting the EU Template 70
4.3 Complex Relational Dynamics 78
4.3.1 AU-REC Relations 78
4.3.2 AU-Member States Relations 86
4.3.3 AU-Civil Society Relations 90
4.4 The Politics of Reforms 93
4.4.1 Powerplay Between the Maximalists and the Minimalists (2005–2011) 94
4.4.2 Pragmatic Incrementalism (2015: Present) 99
4.4.3 The Problematics of Reform Efforts 104
4.5 Conclusion 106
References 107

5 Transcending Member States 115
5.1 Introduction 115
5.2 A Repurposed African Worldview 116
5.3 A Triptych Analysis 119
5.3.1 Internal Dynamics: Repositioning the Centre 119
5.3.2 External Dynamics: Navigating the Shifting Global Geo-Political Landscape 138
5.3.3 Syncretic Dynamics: Towards “Strategic Hybridisation” . . . 143
5.4 Conclusion 151
References 152

6 Conclusion 159
6.1 Summary of Findings 159
6.2 Issues for Further Research and Policy Approaches 161

List of Treaties 165

List of Cases 166

Abbreviations

ACBF	African Capacity Building Foundation
ACDEG	African Charter on Democracy, Election, and Governance
ACHPR	African Charter on Human and Peoples' Rights
ACJ&HR	African Court of Justice and Human Rights
ACP	African Caribbean and Pacific Group of States
ACSO	African Civil Society Organisation
ADIF	African Diaspora Investment Fund
AEC	African Economic Community Treaty
AfCFTA	African Continental Free Trade Area
AfCHPR	African Commission on Human and Peoples' Rights
AfCtHPR	African Court on Human and Peoples' Rights
AfDB	African Development Bank
Afrexim Bank	African Export-Import Bank
Africa CDC	Africa Centres for Disease Control and Prevention
Africom	United States African Command
AGA	African Governance Architecture
AMISOM	African Union Mission in Somalia
AMU	Arab Maghreb Union
APF	African Peace Facility
APRM	African Peer Review Mechanism
APSA	African Peace and Security Architecture
ASF	African Standby Force
ATJ	Andean Tribunal of Justice
AU	African Union
AUDA-NEPAD	African Union Development Agency
AU-YVC	African Union Youth Volunteer Corps
AYC	African Youth Charter
CAF	Central African Federation
CARICOM	Caribbean Community
CDSPAs	Common Defence and Security Policy for Africa

CEMAC	Central African Economic and Monetary Community
CEN–SAD	Community of Sahel–Saharan States
CEPGL	Economic Community of the Great Lakes Countries
CET	Common External Tariff
CIDO	African Citizens' Directorate
CISA	Conference of Independent African States
CMA	Common Monetary Area
COMESA	Common Market for Eastern and Southern Africa
CSOs	Civil Society Organisations
CSSDCA	Conference for Security, Stability, Development and Cooperation in Africa
EAC	East African Community
EACJ	East African Court of Justice
EACSO	East African Common Services Organisation
EAHC	East African High Commission
EC	European Commission
EC	European Community
ECB	European Central Bank
ECCAS	Economic Community of Central African States
ECCJ	ECOWAS Community Court of Justice
ECHR	European Court of Human Rights
ECJ	European Court of Justice
ECOSOCC	Economic, Social and Cultural Council
ECOWAS	Economic Community of West African States
ECSC	European Coal and Steel Community
EEC	European Economic Community
EPA	Economic Partnership Agreement
EPF	European Peace Facility
EU	European Union
FDI	Foreign Direct Investment
FOCAC	Forum of China-African Cooperation
IAFS	India-Africa Forum Summit
ICGLR	International Conference on the Great Lakes Region
IGAD	Intergovernmental Authority on Development
ILO	International Labour Organization
IOC	Indian Ocean Commission
ISS	Institute of Security Studies
MJTF	Multinational Joint Task Force
MRU	Mano River Union
NEPAD	New Partnership for Africa's Development
OAU	Organisation of African Unity
PAIC	Pan-African Investment Code
PanAf	Pan-African Programme
PAP	Pan-African Parliament
PAU	Pan African University

PRC	Permanent Representatives Committee
PSC	Peace and Security Council
RECs	Regional Economic Communities
SACU	Southern African Customs Union
SADC	Southern African Development Community
SDGs	Sustainable Development Goals
STCs	Specialised Technical Committees
TFTA	Tripartite Free Trade Area
TICAD	Tokyo International Cooperation on African Development
UN	United Nations
UNECA	United Nations Economic Commission for Africa
WAEMU	West African Economic and Monetary Union
WTO	World Trade Organization

List of Figure

Fig. 5.1 Interlocking dynamics of continental supranationalism. Source: Author's construction 150

List of Tables

Table 3.1 Comparative table of the OAU and the AU 49
Table 3.2 Assessment of AU supranationalism 60
Table 4.1 Comparison between the EU and the AU 72
Table 4.2 Member states of major sub-regional organisations in Africa 79
Table 4.3 Contributions to the total budget of the African Union (Operational, Programme and Peace Support budgets) (in %) 101
Table 5.1 Chairpersons and deputy Chairpersons of the AU since its formation 122
Table 5.2 The state of freedom in Africa 132

Chapter 1
Introduction

Threading Together the "Africas"

1.1 Background

Africa is currently experiencing one of the most consequential phases of its integrative development. Since 2015, there have been increasing activities around the development of policies and practices around enhancing the African Union (AU) with more assertive powers to coordinate and make binding rules regarding the regional integration process. In other words, these processes aim to cloth the AU with supranational powers, like those exercised by the European Union (EU), which, despite its internal problems, remains the most successful experimentation of supranationalism in the world. This has included efforts such as the decision to finance the AU through an 0.2% tax levy on eligible imports into member states, the decision to reduce the number of AU Commission portfolios from eight to six, the adoption and entry into force (on the 30th of May 2019) of the much touted Agreement establishing the African Continental Free Trade Area (AfCFTA),[1] the adoption of the Protocol to the Treaty Establishing the African Economic Community Relating to Free Movement of Persons, Right to Residence and Right of Establishment, and the adoption of the AU Agenda 2063 policy framework in 2015. How these processes will change the direction of regional integration in Africa is dependent on the existence of quality endowed and driven institutions.

These developments are consequential for several symbolic and practical reasons. Firstly, is that they represent the translation of decades of expressions on the need for stronger regionalism. This is not to say that there have not been other momentous occasions in the history of regionalism but the adoptions of instruments on continental free trade area (and the speed in which it was adopted and eventually ratified

[1] The AfCFTA was initially scheduled to begin operations in July 2020. However, due to the Covid-19 global health pandemic, it began operations on the 1st of January 2021. Ghana hosts the AfCFTA Secretariat. In February 2020, the South African technocrat, Wamkele Mene, was elected as the first secretary-general of the AfCFTA Secretariat.

B. Fagbayibo, *Transcending Member States*,
https://doi.org/10.1007/978-3-031-12451-8_1

by member states) and free movement of persons exhibit some level of traction that has rarely been witnessed before now. Secondly, the fact that moves towards enhanced regionalism in Africa is happening amidst turbulent global dynamics (Brexit, the rise of fascist political parties and elements in Europe and the U.S., and the U.S.—China trade dispute) posit some form of resilience, which if properly managed could prove beneficial. Thirdly, these developments have serious implications for Africa's global positioning, particularly in the context of the rapidly increasing interest (or what some call the new scramble for Africa) of traditional and emerging powers in Africa's geo-strategic advantage. Lastly, these developments speak directly to the possibility of endowing the AU with the much-needed binding and assertive powers to compel member states to act according to organisational norms. The importance of the AU in the matrix of achieving effective continental supranationalism in Africa cannot be overstated. The AU is the largest regional organisation in the world, composed of all the 55 countries on the continent. Despite its many shortcomings, it has come to symbolise the institutionalisation of the vision of an integrated continent through its organs and normative documents. As Edozie puts it, the AU has become

> a vehicle through which Africans are marking their own impact on globalization as they forge a trans-cultural social network of African values, identities and cultures embodies in the symbol of pan-Africa for Africans and African descendants.[2]

Similarly, Tieku highlighted seven areas that have defined the importance and success of the AU thus far. These are: the enhancement of African agency on the world stage; the steady socialisation of the African political class to accept liberal values and norms as the basis for interstate cooperation; the changed attitudes of many governments in Africa from a culture of indifference to a new culture of caring about the African peace and security as a whole; the creation of low-cost, agile, and innovative international decision-making bodies in wide range of issues/areas; success in making international laws that have shaped national legislation and policies; developing wide ranging and effective normative standards in a relatively short period of its existence; and the fact that it has made significant inroads in the areas of nudging African governments to behave appropriately.[3] Also, Wiebusch et al. noted that AU's adoption of more than 40 treaties in less than two decades of its existence (2000–2018) "reflects a greater institutionalization of continental governance mechanism through law. It also suggests a level of confidence within the AU system in the ability of law to engineer social change".[4]

It is this potential that places the AU at an advantageous position to drive the deepening of continental supranationalism in Africa. This is, however, dependent on the extent to which member states are willing to key into this vision by seeing it as an essential geostrategic tool for enhancing Africa's positioning in global *realpolitik*.

---

[2]Edozie (2012), p. 298.

[3]Tieku (2019), pp. 5–13.

[4]Wiebusch et al. (2019), p. 22.

This speaks to the audacity of moving Nkrumah's aphorism of "Africa must unite" from rhetoric to embarking on radical integrative steps. These points are at the heart of this book. The crux of this book is the idea of exploring innovative and context-driven politico-legal policy measures in enhancing the powers of the AU to meaningfully drive the continental integration process. In managing this process, issues of context, political willingness, and innovative and inclusive approaches are essential elements that must be considered. As the 2007 AU Audit report rightly asserted, the question is no longer about whether to unite; rather it speaks to an ideological commitment to devising feasible strategies for ensuring the development of the continent.[5]

1.2 A Diverse Continent

The reference to Africa as "a continent of continents",[6] or what has also been described as "Africas",[7] is one that denotes the expansive landmass of the continent (consisting of 55 countries which roughly covers the same land area as the entire EU, China, India, Mexico, Japan and the United States of America); and the plurality of cultures, languages (there are between 1500 and 2000 spoken African languages[8]), religion; race; and the different interpretations of the ideal politico-legal arrangement for regionalism. It is this kind of diversity that made the poet, Abioseh Nicol, conclude "...that Africa is not a country but a concept/Fashioned in the minds, each to each".[9] Similarly, Dowden rightly observed:

> Who would dare make generalisations about Asia based on Bangladesh? Or about Europe based on Greece? ... Even if you divide Africa in three; Africa north of the Sahara, South Africa and its orbit, and the zone in between, there are few common factors within these regions ... Africa's social systems, beliefs and culture are as diverse as its peoples and as disparate as its climates. West Africa feels quite different from East Africa, and even within West Africa you could never mistake Nigeria for Senegal. And neither of them seems on the same planet as Mali. Every time you say 'Africa is ...' the words crumble and break. For every generalisation you must exclude at least five countries.[10]

Furthermore, in the 1970s, Amin noted that to understand dependence and under-development in Africa, it is important to divide Africa into three micro-regions.[11] The first is the traditional West Africa (Ghana, Nigeria, Sierra Leone, Gambia,

---

[5] African Union (2007), p. 14.

[6] See e.g. The Economist (2010). See also Byiers et al. (2019).

[7] Akinyemi (1982, p. 243), citing Alfred Silbert, had used the term "Africas" to refer to the diversity of the continent, which also speaks to the importance of not engaging in general frames for analysing the continent.

[8] Nations Online (n.d.).

[9] Nicol (1977), p. 76.

[10] Dowden (2008), p. 10.

[11] Amin (1972), p. 504.

Liberia, Guinea-Bissau, Togo, former French West Africa), which he described as "the colonial trade economy".[12] This is further sub-divided into three sub-regions: coastal zone (the rich area that is accessible to the outside world), the hinterland (which serves as a pool of labour for the coast), and Sudan.[13] The second is the traditional Congo River basin (Congo-Kinshasa, Congo-Brazzaville, Gabon, and the Central African Republic), which he defined as "the Africa of the concession-owning companies".[14] The third is the eastern and southern parts of the continent (Kenya, Uganda, Tanzania, Rwanda, Burundi, Malawi, Angola, Mozambique, Zimbabwe, Botswana, Lesotho, Swaziland, and South Africa), which is described as "Africa of the labour reserves".[15] Such diversity in the political economy and social contexts of the continent is imperative for understanding how policies and processes work, which invariably raises the issue of context. This is not to say that there exist no commonalities that could be used to enrich developmental discourses emerging from external or internal sources. It rather asks for a more contemplative approach that seeks to understand how such socio-cultural, political, economic and historical differences shape the present and policy development.

In situating this within the context of continental integration, several points are worth considering. The first is the operational ideology, particularly as it translates to normative and institutional designs. To put it more pointedly, the Eurocentric, neo-liberal basis of continental and sub-regional integration is one that not only misses the goal of an Afrocentric approach but also the opportunity to further subject the "Afrocentric" in regionalism to proper scrutiny. In a "continent of continents", or "Africas", the pursuance of the project of unity should be one that logically provokes questions more than quick fix, "globally accepted" answers.

The second point relates to the question of the meaning of continental integration. In the past six decades of engagement with continental regionalism in Africa, there have been numerous meanings attached to the idea. This ranges from a federal "United States of Africa" (or Union Government), a confederation, sub-regional integration and/or building mega sub-regional blocs, to a supranational African Union. It has also included both neo-liberal and leftist ideological interpretations of the meaning of idea of continental regionalism. The different interpretations are considered in Chap. 2 of this book.

These different viewpoints should be seen as instruments for critically engaging continental regionalism as a more dynamic and non-static concept that should provoke continuous interrogation. Curiously, the AU Agenda 2063 document defers the agreement on the nature and establishment of a continental government to 2030.[16] The logic behind settling on this date is not stated in any AU document or expressed by relevant political elites. However, it could be argued that such

---

[12] Ibid.

[13] Ibid.

[14] Ibid.

[15] Ibid.

[16] AU (2015), p. 5.

postponement is in line with the incremental logic of continental regionalism in Africa, one that prefers a step-by-step approach to arriving at integration objectives. This is also firmly within the purview of the prevailing state-centric or intergovernmental nature of the AU, which emphasises the importance of consensus among member states in arriving at decisions. How this will align or differ with the supranational aspirations of the AU remains to be seen.

The last point speaks to perceptions, or what has been referred to as "mental models",[17] of national and transnational policy-makers, private sector actors and civil society on what is and how should continental integration be imagined and practised. According to North, mental models "are the internal representations that individual cognitive systems create to interpret the environment; institutions are the external (to the mind) mechanisms individuals create to structure and order the environment".[18] The idea of mental models underlines both the operational ideology and meaning of continental integration, which are already highlighted above. It informs the extent to which actors not only design regional norms but also the willingness to implement them. As Kufuor rightly puts it,

> if the mental constructs support regional trade, then African cross-border business interests will be protected from the use and abuse of domestic protectionist interests, and from ideologues in positions of power who pay only lip service to international trade.[19]

For this to happen, Moghalu advocated a strategic review of Africa's worldview, one which bluntly asserts that "Africa's future is rather a foundational understanding that Africans, and no one else, are responsible for the continent's future".[20] This is similar to the oft-stated, but often ignored, mantra of "African solution for African problems".

Diversity, conceptual clarity and positive mental models are at the core of fashioning the desired continental integration in Africa. These issues appear in different forms in the rhetoric and normative instruments underlining regional integration in Africa, albeit the concomitant action has not been forthcoming. This will be further explored in this book.

1.3 Commingling of Law and Politics

At this juncture, it is imperative to situate the normative basis of this book. The reference to "politico-legal" is informed by the interrelationship of politics and law in the operational context of regional integration. As Shivji pointedly noted, "law is

[17] North (1994).

[18] Ibid. 363. This is similar to the German term for worldview, *Weltanschauung* (*Welt* means world while *Anchauung* means perception). The Merriam-Webster dictionary defines *Weltanschauung* as "a comprehensive conception or apprehension of the world especially from a specific standpoint".

[19] Kufuor (2019).

[20] Moghalu (2013), p. 21.

the concentrated form of politics".[21] While the final product of regional integration negotiations often come in the form of legal documents, this is usually preceded by political negotiations and compromises by member states. More importantly, the implementation, or non-implementation, of legal agreements is often shaped by national and regional political currents. Political stability, availability of strong national institutions, friendly neighbouring relations, and integration-friendly national policy approaches are some of the factors that shape political willingness. Recounting a meeting with the late president of Zaire (now the Democratic Republic of Congo), Mobutu Sese Seko, the former head of the United Nations Economic Commission for Africa (UNECA), Adebayo Adedeji, showed how narrow self-interest often obstruct regional integration laws and policies:

> I remember on one occasion, I went to see Mobutu, who was then the president of Zaire . . . At dinner . . . he said to me, "Professor, why do you hate me?" The glass nearly dropped from my hand. I said, "Mr. President, what do you mean by 'I hate you'?" He said, "You know, you are insisting on this trans-African highway being built. I have insurgents. Now if I build the highway, I won't be able to control them. I'll be overthrown." So you can see how personalized public policy is in our countries.[22]

Another aspect of the intersection of law and politics in African integration is the extent to which socio-political forces shape the reaction of African governments to judgments of transnational courts. This is not unique to Africa as authors such as Alter and Helfer have shown how political dynamics sometime enhance or constrain the influence of transnational courts in Europe and Latin America.[23] While the Andean Tribunal of Justice (ATJ) in Latin America has been more cautious in expanding its reach due to the curtailing legal requirements and political situation in the region, the European Court of Justice (ECJ) has been more expansionist based on increasing intra-regional trade and receding political will in member states.[24] In Africa, there have been some backlash against the assertiveness of regional courts in East, West and Southern Africa in recent years. In reaction to the *Mike Campbell* case, where the Tribunal ruled against the Zimbabwean land grab policy,[25] the Southern African Development Community (SADC) decided to first suspend, and eventually whittled down the powers of the Tribunal. In 2009, the then president of The Gambia, Yahaya Jammeh, had pushed for an amendment to the 2005 Economic Community of West African States (ECOWAS) Supplementary Protocol following judgements against his government for serious violations of human rights.[26] The proposal sought to limit the jurisdiction and admissibility of cases to the ECOWAS Court. However, it was unsuccessful due to civil society intervention and the role of

---

[21] Shivji (2020), p. 2.

[22] African Renewal (2002).

[23] Alter and Helfer (2010).

[24] Ibid.

[25] (2/2007) [2008] SADCT 2,

[26] Manneh v. The Gambia; Saidykhan v. The Gambia.

other member states.[27] Following the East African Court of Justice (EACJ) interim ruling[28] against the government of Kenya that barred the East African Community (EAC) from recognising Kenya's legislative nominees, the Kenyan government pushed for the disbanding of the court.[29] The Kenyan government was to later back down from this move.[30] As a reaction to the court's judgement against its mandatory application of death penalty for murder conviction, Tanzania officially withdrew its declaration allowing individuals and NGOs to directly submit applications against it at the African Court on Human and Peoples' Rights (AfCtHPR).[31] Similarly, Cote d'Ivoire withdrew from the AfCtHPR, claiming that the court had undermined its sovereignty by ordering it to suspend the arrest warrant against the opposition leader, Guillaume Soro, and the order to release 19 of his relatives from prison.[32] The government of Benin has also withdrawn from the protocol of the AfCtHPR on individual access due to the court's ruling against it in the *Sébastien Ajavon case*.[33] In this case, the court ruled that the sentencing of Sébastien Ajavon to 20 years in prison with a payment of fine and the exclusion of his party from participating in local elections violated his fundamental rights and ordered the government to pay him compensation.[34]

In his speech at the inauguration of the Organisation of African Unity (OAU) in 1963, Kwame Nkrumah advanced the centrality of politics in achieving African unity:

> African unity, is above all, a political kingdom which can only be gained by political means. The social and economic development of Africa will come only within the political kingdom, not the other way around. The United States of America, the Union of Soviet Socialist Republics, were the political decisions of revolutionary peoples before they became mighty realities of social power and material wealth.[35]

As such, politics and law become intertwined, and applied in different balancing modes or acts in achieving key integration objectives. This understanding should shape the agenda-setting processes and formulation of rational choices on regionalism. In other words, crafting normative documents must be informed by a realistic assessment of strengths and weaknesses, order of preferences and other smart approaches. Essentially, this speaks to the need to centre context (socio-cultural, economic and technological) in the framing of the politico-legal discourse of continental regionalism in Africa.

---

[27] Alter et al. (2016), pp. 288–300.

[28] Anyang' Nyong'o v. AG of the Republic of Kenya.

[29] Alter et al. (2016), pp. 302–303.

[30] Ibid, 303.

[31] Ally Rajabu and Others v United Republic of Tanzania. See also de Silva (2019).

[32] Tih (2020).

[33] Bah (2020).

[34] Application No. 013/2017.

[35] Nkrumah (1963).

1.4 Structure of the Book

This book is organised as follow. The next chapter engages in a conceptual discourse of continental supranationalism in Africa. It starts with the conceptual discussion of the European origin and practise of supranationalism. It then provides a historical excursus of how the idea of pan-Africanism shaped the content and context of African unity. Lastly, it delves into the conceptual categorisation of what continental supranationalism means in Africa. In this respect, three conceptual analytical tools are adopted: pace, nature/type, and context. Pace refers to speed, especially the question on whether continental integration should proceed at a gradual or a much faster speed. Nature speaks to the type of continental integration Africa should pursue: state-centric/intergovernmental or supranational. Context denotes the imperative of continental regionalism responding to an Afrocentric approach, one that is rooted in pan-African knowledge systems and contextual realities.

Chapter 3 examines the supranational status of the AU by using three contextual assessment elements: intention, action and outcome. In the context of this chapter, intention explores how normative provisions and prescriptions support (or even detract) from the ambition of the AU to assert itself over member states. Action denotes the line between stated or implied intentions and outcomes. In other words, the key question is how the AU has engaged in strategic policy choices to ensure that the organisation exercises persuasive and binding powers over its member states. Outcomes is the culmination of the interaction between intention and action. The argument of this chapter is that even if the AU is regarded as an intergovernmental entity, there must be a more nuanced consideration of the interplay of intergovernmental and supranational dynamics in its institutional processes, and how such realisation can be used to advance continental integration.

Chapter 4 explores the way in which law and politics have shaped the aspirations and practice of enhanced continental regionalism in Africa. The key question is the extent to which one has impeded or advanced the other, and how both could in any way reform Africa's approach to the idea of supranationalism. In this respect, three elemental prisms are considered: imitation (the copying of the EU process), relational (AU-RECs, AU-member states, and AU-civil society), and the politics of reform.

Chapter 5 presents a triptych analysis of the feasibility of effective supranationalism in Africa. These include internal (issues such as enhancing the AU's technocratic efficiency, self-restraint mechanisms and bottom-up regionalism), external (the role of global actors in current and future issues that affect regionalism in Africa, including domestic uncertainties determining the global projection of these powers), and syncretic (which speaks to a practical policy position on balancing both internal and external dynamics and determining the suitability of application) dynamics. The chapter argues that a syncretic approach is a desired path for building continental supranationalism in Africa.

The concluding chapter contains a summary of the findings of the book and tease out issues for further research on this pertinent topic.

The intention of this book is not to present a conclusive blueprint on how to organise continental supranationalism in Africa. Rather, it attempts to offer a critical discourse around ideational issues that should frame such ambition. The recommendations offered by the book are intended to stimulate further thinking on this important subject. While the book agrees that there are competing ideologies, framings and narratives on the best path to achieving continental supranationalism in Africa, it is of the view that creating some common ground rules on advancing and deepening continental supranationalism is imperative. The multidimensionality of regionalism is one that seeks inclusive, well-coordinated and pragmatic modes of engagement. This is a point that this book attempts to reinforce.

References

Africa Renewal (2002) You must first set your house in order create the conditions for integration says Prof Adedeji. https://www.un.org/africarenewal/magazine/september-2002/you-must-first-set-your-house-order. Accessed 4 Oct 2021

African Union (2007) Audit of the African Union. https://www.securitycouncilreport.org/atf/cf/%7B65BFCF9B-6D27-4E9C-8CD3-CF6E4FF96FF9%7D/RO%20Audit%20of%20the%20AU.pdf. Accessed 4 Oct 2021

African Union (2015) Agenda 2063: The Africa we want. https://au.int/sites/default/files/documents/36204-doc-agenda2063_popular_version_en.pdf. Accessed 4 Oct 2021

Akinyemi B (1982) Africa – challenges and responses: a foreign policy perspective. Daedalus 111(2):243–254

Ally Rajabu and Others v United Republic of Tanzania. Application No. 007/2015, 28 November 2019. https://africanlii.org/afu/judgment/african-court/2019/7. Accessed 4 Oct 2021

Alter K, Helfer L (2010) Nature or nurture? Judicial lawmaking in the European Court of Justice and the Andean Tribunal of Justice. Int Organ 64(4):563 592

Alter K, Gathii J, Helfer L (2016) Backlash against International Courts in West, East and Southern Africa: causes and consequences. Eur J Int Law 27(2):293–328

Amin S (1972) Underdevelopment and dependence in black Africa – origins and contemporary forms. J Mod Afr Stud 10(4):503–524

Bah A (2020) Benin's partial withdrawal from African Charter of Human Rights is a retreat from democracy. https://globalvoices.org/2020/05/07/benins-partial-withdrawal-from-african-charter-of-human-rights-is-a-retreat-from-democracy/. Accessed 4 Oct 2021

Byiers B, Woolfrey S, Medinilla A, Vanheukelom J (2019) The political economy of Africa's regional 'spaghetti bowl". Synthesis report. European Centre for Development Policy Management (ECDPM). https://ecdpm.org/publications/political-economy-africas-regional-spaghetti-bowl-synthesis-report/. Accessed 4 Oct 2021

Chief Ebrimah Manneh v The Republic of The Gambia. Community Court of Justice of the Economic Community of West African States (ECOWAS) Ruling No. ECW/CCJ/JUD/03/08, 5 June 2008. http://www.worldcourts.com/ecowasccj/eng/decisions/2008.06.05_Manneh_v_Gambia.htm. Accessed 4 Oct 2021

de Silva N (2019) Individual and NGO access to the African Court on Human and Peoples' Rights: the latest blow from Tanzania. https://www.ejiltalk.org/individual-and-ngo-access-to-the-african-court-on-human-and-peoples-rights-the-latest-blow-from-tanzania/. Accessed 4 Oct 2021

Dowden R (2008) Africa: altered states, ordinary miracles. Portobello Books, London

Edozie R (2012) The sixth zone: the African diaspora and the African Union's global era pan-Africanism. J Afr Am Stud 16(2):268–299

Kufuor K (2019) The African Continental Free Trade Agreement and the importance of a two-level approach to its success. https://www.afronomicslaw.org/2019/04/21/the-african-continental-free-trade-agreement-and-the-importance-of-a-two-level-approach-to-its-success. Accessed 4 Oct 2021
Mike Campbell (Pvt) Ltd and Others v Republic of Zimbabwe (2/2007) [2008] SADCT 2, 28 November 2008. http://www.saflii.org/sa/cases/SADCT/2008/2.html. Accessed 4 Oct 2021
Moghalu K (2013) Emerging Africa: how the global economy's 'last frontier' can prosper and matter. Bookcraft, Ibadan
Musa Saidykhan v. Republic of The Gambia. Community Court of Justice of the Economic Community of West African States (ECOWAS) Ruling No. ECW/CCJ/RUL/05/09, 30 June 2009. https://ihrda.uwazi.io/en/entity/froafttgl56tn7350qszzd7vi. Accessed 4 Oct 2021
Nicol A (1977) The meaning of Africa. In: Weaver R, Bruchac J (eds) Aftermath: an anthology of poems in English from Africa, Asia, and the Caribbean. Greenfield Review Press, New York, p 76
Nkrumah K (1963) We must unite now or perish. https://newafricanmagazine.com/3721/. Accessed 4 Oct 2021
North N (1994) Economic performance through time. Am Econ Rev 84(3):359–368
One World Nations Online (n.d.) Languages of Africa. https://www.nationsonline.org/oneworld/african_languages.htm. Accessed 4 Oct 2021
Prof Anyang' Nyong'o & 10 others v. The Attorney General of the Republic of Kenya & 5 Others. Application No. 1 of 2006 (Arising from Reference No. 1 of 2006), 27 November 2006. https://www.eacj.org/?cases=eacj-application-no-1-of-2006. Accessed 4 Oct 2021
Sébastien Germain Ajavon v Republic of Benin. Application No. 013/2017, 28 November 2019. https://africanlii.org/afu/judgment/african-court/2019/6. Accessed 4 Oct 2021
Shivji I (2020) Do constitutions matter? The dilemma of a radical lawyer. Bulletin online. Council for the Development of Social Science Research in Africa (CODESRIA). https://codesria.org/spip.php?article3102. Accessed 4 Oct 2021
The Economist (2010, November 10). The true size of Africa: Africa is bigger than it looks on most maps of the world. https://www.economist.com/graphic-detail/2010/11/10/the-true-true-size-of-africa. Accessed 4 Oct 2021
The Merriam-Webster Dictionary (n.d.) Weltanschauung. https://www.merriam-webster.com/dictionary/Weltanschauung#:~:text=%3A%20a%20comprehensive%20conception%20or%20apprehension,weltanschauung%20that%20is%20unremittingly%20positive%20%E2%80%A6%E2%80%94. Accessed 4 Oct 2021
Tieku T (2019) The African Union: successes and failures. Oxford Res Encyclopedia Polit 5–13. https://doi.org/10.1093/acrefore/9780190228637.013.703
Tih F (2020) Ivory Coast withdraws from African Human Rights Court: West African nation says court has undermined its sovereignty. https://www.aa.com.tr/en/africa/ivory-coast-withdraws-from-african-human-rights-court/1824474. Accessed 4 Oct 2020
Wiebusch M, Aniekwe C, Oette L, Vandeginste M (2019) The African Charter on democracy, elections and governance: past, present and future. J Afr Law 63(1):9–38

Chapter 2
The Idea of Continental Supranationalism

2.1 Introduction

This chapter engages in a conceptual discussion of the term "continental supranationalism". It adopts three analytical frameworks for understanding the ideational underpinnings of this concept, particularly in the African context. These are pace, nature and context. Pace refers to speed, especially the question on whether continental integration should proceed at a gradual or a much faster speed. Nature speaks to the type of continental integration Africa should pursue: state-centric/intergovernmental or supranational. Context denotes the imperative of continental regionalism responding to an Afrocentric approach, one that is rooted in pan-African knowledge systems and contextual realities. These three theoretical perspectives have defined, and continue to define, the politico-legal interventions on African integration by scholars and politicians since the 1950s. For example, while Julius Nyerere advocated an incremental, step by step approach, Kwame Nkrumah insisted that the only panacea for continental development is an immediate establishment of a supranational entity. This chapter begins with a theoretical discussion of the concept of supranationalism. It is followed by a general discussion of the philosophical origins of African unity. This then leads to an exposition of the conceptual contours of "continental supranationalism" in Africa. It ends with a general reflection.

2.2 The Concept of Supranationalism

The post-second World War development of regionalism in Europe gave birth to the idea of supranationalism. This started in 1951, when six countries (France, Germany, Italy, Belgium, Netherlands and Luxembourg) concluded the treaty establishing the European Coal and Steel Community (ECSC), as a post-war initiative aimed at

B. Fagbayibo, *Transcending Member States*,
https://doi.org/10.1007/978-3-031-12451-8_2

enhancing the economy of Europe and recurrence of another war.[1] In 1957, the six founding member states expanded on the ECSC treaty by adopting the treaty establishing the European Economic Community Treaty (EEC), which included a number of supranational initiatives such as a common market of goods, persons, services and capital, commercial policy and other economic activities.[2] Straddling the fields of political science, international law and international relations, the idea of supranationalism helped explain the enhanced powers transferred to the European Community (EC), and how such powers are similar to state-centric competences.

Referred to as a "political-descriptive" concept,[3] supranationalism implies the existence of a multi-level governance structure that grants regional institutions the powers to exercise binding and authoritative powers over member states.[4] It redefines the contours of state sovereignty by ensuring that member states transfer assertive policy and norm making political and economic powers to regional institutions. As such, supranationalism exists at the peak of the evolutionary trend of regional integration, which typically starts with inter-state cooperation and ends, depending on the intention and willingness of member states, with institutions that have exclusive competences over certain state-like powers. According to Hay, the transfer of sovereignty is the "legal-analytical" component of supranationalism.[5]

Although integration is multi-disciplinary, the works of political science/international relations theorists have formed the predominant narrative of integration. This is understandable considering the highly political process that brings about regional integration. However, of equal importance is the legal implication of integration. While political theorists have done extensive work on the theoretical foundation of integration, it is the legal theorists who engage in explaining the evolutionary nature of integration and the consequences of the integration process on national and international politico-legal framework. As Weiler pointedly puts it, any regional integration process is a creation of the law.[6] After the political negotiations and compromises, member states kick-start the process by agreeing on legal instruments such as Treaties, which clearly spell out the rights and obligations of parties involved and the programmes of action.[7] Making a distinction between the juridical and political theories of integration, Weiler averred that:

> Political theories of ... integration [are] largely wedded to a certain notion about the outcome of the process and embodied a certain predictive element about continued progress.

[1]See e.g. O'Neill (1996), p. 10.

[2]Ibid. The European Atomic Energy Community (EAEC or Euratom) Treaty was also signed on the same day as the EEC Treaty.

[3]Hay (1966), p. 69.

[4]Rosamond (2000), p. 204.

[5]Hay (1966), p. 69.

[6]Weiler (1999), p. 221.

[7]Ibid.

> In addition, political theory laid great emphasis on the social, political and economic substantive achievements and less emphasis on the ways and means.[8]

Rather than focus on theoretical assumptions and conclusions, legal analysts investigate the evolution and step-by-step implication(s) of integration arrangements on member states. Legal theories of integration are thus based on a "continuous progress of integration",[9] an analysis which is more concerned with the interpretation and efficacy of treaty provisions dealing with integration, the position of regional bodies in international law and the effects of laws emanating from such regional bodies in member states.[10]

Hay identified the following as the elements of supranationalism: institutional autonomy of an organisation from member states; ability of an organisation to bind its member states by a majority or weighted majority vote; direct binding effect of law emanating from the organisation on natural and legal persons; and the attribution of powers which differs markedly from powers bestowed on other organisations.[11] He further asserted that "supranationalism ... does not depend on express stipulation, but follows from powers and functions actually accorded to an organisation".[12] Building on Hay's analysis, Weiler makes a distinction between normative and decisional supranationalism.[13] He noted that it is the combination of these two features that distinguishes a supranational organisation from other intergovernmental organisations.[14] According to his analysis, normative supranationalism entails "the relationships and hierarchy which exists between the EC [European Community] policies and legal measures on one hand, and competing policies and legal measures of member states on the other".[15] This definition denotes the existence of three situations. Firstly, whether in respect of common interests and competence, the policies and laws of such organisation has direct effect in member states.[16] Secondly, whether the laws of the organisation are superior to the laws of the member states.[17] Lastly, whether member states are pre-empted from enacting contradictory legislation.[18]

[8]Weiler (1981), p. 270.

[9]Ibid.

[10]Hay (1966), pp. 6–8.

[11]Ibid.

[12]Ibid, p. 30.

[13]Weiler (1981), p. 271.

[14]Ibid, p. 305.

[15]Weiler (1981), p. 271.

[16]The doctrine of direct effect is described as "a provision which is clear and unconditional and bestows a legal right on a natural or legal person, exercisable against another natural person, or against the authorities of a member state". Dashwood et al. (2000), pp. 158–159.

[17]The doctrine of supremacy is defined as "the capacity of that norm of Community law to overrule inconsistent norms of national law in domestic law proceedings". See De Witt (1999), p. 152.

[18]In *Commission v Council*, the European Court of Justice (ECJ) highlighted the principle of pre-emption by ruling that

Decisional supranationalism "relates to the institutional framework and decision-making processes by which Community policies and measures are, in the first place, initiated, debated and formulated, then promulgated and finally executed".[19] Pescatore also identified three elements of supranationalism as: the recognition of common values and interests; the creation of an effective power; and the autonomy of these powers.[20] The absence of the aforementioned elements within an institutional framework simply means that such organisation is an intergovernmental organisation.[21] In their analysis of supranational institutional design in the EU, Heisenberg and Richmond highlighted that four points are essential in determining the supranational trajectory: Intentionality (Did the member states intend to create a supranational institution?); Specificity (How concrete is the mandate of the institution?); Relationship to national institution (How much does the supranational institution depend on its national counterpart?); and Institutional copying (Is the supranational institution explicitly modelled on a specific national institution?)[22]

In the matrix of supranationalism, power relations between member states and regional institutions are managed through several mechanisms. One such is the concept of "conservatory principles". Based on the understanding that states remain the primary structure of international relations, the conservatory principles aim to strike a balance between the powers of states and international organisations.[23] The conservatory principles are divided into four:[24] subsidiarity, attribution of powers, proportionality and flexibility. The subsidiarity principle highlights the complementary role of international organisations by prescribing that only matters which cannot be effectively dealt with at the national level should be allocated to international organisations.[25] The principle of attribution of powers simply provides that regional organisations only have powers explicitly or implicitly conferred on it.[26] The principle of proportionality is an enquiry into whether the means employed by regional bodies are suitable and necessary for the attainment of the desired

---

> each time the Community, with a view to implementing a common policy envisaged by the Treaty, adopts provisions laying down common rules, whatever form these may take, the Member States no longer have the right, acting individually or even collectively, to undertake obligations with third countries which affect those rules. As and when such common rules come into being, the Community alone is in a position to assume and carry out contractual obligation towards third countries affecting the whole sphere of application of the Community legal system.

See (Case 22/70) [1971] ECR 263, paras. 17–18.

[19] Weiler (1981), p. 271.

[20] See Pescatore (1974), pp. 51–52.

[21] Ibid; see also Weiler (1981), p. 305.

[22] Heisenberg and Richmond (2002), pp. 204–209.

[23] Dashwood et al. (2000), p. 151.

[24] Ibid, pp. 153–168.

[25] Ibid, pp. 156–162; see also Lenaerts and Van Nuffel (2004), pp. 100–101.

[26] Dashwood et al. (2000), p. 153; Lenaerts and Van Nuffel (2004), p. 90.

objectives.[27] Lastly, the flexibility principle denotes a legal arrangement under which some member states may decide to pursue shared interest outside of the institutional framework.[28]

On the regional integration scale, intergovernmentalism and supranationalism stand at opposite ends. The intergovernmental or state-centric approach posits that nation states remain the dominant players in global or regional affairs.[29] Even when transnational entities are set up, intergovermentalists point to the fact that the representatives of nation states are the primary decision makers and essentially drive the process.[30] According to Schemers and Blokker, there are two defining features of intergovernmentalism: member states as the sole decision-making authority and unanimity or consensus as the formula for arriving at decisions.[31] However, scholars have noted that institutions usually have a mix of both supranationalism and intergovernmentalism, and their designation stems from which of the elements they have in abundance. For example, while the EU is seen as a supranational organisation, it exhibits certain intergovernmental elements. An example is the primary decision-making powers of Council of the European Union, composed of national ministers, in the areas of foreign policy, justice and home affairs.[32] Similarly, a typical intergovernmental organisation like the United Nations (UN) can exercise some supranational powers in terms of voting rules in the General Assembly and sometimes in the Security Council.[33]

There are major procedural differences between intergovernmentalism and supranationalism. Under the former, national elites and their institutions play a central role in the formulation of policies and initiatives while transnational institutions play important role in the latter. It is important to emphasise that supranationalism is not a unipolar process; rather it thrives on the interplay between member states and transnational institutions.

In terms of the political science discourse of supranationalism, there are two main theories: Functionalism and neo-functionalism. However, it is important to emphasise that both theories were underlined by the federal ideas of EU founding fathers: Jean Monnet and Robert Schuman. Both had envisaged the eventual creation of a united, federating Europe, one which encompassed two steps: the pooling together of economic production of coal and steel (establishing and aggregating common interests); and de-emphasising national sovereignty through the integration of national political units under a federal European structure.[34] As such, both

[27] Dashwood et al. (2000), p. 162.

[28] Ibid, p. 164.

[29] Schermers and Blokker (1995), p. 40.

[30] Ibid.

[31] Ibid.

[32] See e.g. Dashwood (1998), pp. 205–206.

[33] Weiler (1981), p. 305.

[34] Burgess (1996), p. 2.

functionalism and neo-functionalism were regarded as pragmatic, means to an end tools for the creation of a federal Europe.

Buoyed by the disastrous aftermath of the Second World War (economic meltdown and absence of peace), the protagonists of the functionalism approach advocated for the creation of technocratic institutions to handle transnational socio-economic problems.[35] Functionalists display an unyielding belief in the ability of technocratic institutions to manage transnational human needs, peace and public welfare.[36] As Mitrany highlighted, these functional bodies will differ from traditional international organisations in the sense that they would be "executive agencies with autonomous tasks and powers".[37] This approach presents an alternative to global governance framework, an attempt to dislocate nation states from matters that border on common (transnational) interests.[38] Furthermore, this idea predicted that the efficient performance of responsibilities by transnational functional agencies would lead to the transfer of loyalty from nation state to these agencies (attitudinal change).[39]

Critics of functionalism argued that this idea ignores the highly political nature of international relations. Mitrany's advocacy of detached and unaffiliated technocratic agencies disregards the state-centric posture of global politics. According to critics, a project which excluded this reality lacked scientific and empirical basis.[40] They also questioned the functionalist assumption of human attitudinal change by arguing that this line of thinking falls within the scope of morality rather than politics.[41] The pervasive and deep-rooted attachment to nationality not only by political actors but individuals essentially rendered the "attitudinal change" theory impractical.

Neo-functionalism was a reaction to the perceived inadequacies of functionalism. Neo-functionalists regarded integration as a more complex process than the apolitical method or "technocratic automaticity" prescribed by functionalism.[42] Neo-functionalism, like its theoretical precursor, highlights the irrelevance of nation states and their inability to maintain peace and security.[43] It, however, acknowledged the primacy of nation states and its political elites (including political parties and interest groups) in the integration process.[44] Thus, this established the empirical foundation of neo-functionalism. At the core of neo-functionalist agenda is the concept of "spillover". This concept refers to situations where integration in one economic sector would lead to further economic integration within and beyond such

[35] Mitrany (1975), p. 126; see also Rosamond (2000), p. 33.

[36] For a detailed analysis of the functionalist theory, see generally, Mitrany (1966), pp. 25–99.

[37] Mitrany (1975), p. 125.

[38] See generally Mitrany (1966).

[39] Rosamond (2000), p. 33.

[40] O'Neill (1996), p. 34.

[41] Ibid, p. 33.

[42] Rosamond (2000), p. 55.

[43] O'Neill (1996), p. 37.

[44] Haas (1958), p. 17; Rosamond (2000), p. 55.

sector (functional spillover).[45] The logic behind "spillover" is that once nation states agree to place the control of a certain sector in the hands of a supranational authority, with success in such sector and with the passage of time, there would be pressures to extend control to other related policy areas. Supranational institutions rather than nation states are seen as the drivers of this process.

Moravcsik, however, argued that spillover into related sectors has not being as consistent as expected.[46] He further notes that neo-functionalism fails to offer an explanation for the domestic dynamics that shape supranational decisions.[47] Neo-functionalism suffered its greatest setback when the then French president, Charles de Gaulle, altered the trajectory of European integration.[48] In sharp contrast to the postulations of functionalist theorists, de Gaulle rejected the European Commission's (EC) modest attempt to reduce the powers of nation states within the community.[49] In reaction to the growing influence of the EC, de Gaulle, in 1965, remarked that only existing European states "had the rights to give orders and power to be obeyed".[50] The European debt crisis (also known as the Eurozone crisis) that started in 2009 was another example of the limitation of this theory. This crisis ensured that EU countries such as Portugal, Ireland, Italy, Greece and Spain (PIIGS) were unable to repay or refinance their debts. This was further worsened by the fact that the European Central Bank (ECB), which exerted supranational monetary powers through the euro, has no powers to regulate the fiscal policies of member states.[51] The rise of "Euroskeptics", who criticise the supranational powers wielded by technocrats in Brussels and favour more national control or even the withdrawal from the EU (as shown by the UK's withdrawal), further threatens the supranational status of the EU.[52] These events expose the empirical limitations and the rigidities of this approach. It brought to the fore the influence of nation states in the integration process. More importantly, it also reinforces the imperative of understanding context, particularly how socio-political and economic peculiarities shape the operationalisation of regionalism in different regions of the world.

[45] Rosamond (2000), p. 60.

[46] Moravcsik (1993), p. 476.

[47] Ibid, p. 477.

[48] Ibid, p. 476.

[49] O'Neill (1996), p. 45.

[50] Cited in Agyemen (1990), p. 19.

[51] Matthijs and Kelemen (2015), p. 104. Although the ECB has no direct powers over EU Member States' fiscal policies, the EU Commission and the Economic and Financial Council (ECOFIN), which is composed of EU economics and finance ministers, can use the 1997 Stability and Growth Pact (SGP) to impose punitive measures of up to 0.5% of national GDP on profligate Member States whose budget deficit exceed 3% of GDP and whose public debt is in excess of 60% of GDP. However, there have been criticisms of the ineffectual enforcement of the SGP. See e.g. Fingland and Bailey (2008).

[52] Ibid, p. 97. It is important to emphasise that Euroskepticism has always been a part of the European integration narrative since the 1950s and has gone through several phases and evolution. See e.g. Bijsmans (2020).

2.3 Pan-Africanism: The Philosophical Underpinning of Unity

The supreme irony, according to Mazrui, is that "it took European colonialism to inform Africans that they were indeed Africans".[53] He further noted that while European colonialism bequeathed Africa with a continental identity, the contact with the Arab world awakened Africa's black consciousness.[54] The consciousness of being an "African", as distinct from being an Ashanti or Yoruba or Zulu, was a reaction to external subjugation either in the form of colonialism or racial prejudice.[55] Julius Nyerere captured this in the following words: "the Africans looked at themselves and knew that vis-à-vis the Europeans, they were one".[56] Along with this racial consciousness was also an awareness of "geographical contiguities", the realisation that Africans inhabit the same territorial space.[57]

The geographic element of pan-Africanism should be understood as not only complementary to the racial consciousness but also an attempt to include Africa North of the Sahara in the discourse on pan-Africanism. Mazrui posited that age-long cultural ties between North and sub-Saharan Africa cannot be discounted.[58] This, he notes, is evident in the vocabulary of some of the most widely spoken languages on the continent.[59] It is noteworthy that the debate on the racial divide between North and sub-Saharan Africa has had little or no impact on programmes aimed at continental integration, as both the Organisation of African Unity (OAU) and its successor, the African Union (AU), are made up of all countries that fall within Africa's geographical boundary.[60] Another controversial element of the

[53] Mazrui (2002), p. 37.

[54] Mazrui (2005), p. 74.

[55] Akinyemi (2008).

[56] Cited in Ibid.

[57] Mazrui (1963), pp. 89–90.

[58] Mazrui (2002) p. 39. Similarly, Nnamdi Azikiwe, a notable Nigerian pan-Africanist, remarked that "...I would like to speak of the peoples of Africa in general terms to include all the races inhabiting that continent and embracing all the linguistic and cultural groups who are domiciled therein ... It would be useless to define 'Pan-Africanism' exclusively in racial or linguistic terms, since the obvious solution would be parochial. And chauvinism, by whatever name it is identified, has always been a disintegrating factor in human society at all known times of human history" Azikiwe (1962).

[59] Mazrui (2002), p. 39.

[60] However, some have questioned this by claiming that North African countries such as Egypt, Libya, Morocco, Tunisia, Algeria and Mauritania are racially, culturally and politically Arab, and not African, countries. See e.g. Chinweizu (1987), pp. 159–171. Mobutu Sese Seko, the then president of Zaire (now the Democratic Republic of Congo), also advocated the creation of an exclusive black sub-Saharan African organisation. Cited in Mazrui (2002), p. 39. Also, Obafemi Awolowo, a prominent Nigerian nationalist, had this to say: "The Sahara Desert is a natural line of demarcation between the Northern and Southern parts of Africa. It is my considered view that the countries of North Africa should, as a first step, constitute a Zone...other territories south of the

geographic component is what Soyinka referred to as "saline consciousness", one that excludes African diaspora from the identity discourse. He queried:

> How can we as intelligent beings submit to the self-imprisonment of a "saline consciousness" which insists that, contrary to all historic evidence, Africa stops wherever salt water licks its shores? Or that, conversely, all that is bound by salt water on the African continent is necessarily African. What other race, especially on the African continent, has lost 200 million of its people through forcible uprooting? Elementary curiosity justifies that we seek out those who survived of that number and inquire in what forms have they survived? What have they achieved? What have they contributed to their environments? What lessons, if any, have their specific genius evolved for those that were left behind?[61]

While this debate may have receded, especially through the institutional recognition of the African diaspora as the "sixth region" of the AU, the AU Constitutive Act is still in line with such "saline consciousness" as it only accords membership to countries within the geographical boundaries of Africa.[62] When Haiti, which was granted an AU observer status in 2012, applied for full membership of the AU in 2016, the AU rejected this application on the basis on its geographical criterion for membership.[63]

The chronological events in Africa's history—the existence of pre-colonial empires, slavery and the arbitrary balkanisation of its territories by European superpowers—proved to be an effective emotive tool for rallying Africans both in the Diaspora and on the continent towards a common purpose.[64] As Legum pointed out, Pan-Africanism is essentially "a movement of ideas and emotions"[65] which lends itself to various manifestations. For Africans in the Diaspora, it represented a bond to a disconnected past, a search for common identity and the restoration of freedom and dignity in an oppressed society.[66] Within the continent, Asante observed that

---

Sahara...should constitute another Zone". Cited in Legum (1962), p. 270. See also, Sangmpam (2018), pp. 58–59.

[61] Soyinka (1985), p. 19.

[62] See Article 29(1) of the AU Constitutive Act. This is a re-affirmation of the membership criterion under Article IV of the 1963 OAU Charter.

[63] See AU (2016b). In the past, some African leaders such as the late Libyan president, Muammar Ghaddafi and the former Senegalese president, Abdoulaye Wade, openly advocated for the inclusion of Caribbean states as members of the AU should also be understood within this context. See e.g. BBC (2009); Reuters (2010).

[64] See e.g. Thompson (1969), p. 33. Nyerere remarks that Africa's pre-colonial history demanded that "African unity must have priority over all other associations". Cited in Mazrui (1963), p. 93.

[65] Legum (1962), p. 14. Murithi refers to it as "an invented idea". Murithi (2005), p. 35. Akinyemi calls Pan-Africanism an "experiential phenomenon (a phenomenon that arises as a reaction to an experience)". Akinyemi (2008). wa Thiong'o views pan-Africanism as "the quest for wholeness' through which Africans within the continent and Africans in diaspora desire "the grandest secular vision for reconnecting the dismembered". See Wa Thiong'o (2009), p. 35.

[66] Thompson (1969), pp. 3–19.

pan-Africanism was "viewed both as an integrative force and as a movement of liberation".[67]

The nationalist resistance to colonialism, however, highlighted a paradox: using the oft-derided colonial boundaries as a legitimate instrument of resistance. While this idea may be perceived as pragmatic, it was to set the tone for a post-colonial attachment to national sovereignty. Once African states "won" their hard-earned independence, the next agenda was to consolidate nationalism rather than focus on integrative matters. Mazrui referred to this attitude as "the nationalism that looks inwardly territorially".[68] In addition, colonial attachments (Francophone versus Anglophone versus Lusophone), differing political ideologies and the inability to see regionalism and national development as interlinked has ensured that efforts of continental integration were consigned to the back seat.[69]

One underlying impetus of pan-Africanism as an "integrative force" was the need to de-emphasise (and/or eliminate) the burdensome political and economic nature of Africa's colonial boundaries. Africa remains the most partitioned continent in the world due to Europe's insensitive cartographic experiments. The lines drawn by European powers were (and still are) illogical to the extent that they, in some cases, separated communities that shared common ancestry, customs and socio-political and economic institutions.[70] For example, Asiwaju observed that:

> In many instances, such as the Uganda-Sudan frontier through the Kakwa territory, the boundaries have separated communities of worshippers from age-old sacred groves and shrines. In other instances, well exemplified by the Somali, the water resources in a predominantly pastoral and nomadic culture area were located in one state while the pastures were in another.[71]

In many cases, European entities used coercive powers and treaties as a pretext for dispossessing Africans of their lands. There were deliberate moves to misinterpret the content of treaties to African chiefs, and in cases where they refused to sign, coercive and brutal measures were employed.[72] Such was the fate of the continent under what is aptly termed "the scramble for Africa". Although some have argued

---

[67] Asante (1997), p. 32; see also Legum (1962), p. 38. According to Jackson et al. (2017), the origins of pan-African integrative agenda can be traced back to the ancient kingdoms of West Africa. Kingdoms such as Ghana, Mali and Songhai encompassed several ethnic groups and created common trade taxes and institutions.

[68] Mazrui (1963), p. 92.

[69] Asante (1997), pp. 34–35.

[70] Asiwaju (1985b), pp. 2–3. For a detailed tabulated list of partitioned ethnic groups in Africa, see Asiwaju (1985a), pp. 256–258. Brownlie, however, argues that the European powers did not always ignore ethnological considerations when delimiting African frontiers. See Brownlie (1979), p. 6.

[71] Asiwaju (1985b), p. 3. For example, the United Kingdom and Ethiopia entered into an agreement in 1954 that nomadic Somali would be allowed to graze their animals across the border (in Ethiopia) but upon the independence of British Somaliland in 1960, Ethiopia decided not to honour the agreement. Oyebode (2003), p. 23.

[72] Oyebode (2003), pp. 90–91; Horchschild (2012), p. 72.

that partitioning is not peculiar to Africa,[73] the resultant effect of this colonial adventure is the designation of Africa as the world's most fragmented region. According to Akonnor, Africa has 165 demarcated borders.[74] The presence of 16 landlocked states in Africa, some of which are not economically viable, is evidence of the arbitrariness of African frontiers.[75] In a bid to forestall conflicts emanating from colonial boundaries, the OAU in 1964 adopted the *uti possidetis* rule, which mandated member states to respect existing frontiers. This, however, failed to stem the tide of border clashes between African states—Somalia and Ethiopia (1964, 1977–1978, and 1982), Libya and Chad (1978–1987), Nigeria and Cameroon (1981–2005), Morocco and Western Sahara (1975 – present), just to mention a few.[76] While most secessionist conflicts in post-colonial Africa have been unsuccessful,[77] the existence of such conflicts is a fundamental consequence of the fault lines imposed by European colonialism.

The earliest manifestation of pan-Africanism as an "integrative force" dates to the 1920s.[78] At that time, a group of intellectuals from the four British dependencies of West Africa—Nigeria, Sierra Leone, Gambia and Gold Coast (later Ghana)—called for closer cooperation and integration of West Africa.[79] One of the principal initiators of this idea, Joseph Casely Hayford (Ghana), presented a demand to the

---

[73] Asiwaju notes that the boundaries of African countries such as Nigeria, Senegal and Mozambique are older than the boundaries of countries like Austria, Hungary, Poland, Greece and Finland. Asiwaju (1985c), pp. 233, 248.

[74] Akonnor (2007), p. 200.

[75] Agyemen (1990), p. 6.

[76] Oyebode (2003), pp. 24–25.

[77] Englebert and Hummel called this the "secession deficit", claiming that only 10 sub Saharan African states have experienced secessionist conflicts despite the plausible rationale for such conflicts in at least 30 African states. Englebert and Hummel (2005), pp. 399–400.

[78] Asante (1997), pp. 34–35. The Jamaican pan-Africanist, Marcus Garvey, was the first person to associate the terminology of the "United States of Africa" with the ambition of uniting the entire continent. In a poem written in 1924, "Hail! United States of Africa", Garvey remarked:

> There is no state left out of the Union-
>
> The East, West, North, South, including Central,
>
> Are in the nation, strong forever,
>
> Over blacks in glorious dominion.
>
> ***
>
> Hail! United States of Africa-free!
>
> Country of the brave black man's liberty;
>
> State of greater nationhood thou hast won,
>
> A new life for the race is just begun.
>
> Garvey (1924).

[79] Thompson (1969), p. 28.

colonial office in London, asking for the establishment of a West African Court of Appeal and a West African University.[80] Although this idea was dismissed by the colonial authorities as "premature", it laid the foundation for the politically-charged activism of the 1940s, with Kwame Nkrumah as a principal player. This era witnessed a renewed focus and an attempt to include Francophone West Africa in the "integrative" agenda.[81] The Nkrumah-led West African National Secretariat, an offshoot of the 1945 Fifth Pan-African congress in Manchester, resolved in 1946 to use the idea of "a *West African Federation* as an indispensable lever for the ultimate achievement of a *United States of Africa*".[82] From this point, the consciousness of continental integration became ingrained in the corpus of the pan-Africanism narrative. Ironically, it also laid the foundation for the idea of integrating Africa on a regional basis. In 1942, Nkrumah remarked that all West African colonies "must first unite and become a national unity, absolutely free from the encumbrances of foreign rule, before they can assume the aspect of international cooperation on a grand scale".[83]

The independence of Ghana in 1957 provided Nkrumah with the solid base to vigorously pursue the African unity project. Nkrumah's assertion that Ghana's independence was incomplete without the total independence of other African states not only reinforced the solidarity message inherent in the pan-Africanist thought, it also demonstrated the readiness to give practical effect to the integrative agenda. Building on the momentum of the 1945 Fifth Pan-African congress in Manchester and the 1946 West African National Congress, Nkrumah convened the first conference of independent African states in 1958. The conference was attended by the eight already independent African states—Ethiopia, Libya, Liberia, Morocco, Sudan, Tunisia, the United Arab Republic and Ghana. The participating states agreed to establish a Joint Economic Research Committee, charged with the responsibility of promoting trade among African countries, coordinate economic planning and investigate the feasibility of an African common market.[84]

The Second Conference of Independent African States (CISA) was held in Addis Ababa in 1960. In addition to the eleven African states already independent,[85] invitations were sent to yet to be independent African states such as Nigeria, Mali Federation, Congo Kinshasa, Madagascar and Somalia.[86] The conference recommended, amongst other provisions, the establishment of a joint African Development Bank, a joint African Commercial Bank and a preferential trade area.[87] The

[80] Ibid.

[81] See Ibid, p. 90.

[82] Legum (1962), pp. 32–33; Thompson (1969), pp. 90–91.

[83] Cited in Asante (1997), p. 32.

[84] Thompson (1969), pp. 348–349.

[85] Cameroon, Ethiopia, Ghana, Guinea, Liberia, Libya, Morocco, Sudan, Togo, Tunisia and the United Arab Republic.

[86] Ajala (1973), p. 25.

[87] Legum (1962), p. 158.

Ghanaian delegation, supported by their Guinean counterpart, advocated a political union while the Nigerian (who had not yet become independent) and Liberian delegations felt such call was premature.[88] The result of this was the emergence of two groups—Casablanca and Monrovia—with differing views on African integration. The Casablanca group was a juxtaposition of two elements: an immediate political union and functional cooperation.[89] The element of political union within this group gave birth to the 1961 Ghana-Guinea-Mali Union (Union of African States) while the functional element was reflected in the provisions of the Casablanca Charter.[90] Conversely, the Monrovia group was united in their call for functional cooperation at regional levels as the best approach.[91] The creation of the OAU in 1963 was the culmination of decades of efforts aimed at giving the debate on unity a practical effect. Although the OAU Charter represented a triumph of a state-centric, functional cooperation, it was able to unite the differing ideologies under the same banner.

While the initiatives outlined above exposed the cleavage that existed, and still exists, in relation to the *modus operandi* of African integration, it helped in forging a template for the on-going debate on integration. The idea of "Africa" might have started as a sentimental attachment to a common heritage, the setting up of institutions both at the regional and continental levels have all contributed to moving pan-Africanism from the realm of romanticism to a realistic and practical objective. Whether through the creation of the AU, Pan-African Parliament (PAP), the New Partnership on Africa's Development (now known as the African Union Development Agency (AUDA) – NEPAD), the African Peer Review Mechanism (APRM), the African Charter on Human and Peoples' Rights (ACHPR), pan-Africanism continues to be expressed in nuanced and adaptive forms.

2.4 Continental Supranationalism in Africa

Since the colonial era, African political elites and intellectuals have, depending on their ideological beliefs and location, offered their views on how to proceed with African integration. If colonialism was the catalyst for the quest for unity, the paradox of Africa's underdevelopment and the need to become a meaningful player in global geopolitics, shaped, and continues to shape, the debate on African integration.

The unanimity of ideas in respect of unity does not, however, extend to the methodology of attaining such goal. The method, especially as it relates to the depth, speed and form remain the defining features of continental integration in Africa. In

[88] Ibid, pp. 46–47.

[89] Nweke (1987), p. 136; see also Legum (1962), pp. 56–57.

[90] *Supra* Nweke (1987), p. 136.

[91] *Supra* Legum (1962), p. 56.

trying to make sense of this understanding, this section employs a three-lens approach in fleshing out the ideational parameters of continental supranationalism.

2.4.1 Pace

The evaluation of the pace of continental integration is one rooted in the robust debates and engagements that preceded the establishment of the OAU in 1963. Kwame Nkrumah's "unite or perish" aphorism came to define the doctrinal approach of those who argued that the only way to counter neo-imperial interference in African affairs, and the diminished continental sovereignty flowing from such interference, is dependent on moving with transnational institutional development at a much faster speed. Nkrumah pushed for continental instead of sub-regional federalism:

> The idea of regional federations in Africa is fraught with many dangers. There is the danger of the development of regional loyalties, fighting against each other. In effect, regional federations are a form of balkanisation on a grand scale . . . the best means . . . is to begin to create a larger and all-embracing loyalty which will hold Africa together as a united people with one government and one destiny.[92]

Agyeman described the philosophy behind the federalist approach as "seek[ing] integration through the vehicle of a political movement powered by political will and dignificatory force toward a redeeming order".[93] Similarly, the Nigerian nationalist, Nnamdi Azikiwe, noted that an African federation or confederation "will raise the prestige of African States in the councils of the world".[94] Although Nkrumah's quest for a much faster and rapid continental integration process failed to materialise, it inspired others such as the late Libyan president, Muammar Ghaddafi to pursue the same line of thought. For example, like Nkrumah, Ghaddafi highlighted the impracticalities of regional federation in the following words:

> The advocates of this theory [regional federations] suggest that we have to wait for Somalia to unite and then Eritrea and Ethiopia. We have to wait for Egypt, Libya, Tunisia, Algeria and Morocco (which is outside the African Union) and Mauritania, and Sahara to become one state. . .it is impossible for these regions to establish one state.[95]

---

[92] Nkrumah (1963), pp. 214–215.

[93] Agyemen (1990), pp. 27–28. On the issue of Africa's maligned dignity, Mazrui observed that "the distinctiveness of the fate of the black people is that they have been the most *humiliated* in recent times. They were the most humiliated in slavery until its abolition in the last century; and have been the most humiliated by racialism and discrimination". Mazrui (1974), p. 36. Similarly, the Ghanaian writer, Ama Ata Aidoo remarked: "When one looks at the contemporary world, one can only be clear by being honest. We African people are at the bottom of the pile. We have to rescue ourselves as our own people. We are not threatening anybody but we need *us*". Needham and Aidoo (1995), p. 126.

[94] Azikiwe (1962).

[95] Ghaddafi (2007), p. 5.

As a counterpoise to the demand for a faster pace is the idea of an incremental approach, one that has become the dominant feature of Africa's continental integration process. The incremental approach advances the imperative of building continental supranationalism from the sub-regional levels, with a phased, incremental transfer of powers to continental organisations. According to Julius Nyerere, the advantage(s) of a regional federation lies in the fact that it would enable the area concerned, "to achieve quickly at least the benefits of greater unity and great strength" and, also, reduce "the number of states which have to sit down together and agree on the final forms of African unification".[96] Similarly, Jomo Kenyatta had asserted that "I want to see first East Africa united and federated, then the whole of Africa as one".[97] The rationale behind this thesis was (and still is) based on the fact that it is easier for states that share similar cultural, administrative and linguistic identities to form a union rather than plunging the whole of Africa, with its internal contradictions and complexities, into a union. Furthermore, this was a tactical recognition of the existing sub-regional organisations that were created by colonial administrations but were then seen (and still seen) as essential postcolonial "special purpose vehicles" for fast-tracking continental unity. Colonial administrations in Africa had established several monetary cooperation arrangements in East Africa, the Federation Rhodesia and Nyasaland, Southern Africa (particularly South Africa, Lesotho, Botswana and Swaziland) and the Franc Zone in west and central Africa. These monetary arrangements were not necessarily aimed to promote exchange rate management and fiscal policy; rather they were designed as an expeditious mechanism for colonial administration, especially in relation to the facilitation of international trade and payments.[98] In East Africa, the British established a customs union between Kenya and Uganda in 1917 (with Tanganyika joining in 1927), then later the East African High Commission (EAHC) in 1948, and then transformed it into the East African Common Services Organisation (EACSO) in 1961.[99] In 1953, the British established the Central African Federation (CAF) in 1953 through the amalgamation of Northern Rhodesia (Zambia), Southern Rhodesia (Zimbabwe) and Malawi. This federation essentially served the economic interest of white settlers, with the introduction of the Common External Tariff (CET), aimed at protecting Southern Rhodesian industries (with Southern Rhodesia receiving two-thirds of the total government expenditure).[100] The French also created the *Union Africaine et Maghreb* (UAM), the French West Africa and the French Equatorial Africa federations, which functioned as customs union and shared the

---

[96] Nyerere (1966), p. 347. Nyerere was not opposed to the idea of a United States of Africa. Writing in 1963, he noted that the idea was Africa's "ultimate destiny", albeit it "does not mean that we must - or that we could - achieve the goal tomorrow, in one step." Nyerere (1963), p. 3.

[97] Legum (1962), p. 65.

[98] See AU & UNECA (2008), pp. 183–186.

[99] EAC website.

[100] Bach (2017), p. 17.

French franc as a common currency.[101] Although some of these organisations no longer exist in their original, colonial forms, existing Regional Economic Communities (RECs) still carry some of their DNA. These include the Southern African Customs Union (SACU), East African Community (EAC), West African Economic and Monetary Union (WAEMU) and the Central African Economic and Monetary Community (CEMAC). Bach described this metamorphosis as "hysteresis": "the continuation, in conjunction with process of adjustment, negotiation and relegitimation, of arrangements that date back to the colonial period".[102]

The incremental ideology shaped the establishment of the OAU in 1963, and that of its successor the AU in 2000. The AU's reference to the eight recognised RECs as the "building blocks" of continental integration further reinforces the gradualist idea.[103] The AU's Agenda 2063 is built around the gradualist ideology, as it encourages the gradual attainment of goals and the deferment of a position on the type of continental government to 2030.[104] Despite the reference to consensus in arriving at the decision of the appropriate continental governance system, the document shows its bias towards supranationalism by noting that "[t]he political unity of Africa will be the culmination of the integration process, which includes the free movement of people and the establishment of continental institutions, leading to full economic integration".[105] Another example is the African Economic Community Treaty (1991), which spelt out a 34-year step-by-step plan to achieving a supranational political and economic union.[106]

It could be argued that since the adoption of the AU Agenda 2063 in 2015, the gradualist approach has encompassed a more pragmatic ideological component.

---

[101] The UAM had functional institutions such as the *Union Africaine et Malgache de cooperation economique*, *Union Africaine et Malgache des postes et telecommunications* and *Air Afrique* (These are economic, postal and air services). As Nweke observes, the UAM contributed immensely to the charting of a continental functionalist trajectory. Nweke (1987), pp. 136–137. See also Bach (2017), p. 14.

[102] Bach (2017), p. 13.

[103] The recognised RECs are: Arab Maghreb Union (UMA), Common Market for Eastern and Southern Africa (COMESA), Community of Sahel–Saharan States (CEN–SAD), East African Community (EAC), Economic Community of Central African States (ECCAS), Economic Community of West African States (ECOWAS), Intergovernmental Authority on Development (IGAD), and Southern African Development Community (SADC).

[104] AU (2015), p. 5.

[105] Ibid.

[106] See Article 6 of The African Economic Community Treaty (1991). Here is an outline of the six-stage process: Strengthening of the RECs (5 years); Removal of tariffs and duties on goods within the RECs (8 years); Establishment of a free trade area and custom union within each REC (10 years); Coordination and harmonisation of tariff and non-tariff systems among the RECs (2 years); Establishment of an African Common Market (4 years); and Consolidation of the common market, the establishment of a monetary union, central bank, parliament and single currency (5 years).

Composed of "Africrats"[107] and national political elites such as the Rwandan president, Paul Kagame, this pragmatic component has introduced far-reaching reform measures; ensured the adoption of the African Continental Free Trade Area (AfCFTA), and the Protocol to the Treaty Establishing the African Economic Community Relating to Free Movement of Persons, Right of Residence and Right of Establishment; and the decision to finance the AU through 0.2% import levy on all "eligible imports" into the continent.[108] These steps will be further explored in subsequent chapters of this book. Suffice to state that these are consequential issues that could, if well managed, shape the course of continental supranationalism in Africa.

2.4.2 Nature

The discourse around the nature of the continental integration process remains the most topical of the three ideational approaches to continental supranationalism. In addressing the question of the nature of the integration process, scholars have employed two analytical prisms: intergovernmental (or state-driven) and supranational (technocratic driven).[109] The former speaks to a state-driven regional integration process where member states are the supreme rule-making structures, while the latter denotes the empowerment of neutral, technocratic, regional institutions to make binding rules and regulations. This binary analysis has defined continental regionalism from the time of the OAU through to recent processes aimed at implementing the AU Agenda 2063. While there exists no consensus on the type of continental government, the recent adoption of norms on free trade, free movement and the need to transfer more powers to the AU indicate a symbolic acceptance of supranational regionalism, albeit in a more manageable and gradual fashion.

The tilt towards supranationalism is informed by Kwame Nkrumah's federalist approach[110] to continental regionalism as it is influenced by the European integration process. The European integration process provided the template for the transformation of the OAU to AU in 2000 and continues to influence continental regionalism through the EU's continued financial assistance and the colonial heritage of regionalism in Africa.[111] The bias towards modelling regional institutions

---

[107] Tieku used this term to describe influential transnational technocrats who worked in the OAU and its successor, the AU. Tieku (2017).

[108] AU (2018, 2016a).

[109] See e.g. Tieku (2017), pp. 221–222.

[110] For example, Nyerere pointed out that the fact that Nkrumah, the major proponent of this idea, went to school in the United States of America largely influenced his ideological position on African unity. He opined: "Kwame [Nkrumah] went to Lincoln University, a black college in the US. He perceived things from a US history, where 13 colonies revolted against the British formed a union". Cited in Mwakikagile (2002), p. 300.

[111] Bach (2017), pp. 81–82; Hansen and Jonsson (2018).

along EU lines is not unique to Africa, and has been described as "downloading the global script".[112] With reference to Eurasian regionalism, Libman identifies four levels of imitation: integration agenda and sequence of integration steps; structure of institutions; formalisation and legalisation of the integration agenda; and explicit reference to individual EU policies and integration steps.[113] These are present in one shape or form in the AU integration agenda. Not only are AU structures modelled along EU institutional lines, the steps for achieving economic and political goals speak to the EU integrative journey and adopts a neo-liberal agenda in crafting institutional policies and aspirations.[114] Similarly, African RECs have also adopted the institutional and regional integration models of the EU, even if they have not been able to integrate as deeply as the latter.[115]

It should, however, be emphasised that there is a range of perspectives on the nature of continental supranationalism. The continental-federalist approach, which advances the establishment of a "United States of Africa", remains the most extreme element of the supranational paradigm. According to Nkrumah, the "United States of Africa" should pursue three objectives: overall economic planning on a continental basis; unified military and defence strategy; and a unified foreign policy and diplomacy.[116] On the institutional architecture of such Union, Nkrumah, in 1964, suggested:

> This Union of Government shall consist of an Assembly of Heads of States and Governments headed by a President elected from among the Heads of State and Government of the Independent African States. The Executive of the Union Government will be a Cabinet or Council of Ministers with a Chancellor or Prime Minister as its head, and a Federal Housing consisting of two Chambers – The Senate and a House of Representatives.[117]

In his address to African leaders at the 1965 OAU Summit in Accra, Nkrumah further proposed that in addition to a Union president, the Assembly should elect a number of Union Vice-Presidents.[118]

Another element is the ideological expectation of a supposed supranational continental government. While some advance a leftist ideology, others argue for a neoliberal approach that is more in tune with globalisation. In terms of the leftist-socialist ideology, Nkrumah, noted that a continental government should be based on a "framework of comprehensive socialist planning and deployment"[119] that for example supervises the pooling together of cash crops produced on the continent in order to determine a common selling policy.[120] He further asserted that "in the case

[112] See generally Libmann (2019), pp. 247–268.

[113] Ibid, pp. 249–250.

[114] This point is further explored in Chap. 4.

[115] Bach (2017), pp. 82–85.

[116] Nkrumah (1963), pp. 218–220.

[117] Nkrumah (1965), pp. 295–296.

[118] Ibid, p. 309.

[119] Nkrumah (1965), p. 11.

[120] Nkrumah (1963), p. 163.

of Africa ... the necessity of a union of independent African states is established, a union integrated by socialism, without which our hard-won independence may yet be perverted and negated by a new colonialism".[121] Similarly, Diop proposed that the constitution of such federalist union should be "so written that no industrial bourgeoisie can come into being. This would prove that we are truly socialist [...]".[122] Conversely, the neo-liberal approach has defined the landscape of transnational policy development processes in Africa since the end of the Cold War.[123] This idea places the objectives of market fundamentalism at the heart of regionalism, advocating the integration of African economies into a global economic system.[124] This logic is evident in AU development documents such as NEPAD, which advocates "the genuine integration of [African countries] into the global economy and politic"[125] and the AU Agenda 2063 which highlights the link between economic growth and the flow of foreign direct investment.[126]

Lastly, is the discursive paradigm that places emphasis on creating supranational institutions with entrance requirements. For example, Ayittey suggested the establishment of the creation of a decentralised "Confederation of African States" with strict admission criteria.[127] This, he noted, should include adherence to democratic practises and internal unity within each African state.[128] In 1962, Azikiwe, made a similar call, by advocating for the establishment of a "concert of African states", a confederation under which "both the external and internal sovereignties of the individual members of the confederation shall remain intact".[129] He then suggested the following as the organs of the confederation: an assembly of heads of state and government, a parliament of African states (similar the UN General Assembly), a pan-African court of international justice, and a pan-African secretariat.[130] Sangmpam also proposed that the AU be dismantled and replaced with an organic based "Unifederation" of sub-Saharan African states. According to him, this is not based on any notion of racial and cultural differences between north and sub-Saharan Africa but mainly due to "the vast differences in socio-economic outcomes between North Africa and SSA that politics imposes and the causes of this differential impact".[131] As he further observed, such "Unifederation" should be able to make binding laws and impose its sovereignty under a decentralised arrangement that also

[121] Nkrumah (2001), p. 118.

[122] Diop (1987), p. 88. Shivji also suggested that such cooperation should focus on fixing of agricultural exports or the repayments of debt. Shivji (2007).

[123] Taylor (2003); Adesina (2004).

[124] Hettne and Soderbaum (2000).

[125] African Union (2001), pp. 8–9.

[126] AU (2013), p. 6.

[127] Ayittey (2010), p. 101.

[128] Ibid. See also Ayittey (2016).

[129] Azikiwe (1962).

[130] Ibid.

[131] Sangmpam (2018), p. 60.

recognises the autonomy of local and sub-regional entities in sub-Saharan Africa.[132]

2.4.3 Context

Context speaks to the imperative of building continental regionalism around Africa's peculiar contexts, and particularly, the adoption of indigenous knowledge systems in the development of policies and processes. Several scholars have emphasised that regional integration is essentially an idea built around the EU's experience and history and has had little successful application elsewhere.[133] As Chabal rightly puts it,

> all concepts are historically and contextually generated and, therefore, bounded by historical circumstances in which they appear. Paradoxically, therefore, they are in this sense local and not universal.[134]

The description of Eurocentric thoughts and processes as universal has been challenged by African scholars for decades. The adoption of theories and practices of European integration, the prescription of either leftist or neoliberal approaches to African integration, and the unbridled attachment to Westphalian sovereignty, are seen as antithetical to achieving an authentic Pan-African integration. As Agyeman noted, the homogeneity of institutional and industrial development is a key feature of European integrative arrangement and has no correlation to the African experience.[135] He further noted that even if Europe was not culturally homogenous, there exists similarities in ideological leanings of political parties and programmes of interest groups across European frontiers.[136] Similarly, Babarinde argued that European and African integration are both spatially and 50 years apart, thereby making institutional imitation problematic.[137]

In the context of international law, Gathii classified such challenge under two schools of thought: contributionists and critical traditionalists.[138] The contributionists school of thought notes that epistemological lessons from pre-colonial African kingdoms and African societies in general on state-building, trade practices, resolution of conflicts and diplomatic processes are essential pointers for rethinking international law, and developing an autochthonous regional

---

[132] Ibid, p. 74.

[133] Agyemen (1990); Acharya (2012); Draper (2012); Silva (2017).

[134] Chabal (2009), p. 177.

[135] Agyemen (1990), p. 8. African states, according to Agyemen (1990, p. 6), are "plagued by the deficiency trilogy of smallness, unnaturalness and illegitimacy".

[136] Ibid, pp. 8–9.

[137] Babarinde (2007), pp. 3–4.

[138] Gathii (2012).

integration process.[139] For example, Ayittey argued that his idea of creating a "Confederal African State" is one that is rooted in an indigenous African model that prioritises the decentralisation of more powers to constituent states.[140] Similarly, Diop linked his proposal of a gendered bicameral legislature for a federated union of African states to an indigenous matriarchal system that encouraged the participation of women in public affairs.[141] Ochonu[142] and Jackson et al[143] respectively show the lessons current efforts at building a continental free trade regime can learn from the practises pre-colonial trans-frontier trade networks and empires.

The critical traditionalists are composed of scholars that "centre their analysis on the structural and economic underpinnings of the place of African States in the world".[144] Mostly belonging to the Third World Approaches to International Law (TWAIL) movement, these scholars highlight the neo-colonial, neo-liberal underpinnings of international law, thereby making it unsuitable for addressing global inequalities and genuine development.[145] In terms of regional integration, critical traditionalists argue that the adoption of neo-liberal institutional mechanisms and norms by regional organisations in Africa only serve as a pretext for "integration in the global capitalist circuits as subordinates".[146]

However, the emphasis on context does not necessarily call for the wholesale abandonment of all external knowledge systems, rather it advocates for what Ndhlovu referred to as "translative adaptation":

> an innovative blending and integration . . . of these development models into home-grown, Africa-centred theories and philosophies that are rooted in endogenous linguistic and material cultures in order to enhance the unlocking of local creative capabilities and potentials for innovation.[147]

Relatedly, Chinweizu noted that:

> [D]ecolonisation does not mean ignorance of foreign traditions; it simply means denial of authority and withdrawal of allegiance to them. Foreign traditions are part of the harvest of human experience. One should certainly know about them, if only because one must know one's environment . . . One should certainly use items from other traditions provided they are consistent with African cultural independence and serve African objectives.[148]

In the same vein, Nkrumah asserted that

---

[139] Ibid; Chinweizu (2011), p. 83; Ani (2019), pp. 145–147; Ochonu (2015); Oluwole (2009), p. 114; Jackson et al. (2017); Levitt (2015); Fagbayibo (2021).

[140] Ayittey (2010), p. 100.

[141] Diop (1987), pp. 33–35.

[142] Ochonu (2015).

[143] Jackson et al. (2017).

[144] Gathii (2012), p. 418.

[145] Ibid.

[146] Shivji (2009), p. 7. See also, Adesina (2004).

[147] Ndhlovu (2017) p. 106.

[148] Chinweizu (1987), pp. 6–7.

> when we study philosophy which is not ours, we must see in the context of the intellectual history to which it belongs, and we must see it in the context of the milieu in which it was born. That way, we can use it in the furtherance of cultural development and in the strengthening of our human society.[149]

Although numerous transnational documents and norms have emphasised the need to recognise and consider African traditional values and principles in the implementation of strategies, there exist no serious measures for achieving this. For example, under Aspiration 5 of AU Agenda 2063, it is stipulated that African cultural heritage will be at the centre of strategies aimed at facilitating Pan-African approaches.[150] The practicalities of achieving this task are missing from the implementation documents of Agenda 2063 and other transnational development blueprints. What remains prioritised is the uncritical adoption of Eurocentric and neoliberal strategies that seek the integration of African economies into global markets.

2.5 Conclusion

This chapter has engaged in a conceptual discourse of the idea of continental supranationalism. Through this discussion, the chapter was able to highlight the different ideational prisms that have shaped the way in which scholars and politicians have interpreted the meaning of continental supranationalism. While there has been some measure of agreement on the need to have a structure that is able to exercise its autonomy and powers over constituent African states, opinions have differed on the nature, pace and context of such entity. Despite this, the concomitant actions for properly situating these perspectives and translating them into a meaningful and transformative continental integration project remains missing. As Udombana aptly surmised:

> African leaders lack the certitude to face the challenges of integration. Integration requires that each constituent party have clearly defined national plans and strategies to achieve economic development. Like a child in a toyshop, most leaders in Africa do not know which way to look. They have been unable to make the changes that will sustain growth and development. Others are not prepared to subordinate immediate national plans to long-term economic regional goals or to cede essential elements of sovereignty to regional institutions.[151]

---

[149] Nkrumah (2001), p. 55. Similarly, Cesaire observed that "whatever its own particular genius may be, a civilization that withdraws atrophies; that for civilizations, exchange is oxygen". Cesaire (2000), p. 33.

[150] AU (2015), p. 8. This position reinforces Art. 3(f) of the Charter for African Cultural Renaissance, which enjoins "cultural cooperation among Member States with a view to the strengthening of African unity, through the use of African languages and the promotion of inter-cultural dialogue".

[151] Udombana (2002), p. 202.

The default intergovernmental mode of continental institutions has always jostled with the supranational aspirations captured in normative and policy instruments, with little political intent to frontally address the gaps. It is not necessarily a bad thing that there exists no consensus on the path continental regionalism should follow, what remains a big concern is the missing ideational purpose. The imperative of grasping the complexities and nuances of currents that drive the theories and praxes of continental regionalism in Africa cannot be overstated. To borrow one of Chinua Achebe's famous aphorisms, it allows us to understand "where the rain began to beat us", and then be able chart a realisable way forward.

References

Acharya A (2012) Comparative regionalism: a field whose time has come? Int Spect 47(1):3–15

Adesina J (2004) NEPAD and the challenges of Africa's development: towards the political economy of a discourse. Soc Transit 35(1):125–144

African Union (2001) New Partnership for Africa's Development (NEPAD). http://www.dirco.gov.za/au.nepad/nepad.pdf. Accessed 4 Oct 2021

African Union (2013) African Union Agenda 2063: A shared strategic framework for inclusive growth and sustainable development: Background note. https://www.au.int/web/sites/default/files/newsevents/workingdocuments/29732-wd-27_08_agenda_2063_background_note_en_0.pdf. Accessed 4 Oct 2021

African Union (2015) Agenda 2063: The Africa we want. https://au.int/sites/default/files/documents/36204-doc-agenda2063_popular_version_en.pdf. Accessed 4 Oct 2021

African Union (2016a) Frequently asked questions about financing the Union. https://au.int/sites/default/files/pages/31953-file-faq.pdf. Accessed 4 Oct 2021

African Union (2016b, May 18) Haiti will not be admitted as African Union Member State at next Summit in Kigali, Rwanda. https://au.int/en/pressreleases/20160518-0. Accessed 4 Oct 2021

African Union (2018, March 21) AU member countries create history by massively signing the AfCFTA agreement in Kigali. https://au.int/en/pressreleases/20180321/au-member-countries-create-history-massively-signing-afcfta-agreement-kigali. Accessed 4 Oct 2021

African Union & United Nations Economic Commission for Africa (2008) Assessing regional integration in Africa III: Towards monetary and financial integration in Africa. https://repository.uneca.org/bitstream/handle/10855/15035/58271.pdf?sequence=1&isAllowed=y. Accessed 4 Oct 2021

Agyemen O (1990) Pan Africanist- federalism. https://msuweb.montclair.edu/~lebelp/CERAFRM035Agyeman1991.pdf. Accessed 4 Oct 2021

Ajala A (1973) Pan Africanism: evolution, progress and prospects. St. Martin Press, London

Akinyemi B (2008) Ghana: Kwame Nkrumah and pan-Africanism. https://allafrica.com/stories/200810150524.html. Accessed 4 Oct 2021

Akonnor K (2007) Stuffing old wine in new bottles: the case of the African Union. In: Mazama A (ed) Africa in the 21st Century: toward a new future. Routledge, London, pp 191–210

Ani A (2019) Three schools of thought on 'African solutions to African problems'. J Black Stud 50(2):135–155

Asante S (1997) Regionalism and Africa's development. Macmillan, London

Asiwaju A (1985a) Partitioned cultural areas: A checklist. In: Asiwaju A (ed) Partitioned Africans: ethnic relations across Africa's international boundaries 1884-1984. University of Lagos Press, Lagos, pp 252–259

Asiwaju A (1985b) The conceptual framework. In: Asiwaju A (ed) Partitioned Africans: ethnic relations across Africa's international boundaries 1884-1984. University of Lagos Press, Lagos, pp 1–18
Asiwaju A (1985c) The global perspective and border management policy option. In: Asiwaju A (ed) Partitioned Africans: ethnic relations across Africa's international boundaries 1884-1984. University of Lagos Press, Lagos, pp 233–251
Ayittey G (2010) The United States of Africa: A revisit. Ann Am Acad Polit Soc Sci 632(1):86–102
Ayittey G (2016) Disband the African Union. https://foreignpolicy.com/2016/07/10/disband-the-african-union/. Accessed 4 Oct 2021
Azikiwe N (1962) The future of pan-Africanism. https://www.blackpast.org/global-african-history/1962-nnamdi-azikiwe-future-pan-africanism/. Accessed 4 Oct 2021
Babarinde O (2007) The EU as a model for the African Union: The limits of imitation. Paper presented at The European Union, fifty years after the treaty of Rome conference, University of Miami, March 26. http://aei.pitt.edu/8185/1/BabarindeEUasModellong07edi.pdf. Accessed 4 Oct 2021
Bach D (2017) Regionalism in Africa: genealogies, institutions and trans-state networks. Routledge, London
BBC (2009) Ghaddafi wants Caribbean in Africa. http://news.bbc.co.uk/2/hi/africa/7883178.stm. Accessed 4 Oct 2021
Bijsmans P (2020) Euroskepticism, a multifaceted phenomenon. The Oxford Research Encyclopedia of Politics. https://oxfordre.com/politics/view/10.1093/acrefore/9780190228637.001.0001/acrefore-9780190228637-e-1062#acrefore-9780190228637-e-1062-div1-2. Accessed 4 Oct 2021
Brownlie I (1979) African boundaries: a legal and diplomatic encyclopaedia. University of California Press, Berkeley
Burgess M (1996) Federalism and building the European Union. Publius 26:1–15
Cesaire A (2000) Discourse on colonialism, translated by J. Pinkham. Monthly Review Press, New York
Chabal P (2009) Africa: the politics of suffering and smiling. Zed Books, London
Charter for African Cultural Renaissance (2006). https://au.int/en/treaties/charter-african-cultural-renaissance. Accessed 4 Oct 2021
Chinweizu. (1987) Decolonising the African mind. Pero Press, Lagos, p 1987
Chinweizu. (2011) Pan Africanism: rethinking key issues. In: Bankie F, Zimunya V (eds) Sustaining the new wave of Pan Africanism. National Youth Council of Namibia, Windhoek, pp 62–95
Commission v. Council. (Case 22/70) [1971] ECR 263 https://eur-lex.europa.eu/legal-content/EN/TXT/PDF/?uri=ecli:ECLI%3AEU%3AC%3A1971%3A32 Accessed 04 October 2021.
Constitutive Act of the African Union (2000). https://au.int/sites/default/files/pages/34873-file-constitutiveact_en.pdf. Accessed 4 Oct 2021
Dashwood A (1998) States in the European Union. Eur Law Rev 23:201–216
Dashwood A, Wyatt D, Arnull A, Ross M (2000) European Union law. Sweet & Maxwell, London
De Witt B (1999) Direct effect, supremacy, and the nature of the legal order. In: Craig P, De Burca G (eds) The evolution of EU law. Oxford University Press, Oxford, pp 187–227
Diop C (1987) Black Africa: the economic basis for a federated state. Lawrence Hill Books & Africa World Press, Chicago IL & Trenton NJ
Draper P (2012) Breaking free from Europe: why Africa needs another model of regional integration. Int Spect 47(1):67–82
East African Community (n.d.) History of the EAC. https://www.eac.int/eac-history. Accessed 4 Oct 2021
Englebert P, Hummel R (2005) Let's stick together: understanding Africa's secessionist deficit. Afr Aff:399–427
Fagbayibo B (2021) Studying the past in present tense: international law in the Benin empire. Politikon 48(3):468–485

Fingland L, Bailey S (2008) The EU's stability and growth pact: its credibility and sustainability. Public Money Manage 28(4):223–230

Garvey M (1924) Hail! United States of Africa. http://marcusgarvey.com/?p=199. Accessed 4 Oct 2021

Gathii J (2012) Africa. In: Fassbender B, Peters A (eds) The Oxford handbook of the history of international law. Oxford University Press, Oxford, pp 407–428

Ghaddafi M (2007, June 5) Address by the leader of the revolution at the opening session of the north African popular activists' forum in Tripoli, Libya

Hansen P, Jonsson S (2018) Eurafrica: History of European integration, "compromise" of decolonization. https://www.europenowjournal.org/2018/02/28/eurafrica-history-of-european-integration-compromise-of-decolonization/. Accessed 4 Oct 2021

Haas E (1958) The uniting of Europe: political, social and economic forces 1950–1957. Stanford University Press, Stanford

Hay P (1966) Federalism and supranational organisation: patterns of new legal structure. University of Illinois Press, Urbana

Heisenberg H, Richmond A (2002) Supranational institution-building in the European Union: a comparison of the European Court of Justice and European Central Bank. Eur Public Policy 9(2):201–218

Hettne B, Soderbaum F (2000) Theorising the rise of regionness. New Polit Econ 5(3):457–473

Horchschild A (2012) King Leopold's ghost: a story of greed, terror and heroism in colonial Africa. Pan Books, Oxford

Jackson K, Potts D, Bah E (2017) West Africa: Empirehood and colonialism offer lessons in integration. https://theconversation.com/west-africa-empirehood-and-colonialism-offer-lessons-in-integration-87470. Accessed 4 Oct 2021

Legum C (1962) Pan Africanism: a short political guide. Pall Mall Press, London

Lenaerts K, Van Nuffel P (2004) Constitutional law of the European Union. Sweet & Maxwell, London

Levitt J (2015) African origins of international law: myth or reality? UCLA J Int Law Foreign Aff 19:113–165

Libmann A (2019) Learning from the European Union? Eurasian regionalism and the "global script"'. Outlines Glob Transfor Polit Econ Law 12(2):247–268

Matthijs M, Kelemen R (2015) Europe reborn: how to save the European Union from irrelevance. Foreign Aff 94(1):96–102

Mazrui A (1963) On the concept of "We are all Africans". Am Polit Sci Rev 57(1):88–97

Mazrui A (1974) World culture and the black experience. University of Washington Press, Seattle

Mazrui A (2002) Who are Africans: identity in search of unity. In: Falola T, Laremont R, Seghatolislami T (eds) African redefined: collected essays of Ali. A. Mazrui, Vol 1. Africa World Press Incorporated, New Jersey, pp 37–42

Mazrui A (2005) The re-invention of Africa: Edward Said, V.Y. Mudimbe and beyond. Res Afr Liter 36(3):68–82

Mitrany D (1966) A working peace system. Quadrangle Books, Chicago

Mitrany D (1975) The functional theory of politics. St. Martin's Press, New York

Moravcsik A (1993) Preferences and power in the European Community: A liberal intergovernmentalist approach. J Common Mark Stud 31(4):473–524

Murithi T (2005) The African Union: Pan-Africanism, peace-building and development. Ashgate, Hampshire, England

Mwakikagile G (2002) Nyerere and Africa: end of an era. Protea Publishing, Las Vegas

Ndhlovu F (2017) Southern development discourse for Southern Africa: linguistic and cultural imperatives. J Multicult Discour 12(2):89–109

Needham A, Aidoo A (1995) An interview with Ama Ata Aidoo. Massachusetts Rev 36(1): 123–133

Nkrumah K (1963) Africa must unite. Praeger, New York

Nkrumah K (1965) Neo-colonialism: the last stage of imperialism. International Publishers, New York

Nkrumah K (2001) Consciencism: philosophy and ideology for decolonization. PANAF, London

Nweke G (1987) The organisation of African Unity and intra-African functionalism. Ann Am Acad Polit Soc Sci 489(1):133–147

Nyerere J (1963) A United States of Africa. J Mod Afr Stud 1(1):1–6

Nyerere J (1966) Freedom and unity uhuru na umoja: a selection from writings and speeches 1952-1965. Oxford University Press, Oxford

O'Neill M (1996) The politics of European integration. Routledge, London

Ochonu M (2015) The Wangara Trading Network in precolonial West Africa: an early example of Africans investing in Africa. In: McNamee T, Pearson M, Boer W (eds) Africans investing in Africa: understanding business and trade, sector by sector. Palgrave Macmillan, London, pp 9–27

Oluwole S (2009) Socrates and Orunmila: two patron saints of classical philosophy. Ark Publishers, Lagos

Organisation of African Unity Charter (1963). https://au.int/sites/default/files/treaties/7759-file-oau_charter_1963.pdf. Accessed 4 Oct 2021

Oyebode A (2003) International law and politics: an African perspective. Bolabay Publications, Lagos

Pescatore P (1974) The law of integration. Sijthoff, Leiden

Reuters (2010) African Union to consider "land for Haitians" plan. http://www.reuters.com/article/idUSTRE60U0IV20100131. Accessed 4 Oct 2021

Rosamond B (2000) Theories of European integration. McMillan, London

Sangmpam S (2018) Why the African Union should be dismantled and buried with Gaddafi. Afr Dev XLIII(3):53–82

Schermers H, Blokker N (1995) International institutional law: unity within diversity. Martinus Nijhoff, The Hague

Shivji, I. (2007). The essential building blocks of the pan-African vision. https://www.pambazuka.org/pan-africanism/essential-building-blocks-pan-african-vision. Accessed 4 Oct 2021

Shivji I (2009) Pan-Africanism and the challenge of East African integration. http://repository.eac.int/bitstream/handle/11671/319/Pan%20Africanism%20and%20the%20Challenge%20of%20EAC%20Integration.pdf?sequence=1. Accessed 4 Oct 2021

Silva K (2017) Beyond the border between the North and the South: towards a decolonization of epistemologies and fields of research on Mercosur. Revista de Direito Internacional Brasilia 14(2):413–429

Soyinka W (1985) The African world and the ethnocultural debate. In: Asante M, Asante K (eds) African culture: the rhythms of unity. Greenword Press, Westport, pp 13–38

Taylor I (2003) Globalization and regionalization: reactions to attempts at neo-liberal regionalism. Rev Afr Polit Econ 10(2):310–330

Thompson V (1969) Africa and unity: The evolution of pan-Africanism. Longman, London

Tieku T (2017) Governing Africa: 3D analysis of the African Union's performance. Littlefield, Rowman and New York and London

Treaty Establishing the African Economic Community Treaty (1991). https://au.int/en/treaties/treaty-establishing-african-economic-community. Accessed 4 Oct 2021

Udombana J (2002) A harmony or a cacophony? The music of integration in the African Union treaty and the New Partnership for Africa's Development. Indiana Int Comp Law Rev 13(1): 185–236

Wa Thiong'o, N. (2009) Something torn and new: an African renaissance. BasicCivitas Books, New York

Weiler J (1981) The community system: the dual character of supranationalism. Yearb Eur Law 1(1):267–306

Weiler J (1999) The constitution of Europe: do the new clothes have an emperor? And other essays on European integration. Cambridge University Press, Cambridge

Chapter 3
The African Union

Navigating the Intergovernmental/Supranational Terrain

3.1 Introduction

Unlike its predecessor, the Organisation of the African Unity (OAU), the African Union (AU) was designed as a vehicle for the attainment of closer continental integration. The institutional architecture of the AU coupled with its ambitious developmental strategies evinces a determination to transcend the realms of national politics. It also represents an attempt to place Africa in the mainstream of global *realpolitik.* The keen negotiations leading to the establishment of the organisation, including the moves by the founders to change the discourse on how Africa should handle its own affairs and engage with external parties indicated the willingness to change course. In addition, it pushed to the fore the discourse on how to move from intergovernmental cooperation to continental supranational regionalism in Africa. In his assessment of the AU after its 10 years of existence, the former South African president, Thabo Mbeki echoed this sentiment by highlighting the organisation's mandate of ensuring that the mission of continental unity and development must no longer be deferred.[1]

At the launch of the AU in 2002 in Durban, South Africa, Mbeki had expressly designated the AU Constitutive Act as "the supreme law of the continent" because of its express approval by the entire national parliaments across the continent.[2] Such designation evokes two fundamental points. One is what international lawyers refer to as the "internationalisation of constitutional law" or "constitutionalisation of international law".[3] Although these two concepts have different meanings, they both have similar results. While the former denotes the emergence of international parallel constitutions due to transfer of functions to regional institutions, the latter

[1] Mbeki (2012), p. 24.

[2] Mbeki (2002).

[3] Cottier and Hertig (2003), pp. 269–270.

B. Fagbayibo, *Transcending Member States*,
https://doi.org/10.1007/978-3-031-12451-8_3

explains the transformation of treaties into domestic-like constitutions.[4] These concepts jointly highlight the growing influence of international organisations and the possibility (or existence) of an overarching framework by which domestic constitutions should be measured.[5] The second relates to the practicalities of transnational norms in achieving express and/or implied goals. In the context of the AU, this continues to raise questions such as whether the AU Constitutive Act can be an instrumental tool for achieving supranationalism, the contextual assessment of the AU as either an intergovernmental or supranational entity, and the kind of reforms needed for enhancing the powers of the AU. These issues are at the heart of ongoing governmental and non-governmental efforts and initiatives aimed at sharpening the role of the AU. In addressing this, the chapter begins with a narrative of the circumstances surrounding the creation of the AU. It is then followed by a discussion of the AU Constitutive Act. It concludes with an assessment of AU's supranational status.

3.2 The Establishment of the AU

The continued inability of the OAU to respond to intra-African conflicts, curtail the deluge of gross human rights violations and address contemporary challenges facing the continent prompted the need for a radical revamp of the organisation.[6] More importantly, the view was held that the organisation had completed its primary functions namely eradicating colonialism, ending *Apartheid* and establishing the independence of African states.[7] The journey towards the creation of the AU started at the 35th ordinary session of the OAU Assembly held in Algiers, where the late Libyan leader, Muammar Ghadaffi, proposed to convene an extra-ordinary summit to be held in Sirte, Libya in September 1999. Touray, however, noted that while Ghaddafi may have appeared to be the most vociferous advocate of reforming the OAU at that time, other reform ideas, largely championed by Thabo Mbeki (South Africa) and Olusegun Obasanjo (Nigeria), were already in motion and slated for debate at the Algiers summit.[8] Several reasons have been advanced for Ghadaffi's leading role in the quest for African unity. One of the major reasons include Ghadaffi's tactical shift to Sub-Sahara African affairs after his abortive

---

[4] Ibid, pp. 270–271.

[5] See e.g. Werner (2007), pp. 19–22.

[6] According to Jeng (2012, pp. 128–134), the OAU's institutional (lack of institutional mechanism to enforce and compel member states to act accordingly) and normative weaknesses (the principle of non-interference in member states' affairs) to confront the spate of armed conflicts across the continent attracted the most condemnation.

[7] Packer and Rukare (2002), p. 366.

[8] Touray (2016), pp. 38–39.

attempt at establishing an Arab union.[9] Others point to Ghadaffi's gratitude to Africa for the OAU's collective support throughout Libya's dispute with the United States of America and the United Kingdom over the Lockerbie affair.[10]

At the Sirte summit, Libya circulated a draft document titled a "draft Sirte Declaration" for consideration.[11] The draft Treaty called for the establishment of an "African Union" with organs such as the African Congress; the Summit Council; the Executive Council; the General Secretariat; the Specialised Executive Committees; the Supreme African Court; and the African Monetary Fund.[12] However, the OAU General Secretariat had prepared a draft treaty which was totally different from the Libyan document.[13]

A ministerial group was tasked with preparing a compromise document.[14] Following an extensive discussion and debate among the heads of state, the Sirte Declaration was adopted. The preamble reads:

> Having discussed frankly and extensively on how to proceed with the strengthening of the unity of our continent and its peoples...we decided to establish an African Union, in conformity with the ultimate objectives of the Charter of our continental Organisation and the provisions of the Treaty establishing the African Economic Treaty.[15]

Furthermore, the Sirte Declaration provided timelines relating to the adoption of the Constitutive Act (June 2000), completion of the ratification process (December 2000), formal launch of the AU (January 2001), and the establishment of the Pan-African Parliament (by 2000).[16] Since this declaration did not specify the form or shape the new AU was to take, it was left to a team of legal experts to decide on the following questions: whether the new organisation should exist alongside the OAU and the African Economic Community (AEC); if the new organisation could be merged with the OAU and the AEC; the replacement of the OAU while keeping the AEC intact; or whether the institutional architecture of the new organisation should be modelled on the EU.[17] With regard to the relationship between the OAU and the new organisation, three views emerged: that the AU should be a strong institution that should transcend the existing institutional framework; that the proposed AU should be a part of the continental organisations in which the OAU provides the framework and the AEC and the union become pillars;

---

[9] See generally, Hugo (2007). At the Sirte Summit, Ghadaffi intoned, "I wasted over 30 years advocating for Arab unity in vain. I gave up and now I came to Africa. If you are going to similarly fail me, I would have no choice but to go to the Mediterranean!" Cited in Dagash (2006), p. 105.

[10] Huliaras (2001), pp. 10–13. See also Maluwa (2001), p. 9.

[11] Maluwa (2001), p. 17.

[12] Ibid.

[13] Ibid.

[14] Ibid.

[15] AU (1999), p. 3.

[16] Ibid, p. 4.

[17] Maluwa (2001), p. 20.

and the need to amend the OAU Charter with a view to establish a new institutional framework.[18]

After much deliberation and debate, the team of experts could not agree on the relationship between the OAU and the new organisation. A draft legal text establishing the AU was, however, adopted by the experts and later submitted to the Tripoli ministerial meeting, which was held between 31 May and 2 June 2000.[19] However, the ministerial meeting was able to settle the critical questions surrounding the nature and shape of the proposed organisation.[20] To resolve this impasse, an ad-hoc committee of 15 members, headed by the Malian Foreign Affairs minister, Modibo Sidibe, was set up to examine and submit a report on the draft legal text.[21] The committee then set up another sub-committee of three, composed of Libya, Mali and the Secretary General of the OAU, which then came up with the draft Constitutive Act.[22] It was concluded that the OAU would evolve into the AU.[23] The Constitutive Act was subsequently adopted by the Assembly on July 11, 2000. By March 2001, all the member states of the OAU had acceded to the Constitutive Act, and the organisation was formally launched in 2002.[24]

3.3 The AU Constitutive Act

In terms of the categorisation provided by Maluwa, the Constitutive Act (together with Treaty Establishing the African Economic Community, Protocol to the Treaty Establishing the African Economic Community relating to the Pan-African Parliament, Peace and Security Council Protocol, Protocol of the Court of Justice of the African Union, and the Statute of the African Union Commission on International

---

[18]Touray (2016), p. 41.

[19]Maluwa (2001), p. 20.

[20]Touray (2016) 42.

[21]Ibid.

[22]Ibid.

[23]Ibid.

[24]One could thus expand Kennes' thesis by stating that the creation of the AU is a continuation of the second wave of integration in Africa, as the first wave started in the 1960s through to the 1980s. Kennes (1999), p. 27. Also, Adebayo Adedeji classified African integration into five phases: The first phase, in the early twentieth century, was the historic struggle for Pan-Africanism led by African leaders and Africans in the Diaspora. In parallel, colonial administrators established colonial federation in west, central and eastern Africa; The 1960s represented a second phase, in which numerous intersectoral and multilateral organisations were set up mostly at sub-regional level; The third stage was the period between 1975 and 1983, during which a number of breakthroughs led to the establishment of sub-regional entities; The fourth stage was in the 1980s and 1990s during which notable documents such as the Lagos Plan of Action (LPA) and the Abuja Treaty were adopted; and the creation of the AU represents the fifth stage. UNECA (2002), p. 9.

Law) form the foundational legal instruments of the AU.[25] Other categories include Trade, economic and technical cooperation (Civil Aviation Constitution, Rehabilitation Institute Agreement; and Convention of the African Energy Commission); Privileges and immunities of the organisation (General Convention on the Privileges and Immunities of the OAU and Additional Protocol to the OAU General Convention on Privileges and Immunities); Human rights and refugee rights (OAU Convention Governing the Specific Aspects of Refugee Problems in Africa, African Charter on Human and Peoples' Rights, Protocol to the African Charter on Human and Peoples' Rights on the Establishment of an African Court on Human and Peoples' Rights, and Protocol to the African Charter on Human and Peoples' Rights relating to the Rights of Women in Africa); Environment (African Convention on the Conservation of Nature and Natural Resources and Bamako Convention on the Ban of the Import into Africa and the Control of Transboundary Movement and Management of Hazardous Wastes within Africa); international security and crime (OAU Convention for the Elimination of Mercenarism in Africa, African Nuclear-Weapon-Free Zone Treaty, OAU Convention on the Prevention and Combating of Terrorism, African Union Convention on Preventing and Combating Corruption and the African Union Non-Aggression and Common Defence Pact); and Culture (Cultural Charter for Africa and the African Youth Charter).[26] Amao added two more categories to these: soft laws (non-binding instruments such as the New Partnership for Africa's Development, African Peer Review Mechanism, and guidelines on elections, fundamental rights and culture) and judicial decisions (decisions of the African Commission on Human and Peoples' Rights and the African Court on Human and Peoples' Rights).[27] These, together with the institutions enumerated below, form legal order of the AU, and the source through which its powers, intergovernmental and/or supranational, are to be exercised.

As Olowu rightly observed, the Constitutive Act is "[a] mere roadmap to the required regional understanding for future continent-wide cooperation and integration in Africa".[28] Similarly, Udombana remarked that "the AU Treaty ... is not a global programme of action. It only defined a general framework that is aimed at taking up the challenges facing the continent".[29] In response to global realities, the Constitutive Act symbolises a necessary and ambitious plan to help solve continental problems and to fast track the process of integration. In this regard, it provides for

---

[25] Maluwa (2012), p. 20. In an assessment of how African states have contributed to the development of international law, Maluwa (2020, pp. 331–332) provided three categories of OAU/AU laws: norms that are original and distinct from existing international law norms (e.g. the AU Convention for the Assistance and Protection of Internally Displaced Persons 'Kampala Convention' 2009); norms established to supplement legal norms that already exist under international treaties (OAU Convention Governing the Specific Aspects of Refugee Problems in Africa, 1969); and norms adopted under the auspices of sub-regional organisations in Africa.

[26] Ibid, pp. 21–26.

[27] Amao (2019), pp. 37–42.

[28] Olowu (2003), p. 223. See also Maluwa (2003), p. 168.

[29] Udombana (2002), p. 218.

democratic ideals and institutions charged with steering Africa towards the "promised land" of continental integration.[30] In the same breadth, it builds on the socio-political realities on the continent by incorporating mechanisms aimed at preserving the hegemonic influence of autocratic regimes on the continent. It is this contradictory (perhaps balancing) act that continues to frustrate or limit the organisation from living up to its espoused ideals.

Here is an exposition of the content of the Constitutive Act. Articles 3 and 4 deal, respectively, with the objectives and principles, which mirror the objectives found in Article II of the OAU Charter except for the new added objectives which include—the promotion of good governance; the promotion and protection of human rights; the promotion of peace, security and stability on the continent; promotion of democratic principles and institutions; the promotion of sustainable development at the economic, social and cultural levels; the establishment of the necessary conditions for the continent to play its rightful role in the global economy and in international negotiations; and the coordination and harmonisation of policies between the various African RECs. All these objectives reflect the understanding and the need to tackle the contemporary challenges facing the continent.

Article 4(h) provides a caveat to the principle of non-interference by stipulating the right of the Union to intervene in Member States under the following conditions: war crimes, genocide and crime against humanity and, through a 2003 amendment that is yet to come into force, a serious threat to legitimate order. The inclusion of Article 4(h) is justified by the need to prevent a recurrence of the Rwandan genocide and a need to put a stop to the incessant conflicts ravaging the continent. During the negotiations of the AU Constitutive Act, Article 4(h) was one of the most contentious issues as some member states saw it as an avenue for interference in national affairs.[31] The AU is, however, yet to activate Article 4(h).[32] In terms of Article 4(j), member states have the right to request for intervention from the Union in order to restore peace and security. Intervention by the Union, however, requires a decision by the Union's Assembly of Heads of State and government.

In a marked departure from the OAU Charter, article 30 of the Constitutive Act provides for the prohibition from the participation in the activities of the organisation where the government of a member state has come to power through unconstitutional means. This provision, read together with the objectives to promote human rights, social justice, gender equality and good governance, once again buttress the idea that these elements are essential ingredients, not only for the development of the continent but also for a solid and viable integration process. It is pertinent that an organisation responsible for overseeing continental integration process is bestowed

[30]Maluwa (2003, p. 163) highlighted the absence of deep discussion and understanding among political elites on the meaning of "union". He further notes, "some leaders regard it as the panacea for all Africa's economic and political problems, while yet others still view it as the thin end of the wedge in a move towards the creation of a "United States of Africa"."

[31]Welz (2020), pp. 168–170.

[32]One reason is that this inaction stems from the lack of common understanding and adherence to stipulated shared norms. See e.g. Fagbayibo (2017), p. 166.

with adequate powers and resources indispensable for the discharge of its functions. Article 23(2) of the Constitutive Act also provides for the imposition of sanctions on member states which fail to comply with the decisions and policies of the AU. It further provides for the imposition of sanctions on members that defaults in the payments of its contribution. At the extraordinary summit of the AU Assembly in November 2018, a decision was made to apply more stringent sanction measures against defaulting member states.[33] The categories of sanctions include cautionary (which applies to member states that have not paid 50% of their assessed dues in six months and deprives such member states the right to contribute to AU meetings), intermediate (which applies to member states in arrears for one year and suspends the member states from nominating their nationals for appointment or participation in AU activities and employment), and comprehensive (which applies to member states that have defaulted payments for two years and are liable for a combination of cautionary and intermediary sanctions plus suspension from participating in AU meetings).[34] On the 16th of June 2020, the AU applied the comprehensive sanction against South Sudan for the failure to pay over three years of its membership dues.[35]

The Constitutive Act builds on the socio-political realities of the continent by putting in place measures aimed at preserving the *status quo* either through maintaining colonial boundaries or the protection of African leaders. Article 4 (b) reasserted the *uti possidetis* principle by stating the respect of borders existing on the achievement of independence. Article 4 re-affirms four of the seven principles stipulated in Article III of the OAU Charter. They are—sovereign equality; non-interference in the internal affairs of member states; peaceful settlement of disputes; and the condemnation of political assassination and subversive activities. The 2003 amendment to article 4(h), which provides for intervention in order to prevent serious threat to serious legitimate order, should be understood as a measure of protecting and preserving all regimes, regardless of their nature. This reasoning stems from two positions. Firstly, the AU Constitutive Act did not define the term "legitimate order". Secondly, the premature ratification of questionable election results, without any serious investigation into the substance of the process, points to a tacit acknowledgment of the weak institutionalisation of democracy in Africa. This also applies to the principles of non-interference and condemnation of subversive activities. As benevolent as these provisions appear, the fact remains that the political leadership in some African countries lack legitimacy. To guarantee the preservation of such regimes, without addressing the question of legitimacy, smacks of contradiction and an avenue for inaction.

Article 5 spells out the internal institutional architecture of the African Union. It is composed of the Assembly of the Union; the Executive Council; the Pan-African

[33] AU (2018).

[34] Ibid. According to Mattheis and Staeger (2020), as at October 2020, 14 countries have been sanctioned under cautionary sanction, two countries under intermediate sanctions, and two countries under comprehensive sanctions.

[35] Shaban (2020).

Parliament; the Court of Justice; the Commission; the Permanent Representative Committee; the Specialised Technical Committees; the Economic, Social and Cultural Council; and the financial institutions (consisting of the African Central Bank, the African Monetary Fund and the African Investment Bank). Other notable bodies which are not listed here include the Peace and Security Council (PSC), the African Union Development Agency—New Partnership for Africa's Development (AUDA-NEPAD) (formerly NEPAD), the African Peer Review Mechanism (APRM), the African Continental Free Trade Area (AfCFTA) secretariat, the African Commission on Human and Peoples' Rights (AfCHPR), the Africa Centres for Disease Control and Prevention (Africa CDC) and the African Capacity Building Foundation (ACBF).

The Assembly of the Union is the supreme governing body of the Union. It is composed of 55 heads of state and government. The Assembly meets once a year in an ordinary session with the possibility of extraordinary sessions called by a two-thirds majority. Decision and resolutions are by two-thirds majority while questions of procedure require only a simple majority. The functions of the Assembly include the determination of common policies, take decisions on reports and recommendations of other organs of the AU, consider requests for membership, establish any organ of the AU, monitor the implementation and ensure compliance by member states, and adopt the budget of the AU.[36] The Assembly can also delegate its powers and functions to any organ of the AU.[37]

The Executive Council is made up of ministers designated by the member states (mainly ministers of foreign affairs). It meets twice in a year with the possibility of extraordinary sessions. It coordinates and takes decisions on common policies such as foreign trade, transport, agriculture, social security, immigration, environmental protection, and communication.[38] The Executive Council can delegate any of its functions to the Specialised Technical Committees (STCs).[39]

The Pan-African Parliament is the legislative body of the African Union. It presently has advisory and consultative powers which will last for the first 5 years of its existence—it was inaugurated in March 2004—after which it will start exercising full legislative powers. Member states have refused to grant it full legislative powers. Rather, the 2001 protocol has been amended to merely grant it the right to "propose draft model laws".[40] The parliament is composed of representatives elected by the national legislature of AU member states rather than being directly elected in their own capacity. Article 5(3) of the amended protocol envisages the possible adoption of a code that allows for the direct election of parliamentarians.

[36] Article 9(1) of the AU Constitutive Act.

[37] Ibid, Article 9(2).

[38] Ibid, Article 13(1).

[39] Ibid, Article 13(2).

[40] Article 8(1) of the Protocol to the Constitutive Act of the African Union relating to the Pan-African Parliament (2014).

The Court of Justice is to be merged with the African Court on Human and Peoples' Rights and will be known as the African Court of Justice and Human Rights (ACJ&HR). It will be made up of two sections: a General Affairs Section composed of eight judges and a Human Rights Section composed of eight judges.[41] The Court shall be responsible for the interpretation and application of the AU Constitutive Act, any questions on international law, other Union treaties and all subsidiary legal instruments adopted by the AU and the OAU.[42] While the Human Rights section is already operational (in the form of the African Court of Human and Peoples' Rights [AfCtHPR]), the General Affairs section of the court is yet to come into existence due to the lack of the requisite 15 ratifications. The AU has, however, gone ahead to further amend the unratified protocol by adding a third section: the International Criminal Law section, which excludes heads of state or government or other senior government officials from prosecution for acts of genocide, war crimes, and crimes against humanity.[43]

The AU Commission functions as the executive arm and the bureaucracy of the AU. It implements AU policies. The Commission is headed by a Chairperson, deputy Chairperson and eight commissioners dealing with different policy areas. This includes peace and security, political affairs, infrastructure and energy, social affairs, trade and industry, rural economy and agriculture, economic affairs, and human resources, science and technology. As part of the AU reforms (which is discussed in Chap. 4), the number of commissioners has been reduced from eight to six. The new portfolios are: Agriculture, Rural Development, Blue Economy and Sustainable Environment (ARBE); Economic Development, Trade, Industry and Mining (ETIM); Education, Science, Technology and Innovation (ESTI); Infrastructure and Energy; Political Affairs, Peace and Security (PAPS); Health, Humanitarian Affairs & Social Development (HHS). The AU Commission has the following policy initiation and implementation functions: Represent the Union and defend its interests under the guidance of and as mandated by the Assembly and the Executive Council; Initiate proposals for consideration by other organs; Coordinate and monitor the implementation of decisions taken by organs; Organise and manage the meetings of the Union; Act as the custodian of the Constitutive Act, its protocols, the treaties, legal instruments, decisions adopted by the Union and those inherited from the OAU; Assist member states in the implementation of Union programmes and policies; Prepare the Union's programme and budget for approval by the policy organs; Prepare strategic plans and studies for the consideration of the Executive

[41] Article 16 of the Protocol on the Statute of the African Court of Justice and Human Rights (2008).

[42] Ibid, Article 28. The AfCtHPR noted in the *Mtingwi case* that it does not have jurisdiction to hear appeals from national courts. See Application 001/2013, paras. 14–16. However, in the *Thomas* case, the court averred that the lack of appellate jurisdiction "does not preclude the Court from examining whether the procedure before national courts are consistent with the international standards established by the Charter or other applicable human rights instruments". See Application 005/2013, para. 130.

[43] Protocol on Amendments to the Protocol on the Statute of the African Court of Justice and Human Rights (2014).

Council; Promote integration and socio-economic development; and Strengthen cooperation and coordination of activities between member states in fields of common interests.[44]

The Permanent Representatives Committee (PRC) consists of nominated permanent representatives of member states. It serves as the secretariat of the Executive Council by preparing the work of the Executive Council.[45]

The Specialised Technical Committee (STCs) prepares the background work on common policy projects falling within their competence. These include rural economy and agriculture, science and technology, energy, education, environment, health, transport, trade and natural resources.[46] The STCs is composed of ministers or senior officials responsible for areas falling within their competence.[47]

The Economic, Social and Cultural Council (ECOSOCC) is an advisory organ composed of Civil Society Organisations (CSOs) on the continent. It is aimed at ensuring the participation of the peoples of Africa in the AU process. Furthermore, the Constitutive Act makes provision for three financial institutions: the African Central Bank, the African Monetary Fund and the African Investment Bank. Like the ACJ&HR, these institutions are yet to become operational.

3.4 How Supranational Is the AU?

As indicated in the previous chapter, supranationalism entails the existence of an organisation that operates above the framework of nation states. While international relations is essentially state-centric, the concept of supranationalism seeks to craft the ideology of resolving common and related problems through neutral and technocratic institutions. The corollary of this is the existence of an insulated decision-making body which takes binding decisions and responsible for the supervision and implementation of such decisions. Considering the primacy of nation states in global *realpolitik*, the architecture of supranationalism includes states as privileged players in the integration process.[48]

At the heart of the assessment of the supranational status of the AU are two narratives. The first speaks to the Eurocentric worldview of regionalism, and how it continues to shape the theories and praxis of assessment. As shown in Chap. 2, the theoretical discourse of supranationalism is tied to post-second World War political development in Europe, and how this underlined the establishment of transnational institutions in Europe. As many regional institutions in Africa, Latin America and Asia have adopted the institutional and procedural format, mainly in form but not

[44] Art. 3(2) Statutes of the Commission of the African Union.

[45] Art. 21 of the AU Constitutive Act.

[46] Ibid, Art 14(1).

[47] Ibid, Art. 14(3).

[48] Weiler (1999), p. 273.

necessarily in substance, of the EU, this narrative thus suggests that the assessment of their development should mirror a Eurocentric neo-liberal perspective of regionalism.[49] The second is the narrative that emphasises context. As Dirar noted,

> classical theories of integration seem to lack the capacity to fully explicate African integration schemes, either due to lack of empirical data in the African context or due to the fact that they were developed in relation to integration schemes of developed north.[50]

Similarly, Agyeman argued that the homogeneity of institutional and industrial development is a key feature of European integrative arrangement, a factor that is absent in the African situation.[51] As shown in the previous chapter, the notion of context also encompasses the idea of developing and measuring African integration schemes against Afrocentric values and norms. The emphasis on context thus paves the way for two possible kinds of assessment. The first is an assessment solely based on traditional pan-African mechanics, completely excluding any traces of Eurocentric conceptual tools. This approach is what Taiwo referred to as "occident anxiety":

> Occident anxiety is what leads us always to think that if we cannot show that it is "homegrown", it cannot be authentic – as if being authentic is a synonym for being right or effective. African intellectuals think that authenticity must mean defining themselves against the West. Whatever it is they take the West to be, Africa must be the opposite or, minimally, unlike it.[52]

As such, the problem with this kind of assessment is that it ignores the confluence of thoughts and the possibility of learning and adapting ideas for optimal and beneficial solutions.

The second, which is a more pragmatic and feasible path, suggests the imperative of strategic adaptation of assessment tools. In other words, while the intellectual contributions and usefulness of the European basis of regional integration are acknowledged, it seeks to expand the focus of assessment by centring pan-African realities. For example, Tieku noted that a contextual assessment of AU's supranational drive should consider the critical role of non-governmental actors in influencing decisions through consultancy services, advocacy and access to decision-makers.[53] In addition, the role of AU technocrats as active political players rather than mere international bureaucrats should also be factored into the assessment.[54] Similar to Tieku's proposition, it has also been suggested that factors such as the level of participation of Africans in the integration process through civil society, teaching of integration in African schools, and an intensive skills development programme for regionalism should form part of the assessment.[55] Gathii noted that

---

[49] Dirar (2014), p. 157. See also Silva (2017), p. 414. Fagbayibo (2013), p. 70.

[50] Dirar (2014), p. 157.

[51] Agyemen (1990), p. 8.

[52] Taiwo (2019).

[53] Tieku (2017), p. 228.

[54] Ibid.

[55] Fagbayibo (2013), pp. 65–68.

a better way of understanding regional integration arrangements, particularly regional trade agreements, in Africa is through the prism of flexibility.[56] He argued that African governments prefer "flexible regimes of cooperation as opposed to containing rules requiring scrupulous and rigorous adherence".[57] Furthermore, Schoeman propositioned that the assessment of regionalism in Africa should go beyond the quantity-oriented (increased volume of intra-community trade) by focusing on the quality based (the quality of collective bargaining and common position in the international area) aspects of integration.[58]

Based on the foregoing, the next question is what should form the paradigms of assessing the supranational status of the AU? While it is important to engage in a broader and contextual assessment, it is equally important to test the AU against the stated objectives and processes. In other words, the necessary departure point should be the link between its institutional set-up and how this has translated (or should have translated) into the goal of exercising meaningful and binding powers over its member states. Through such assessment, not only will the shortcomings become more apparent, but it can also pave the way for forging a context-driven way forward. In this respect, three measurable assessment paradigms are necessary: *intention, action and outcomes.*

3.4.1 Intention

In terms of intention, it is important to explore how normative provisions and prescriptions support (or even detract) from the ambition of the AU to assert itself over member states. As explained above, the AU was created against the background of the realisation that the OAU was ineffectual in addressing continental problems and more importantly, continental integration. In addition, the reform process that has been embarked on since its establishment indicates the intention, even if this has not been matched by concomitant political will, to position the AU as a meaningful supranational entity. At the institutional level, the AU is a clear departure from the OAU era, as its institutions have been established to address specific challenges ranging from security, human rights, globalisation, socio-economic development, harmonisation of policies of member states and RECs, and political and democratic governance (see Table 3.1 above).

What the table above highlights is not so much the difference between intergovernmentalism and supranationalism as it is the potential of the AU to engage in more supranational activities than the OAU. The powers of the AU institutions to make decisions, assess compliance standards, and initiate policies on common

[56] Gathii (2009).

[57] Ibid, p. 573.

[58] Schoeman (2002), pp. 13–14.

Table 3.1 Comparative table of the OAU and the AU

Parameters	OAU	AU
Source of authority	The Assembly of Heads of State and Government exercised sole authority	The Assembly of Heads of State and Government remain the primary decision-making organ but other organs such as the African Court, PSC, PAP can exercise varying decision-making powers. Civil society is also allowed to play some role. Unlike the OAU, the AU has more institutions dealing with issues ranging from health, capacity-building, economic development, assessment of governance standards etc.
National sovereignty	Non-interference in the internal affairs of member states.	The principle of non- indifference: right to intervene in grave circumstances. There is also the power to suspend governments that have come to power through unconstitutional means. However, the AU Constitutive Act still stipulates the sanctity of colonial boundaries.
Objectives	Liberation of African countries from colonialism and the defence of national sovereignty. There was no intention of creating a supranational structure.	Enhance Africa's positioning in global *realpolitik;* adopt common position on global and regional issues; establish a continental FTA, customs union and common market; strengthen democratic principles in member states; gender equality.
Funding	Solely relied on member states for the funding of its programmes	Dependence on external sources such as the EU, China and IFIs for the funding of its programmes.
Secretariat	Headed by a secretary-general and Assistant secretary generals. The SG had no powers to take initiatives until the later years of the organisation. No attention was paid to gender equality in the composition of the top management of the secretariat.	The AU Commission is headed by a Chairperson, a deputy Chairperson and six Commissioners. The rule stipulates gender equality in the composition of the top management of the Commission. The Chairperson and the Commissioners have powers to initiate policies and programmes.

Source: Author's compilation from the following sources: AU (2004), pp. 23–24; AU website; Mattheis and Staeger (2020); Packer and Rukare (2002)

position, are all references to such potential. The next section assesses the extent to which the AU can be described as a supranational entity.

A closer look at the functions of these institutions reveals an intention on the part of the drafters of the Constitutive Act to confer some degree of powers that transcend mere interstate cooperation. For example, the AU Assembly has the powers to determine common policies, monitor implementation of these policies, ensure compliance by member states and impose sanctions on member states that fail to comply with these common policies.[59] Under Rule 33 of the Rules of Procedure of the AU Assembly, the decisions of the Assembly are categorised under three rubrics: Regulations; Directives; and Recommendations, Declarations, Resolutions and Opinions.[60] Regulations are applicable in member states and member states must implement them.[61] Directives are binding rules addressed to any or all member states, with member states having the flexibility to determine the mode of implementation.[62] Recommendations, declarations, resolutions and opinions are not binding, they are only intended to guide and harmonise the viewpoints of member states.[63] In addition to member states, regulations and directives are also binding on organs of the AU and RECs.[64] Regulations and Directives become enforceable 30 days after their publication in the official journal of the AU or as indicated in the decision.[65]

Another important element of intention is the Assembly's power of delegation under Article 9(2) of the Constitutive Act. The implication of this is that if the requisite political will exists, the Assembly is in a position to empower any of the AU organs or agencies to exercise assertive, binding powers over member states. This could be in terms of either expressed or implied provisions of the Constitutive Act and/or other normative instruments of the AU. The expansive coordinating functions assigned to the Executive Council is another indication of intention. These include issues ranging from foreign trade, immigration, energy, social security and transportation.[66] In furtherance of this mandate, the Executive Council is empowered to take a decision on the nomination of African candidates for positions in the international system.[67] The office of the Legal Counsel of the AU, in its legal opinion on Nigeria's substitution of its candidate for the secretary general of the World Trade Organisation (WTO) after a decision had been made by the Executive Council, stated that the decision of Executive Council in this regard is binding on member states.[68]

Similarly, the AU Commission's power to initiate and implement policies and norms speaks to the will of member states to grant the organisation some modicum of binding powers.[69] In addition, Article 3(l) of the AU Constitutive Act mandates the organisation to coordinate and harmonise the policies of the RECs as a key

[59] Articles 9 and 23(2) of the AU Constitutive Act.

[60] AU (2002).

[61] Ibid, Rule 33.

[62] Ibid.

[63] Ibid.

[64] Ibid, Rule 34(2).

[65] Ibid, Rule 34(1).

[66] Article 13(1) of the AU Constitutive Act.

[67] AU (2014).

[68] AU (2020a).

[69] Article 3(2) Statutes of the Commission of the African Union.

element of attaining the desired supranational goal. This mandate is in tandem with the envisaged vision of creating an African Economic Community.[70]

The jurisdictional powers of the proposed ACJ&HR over matters relating to the interpretation of the Constitutive Act, disputes between states, acts and functions of the organs of the AU, and human rights matters also speak to the intention of supranationalism.[71] Articles 46 (1) and (2) of the ACJ&HR Protocol further explicitly provides that the decision of the court is binding on both state and non-state actors.[72] Intention also exists in the kind of role the quasi-judicial African Commission of Human and Peoples' Rights (AfCHPR) plays in the promotion and protection of human rights in Africa. In terms of its protective powers, the Commission receives and adjudicates on communications and complaints from states and non-state actors.[73] The binding nature of the decision of the Commission has been a source of debate over the years. Although the Commission has in some cases indicated the binding nature of its decisions,[74] this position has been criticised by some authors.[75] However, it has been argued that the subsequent approval of the finalised communications of the Commission by the AU Assembly, under article 59 of the Charter, is a key indication of the intention of its binding nature.[76]

The inclusion of article 4(h) in the Constitutive Act of the AU, with the parallel conception of the African Peace and Security Architecture (APSA), provided the impetus for viewing intervention through a supranational paradigm. The normative authority of the AU to make binding rules and act upon such is at the core of the APSA. The Constitutive Act circumscribes the provision on sovereignty and territorial integrity of member states by stipulating the right of intervention under the following conditions: war crimes, genocide, crime against humanity and, through a 2003 amendment, a serious threat to legitimate order. Through the AU Constitutive Act, and more importantly, its Protocol on Peace and Security Council (PSC), there exists the mandate for the creation of the African Standby Force (ASF) as a rapid response brigade.[77] The ASF is expected to be composed of five regional brigades, each composed of between 3500–5000 troops, to be deployed in conflict situations.[78] While the AU Assembly makes the ultimate decision on intervention

[70] See Article 6 of the AEC Treaty (1991).

[71] Article 28 of the ACJ&HR Protocol.

[72] Ibid, Articles 46(1) & (2).

[73] Articles 47-58 of the ACHPR.

[74] *International PEN, Constitutional Rights Project, Civil Liberties Organisation and Interights on behalf of Ken Saro-Wiwa v. Nigeria.*

[75] See e.g. Murray (2000), pp. 54–55.

[76] Viljoen and Louw (2004), p. 9.

[77] Article 13 of the PSC Protocol.

[78] The envisaged brigades include: Southern African Development Community Brigade (SADCBRIG), which is now referred to as SADC Standby Force; East African Standby Brigade (EASBRIG); Economic Community of West African States Brigade (ECOBRIG); North African Standby Brigade (NASBRIG); and Economic Community of Central African States Brigade (ECCASBRIG).

under Article 4(h), the role of the 15-member PSC in the decision-making process signify the intention to cloth the organisation with supranational powers. In this regard, the PSC arrives at a decision on intervention, which is then forwarded to the AU Assembly for ratification, either through consensus, or if that fails, two-thirds majority voting.[79]

The foregoing analysis demonstrates that there exists the intention to set the AU apart from its predecessor, the OAU, by putting in place normative measures and standards that paves a supranational path for the former. However, mere intention is insufficient as there must be deliberate and measurable actions to effect such will. This is where the next analytical element of assessment, action, comes into the picture.

3.4.2 Action

Action denotes the line between stated or implied intentions and outcomes. In other words, the key question is to what extent has the AU engaged in strategic policy choices to ensure that the organisation exercises persuasive and binding powers over its member states? The politico-legal complexities of regionalism in Africa requires a more broad and nuanced way of assessing the level of action. In this respect, two tracks of assessment are necessary: macro-normative and micro-normative. The macro-normative angle considers how express and implied intentions in legal documents have translated into institutional activities aimed at enhancing the AU. The micro-normative element speaks to processes within and outside the purview of legal instruments that may not have legal force but contributes to the overall principles and objectives of deeper regionalism.

From the macro-normative angle, the question typically revolves around how AU organs have been able to exercise express or implied assertive powers. In other words, do AU organs such as PAP, ACJ&HR, and the AU Commission dispense decisions that are binding on member states?

For example, in terms of the implementation of Article 4(h), designated organs such as the PSC has in the past recommended to the Assembly to activate the provision, especially in the case of Burundi, but the latter refused to do this.[80] However, the AU has been able to exercise supranational authority in promoting democracy through the suspension of member states for incidences of military coups and the unconstitutional take-over of government.[81] These include: Madagascar (2002), Mauritania (2005), Guinea (2008), Egypt (2013), Central African Republic (2013), Zimbabwe (2017), Sudan (2019), Mali (2020), and Guinea (2021).

---

[79] Article 8(13) of the PSC Protocol.

[80] Connolly (2016).

[81] The decision to implement this corrective measure has often directly or indirectly come from AU organs such as the PSC, AU Commission, and the ACHPR.

In the case of PAP, the AU Assembly is yet to grant it binding legislative powers as it still exercises consultative and advisory powers. If the 2014 amended Protocol comes into effect, PAP will only be able to make model, not binding, laws. The AU Assembly remains vested with full legislative powers. While the ACJ&HR is yet to come into existence as a single court, the human rights section, in the form of the African Court of Human and Peoples Rights (AfCtHPR), has started exercising judicial powers. As of October 2021, the court has received 299 applications from individuals, 21 from NGOs, and three from the Commission in Banjul.[82] In addition, there have been 127 finalised applications out of a total of 334 applications.[83] Thus far, the court has made 270 decisions (141 judgements and 129 orders).[84] The court has made some far-reaching, supranational decisions on issues relating to democratic governance in member states. In *APDH v Cote d'Ivoire,* the court ruled that the state should bring its electoral law, in particular the independence of the electoral management body, in line with international instruments, including the African Charter on Democracy, Election, and Governance (ACDEG), the ACHPR, and the Economic Community of West African States (ECOWAS) Democracy Protocol.[85] Similarly, in *Mtikila v Tanzania,* the court held that the ban on independent candidacy is a violation of the applicant's rights to free association and political participation under the ACHPR, and ordered the amendment of the constitution to this effect.[86] Despite Cote d'Ivoire's April 2020 withdrawal of the declaration to allow the court receive applications from individuals, the AfCtHPR, on the 15th of September 2020, ruled in the *Soro* case that the state must remove all obstacles preventing the Applicant from participating in the presidential elections.[87] However, some of its decisions have already raised some political backlash, through withdrawal of the right of individual access to the court, from member states such as Rwanda, Tanzania, Benin and Cote d'Ivoire.[88] Additionally, there remains a serious non-compliance crisis with the decisions of the court. Member states have not complied with about 75% of the court's decision.[89] The quasi-judicial African Commission has over the years issued assertive and defining decisions on the protection and promotion of political, economic and socio-cultural rights in member

[82] See generally, the AfCtHPR's website.

[83] Ibid.

[84] Ibid.

[85] App. No. 001/2014 (2016).

[86] *Tangayika Law Society, The legal and Human Rights Centre v The United Republic of Tanzania* and *Rev. Christopher R. Mtikila v. United Republic of Tanzania.*

[87] *Guillaume Kigbafori Soro and Others v Republic of Cote d'Ivoire.*

[88] Other AU organs such as PAP have also experienced political backlash from member states for trying to assert their powers. Welz (2014, pp. 7–8) pointed out that after PAP election observers questioned the credibility of elections in Kenya (2007) and Zimbabwe (2008), AU member states agreed to cut its budget by 22% in 2009.

[89] Chenwi (2021).

states.[90] As Amao rightly noted, the decisions of the African Commission constitute an integral part of the jurisprudence and sources of AU law.[91] The implication of this is that it could feed into the framework of expressing, and implementing, the supranational powers of the AU in the areas of free movement of persons and goods, upholding of democratic and fundamental rights, and the relationship between AU laws and domestic laws.

Other activities under the macro-normative purview include the adoption and ratification of key instruments that are at the heart of the AU exercising supranational powers. One such is the adoption of the Agreement Establishing the African Continental Free Trade Area (AfCFTA), and the Protocol to the Treaty Establishing the African Economic Community Relating to Free Movement of Persons, Right to Residence and Right of Establishment in March 2018. While the AfCFTA Protocol has entered into force, with ongoing negotiations regarding its implementation, the Protocol on free movement is yet to be ratified.[92] The little attention paid to ratifying the free movement protocol reflects the politics of restrictive and stringent migration policies in many African countries. Africa is the continent with the highest use of intra-continental visas. According to the 2018 "Africa Visa Openness Report", 51% of African states still demand visas from other African citizens (it used to be 60%), only 24% of African countries offer visa on arrival to other Africans, and just 25% of African countries have no visa requirements for other Africans.[93] In terms of the flexibility and openness of free movement in the RECs, ECOWAS leads the way by having 100% reciprocity of visa policies, followed by 90% in the East African Community (EAC), 60% in Arab Maghreb Union (AMU), and 56% in Southern African Development Community (SADC).[94]

It is projected that the AfCFTA will be the largest free trade arrangement in the world, increase intra-African trade by 52% by 2022, with a positive impact on Africa's economic development and global positioning.[95] Intra-African trade currently stands at 17%, which is the lowest of any continent. Comparatively,

---

[90] This includes decisions on the right of indigenous people and development (*Centre for Minority Rights Development (Kenya) and Minority Rights Group International on behalf of Endorois Welfare Council v Kenya The Nubian Community in Kenya v. The Republic of* Kenya), the right of people to freely elect and choose their leaders (*Constitutional Rights Project and Another v Nigeria*), the violation of self-determination (*Democratic Republic of the Congo v Burundi, Rwanda and Uganda*; *Gunme and Others v Cameroon*; Katangese Peoples' Congress v Zaire), death penalty as torture and inhumane punishment (*Interights & Ditshwanelo v Botswana*), illegality of the expulsion of foreign nationals (*Institute for Human Rights and Development in Africa v Angola*; *Recontre Africaine pour la Défense des Droits de l'Homme v Zambia*), and the supremacy of the African Charter over conflicting domestic norms (*Media Rights Agenda and Others v Nigeria*).

[91] Amao (2019), pp. 38–42.

[92] AU (2019).

[93] AfDB & AU (2019), p. 20.

[94] In the top 20 most visa-open countries, 8 countries are in East Africa, 7 in West Africa, 4 in Southern Africa, and only 1 in North Africa. See Ibid, p. 13.

[95] UNECA & AU (2018).

intra-regional trade in Europe is 69%, 59% in Asia, and 31% in North America.[96] The AfCFTA was officially launched on the 1st of January 2021, with its Secretariat, which will operate separately from the AU Commission, hosted by Ghana.[97] The AfCFTA Agreement stipulates the establishment of a supranational Dispute Settlement Body to give binding decisions regarding matters between state parties.[98] This means that trade matters will fall outside of the ACJ&HR jurisdictional reach. However, it can be argued that where trade matters have implications for human rights, the ACJ&HR, particularly the Human Rights section, will have jurisdiction. This is a recognised jurisprudential approach in some of Africa's sub-regional courts, especially in terms of exercising express and/or implied jurisdiction over human rights.[99] Another possibility is Mutubwa's proposition of endowing a section of the ACJ&HR, through the Pan-African Investment Code (PAIC), with jurisdiction over investment matters between investors and state parties, and individuals *inter se*.[100] Ngobeni is less sanguine about the possibility of the PAIC opening the door for jurisdiction over investor-state dispute as the recent trend in many African countries favour state to state arbitration.[101]

The micro-normative angle is the soft law element of action. In this respect, it speaks to non-binding institutional and non-state actors' activities aimed at reinforcing and enhancing the powers of the AU. The AU Commission is a crucial player in this respect. Since its inception, the AU Commission, either through its own initiative or mandate from the AU Assembly, has introduced several initiatives aimed at channelling the organisation towards a supranational path. An example the important "Strategic Plan of the AU Commission (2004–2007; 2009–2012; 2014–2017)" through which the AU Commission has been able to set out processes and steps towards supranational integration.[102] The key planks of this documents are issues such as the institutional strengthening of the AU Commission, intra-AU institutional relations and relations with development partners, and a "Minimum Integration Programme" that places emphasis on the gradual attainment of continental supranationalism.[103] This has further led to guidelines and normative documents on trade, infrastructure development, free movement and the AU Agenda 2063 framework. The AU Agenda 2063 is further discussed in the next chapter.

---

[96] Songwe (2019). See also, Afrexim Bank (2019), p. 15.

[97] In February 2020, Wamkele Mene was elected as the first secretary-general of the AfCFTA Secretariat and was sworn in on the 18th of April 2020. AU (2020b).

[98] Article 20 of the AfCFTA Agreement. For a critical perspective on the AfCFTA dispute settlement mechanism, see e.g. Akinkugbe (2020).

[99] Ali (2012); Helfer (2018); Ebobrah (2009).

[100] Mutubwa (2020).

[101] Ngobeni (2019), p. 8.

[102] AU (2004, 2009, 2013).

[103] See generally, AU (2004, 2009, 2013).

The role of the epistemic community in the micro-normative space of the AU has also been critical. Despite the shortcomings of the ECOSOCC,[104] civil society has played and continue to play influential role in the process of enhancing the powers of the AU. Tieku identified three key ways in which the epistemic community have played important roles in the AU. One is the role of international consultants from the International Labour Organisation (ILO) and Ernst and Young played in designing the structure of the AU Commission at its inception, and the selection of the first set of commissioners for the AU Commission.[105] The second is the involvement of experts in the AU through short-term contract employment system.[106] Some of these experts end up becoming permanent employees, and provide vital support in writing reports, analysis and studies on the effective functioning of the organisation.[107] Lastly, is the way in which the AU utilises the expertise of civil society in crafting policy measures.[108] Organisations such as the Institute of Security Studies (ISS), Electoral Institute for Sustainable Democracy in Africa (EISA), and the African Centre for the Constructive Resolution of Disputes in Africa (ACCORD) play diverse roles in writing reports and providing epistemic support for AU activities on democracy, elections, peace and security, and human rights.[109] Other civil society actors have played a more assertive role in presenting independent reports and programmes on the normative shape of an envisaged supranational AU. One such example is the African Civil Society Organisation (ACSO), which in 2005 proposed a draft "Constitution of the United Africa (CUA) (The United States of Africa)".[110] This document covered issues ranging from the institutional structure of the proposed union, democratic participation of African people in the integration process, mode of self-financing of the process, and relations between AU organs and member states.[111] The works of civil society have ended up forming the basis and framework upon which the AU Commission has been able to provide solid ideational path for reforming the organisation.

Another element of the micro-normative aspect is the role of the APRM. Established in 2003, the APRM is a voluntary peer review process that assesses four thematic governance standards in member states: democracy and political governance; economic governance and management; socio-economic governance;

[104]The actualisation of this ideal continue to be hampered by factors such as lack of awareness, limited funding, ambiguous election process to the body and the fact that the body only has an advisory status. See AFRODAD et al. (2007), pp. 6, 37; Finizo (2018), p. 314.

[105]Tieku (2017), p. 47.

[106]Ibid.

[107]Ibid, 48.

[108]Ibid.

[109]Ibid.

[110]ACSO (2005). For a discussion on how CSOs have contributed to the political agenda of continental integration, see Finizo (2018), pp. 307–309.

[111]ACSO (2005).

and corporate governance.[112] There are four kinds of review. The first review is the base review, which will be carried out within eighteen months of a country becoming a member of the APRM process. The second review is a periodic review which takes place every 2 to 4 years. Thirdly, a member country can, for its own reasons, ask for a review that is not part of the periodically mandated reviews. And lastly, participating Heads of States and Government, on sensing signs of an impending political and economic crisis in a member country, can call for a review.[113] Each of the review has five complex and time-consuming stages. The five-stage process is set out below:[114]

- **Stage 1**: At this stage, the APRM Secretariat prepares a background research paper on the country to be reviewed in relation to the four thematic areas: Democracy and Political Governance, Economic Governance and Management, Corporate Governance and Socio-economic Governance.
- **Stage 2**: This is the Country Review Mission. Based on the background research paper, the country review team, led by a panel member visits the country to be reviewed. The team is usually composed of about 15–25 experts and is expected to spend between two to three weeks in the country. During the visit, the team will engage in the widest range of consultations with government officials, political parties, and civil society including the media, academia and trade unions.
- **Stage 3**: After the Country Review Mission, the team is expected to discuss the issues observed during the visit and then prepare a draft Country Review Report. This report is sent back to the government of the country in question for comments. The government cannot amend the report; it can only append its comments to the report.
- **Stage 4**: The Secretariat then submits the final Country Review Report to the APR Forum, Heads of States and Government, for peer review. The time allotted for this process is a modest two hours.
- **Stage 5**: Six months after the discussion by the Forum, the report is tabled before the relevant institutions: the PAP, RECs, African Commission on Human and Peoples' Rights, AU PSC and ECOSOCC.

Thus far, 21 countries, out of the 40 AU member states that have acceded to the APRM document, have successfully completed the five stages review process (base review).[115] Although the process does not have binding effect, the APRM reviews have sensitively, yet boldly and critically, dissected relevant issues stagnating national, and to some extent, continental development. National issues such as revenue and fiscal allocation, corruption, constitutional reform, independence of the separate branches of government, and public participation were for the first

[112]NEPAD (2003).

[113]Ibid, para 14.

[114]Ibid, para 18–25.

[115]See generally, APRM website.

time handled by a continental body.[116] As part of the AU reform efforts, the APRM is now officially recognised as a specialised agency of the AU, with the added mandate of tracking member states' progress regarding the AU Agenda 2063 and the UN Sustainable Development Goals (SDGs).[117] A key implication of this mandate is that the APRM will now have the mandate to assess all 55 AU member states. In a bid to cloth the APRM process with legal teeth, the APR Forum, made up of the Committee of Participating Heads of State and Government, adopted the Statute of the African Peer Review Mechanism in 2016.[118]

3.4.3 Outcomes

Outcomes is the culmination of the interaction between intention and action. The dominant narrative is that the AU is essentially an intergovernmental organisation, where member states play the key decision-making role. The institutional process and interaction between AU technocratic organs and member states (either through the AU Assembly or directly with individual/group of member states) often show that the balance power is firmly in the hands of the latter. The question is not so much about the terminology of the designation as it is about engaging in a multi-perspectival analysis, one which may eventually arrive at the intergovernmental description but is informed by nuances. The AU itself is cognisant of its intergovernmental description, a factor that has led to ongoing reform efforts. However, it is problematic to not consider the fact that while the AU may be intergovernmental, it is also a platform through which multidimensional activities shape its supranational aspirations. In other words, it is important to weigh both normative and non-normative inputs, and how these have shaped certain outcomes. For example, the role of technocrats in the AU, with important support from civil society entities in drawing up reform paths, and how some of these have translated into normative documents and processes is an important point. This is not to discount the continued obstructive actions of member states, where political issues have been prioritised over the bigger picture of deepening continental integration, the elitist construct of regional integration, and the routine flouting of stipulated norms by member states. The idea is to show that a one-sided story cannot fully capture the narrative of continental integration. This position allows for a much broader, contextual and nuance appraisal of the AU's supranational drive.

At the heart of such assessment is the question of the legitimacy of the AU. As the primary regional institution on the continent, with enough level of recognition as the key driver of the continental integration process, the AU enjoys a significant

[116] See generally, Akoth (2007); Herbert and Gruzd (2008), pp. 157–313.

[117] Turianskyi (2019).

[118] For a critical perspective on the plan to ensure a universal accession of the APRM instrument, see Gruzd and Turiansky (2020).

symbolic legitimacy. In addition to this are politico-normative activities aimed at positioning the organisation as the ultimate continental voice. The ongoing institutional reform efforts on self-financing, negotiating with external parties as a single unit, enhancing the powers of the AU Commission, and the adoption of the AfCFTA Agreement are key examples. On the converse is the legitimacy deficit and how this translates into negative outcomes. The optics and actual implications of lack of compliance with AU norms and decisions represent a major detracting factor. As bluntly highlighted in the report of the Paul Kagame led process on the institutional transformation of the AU, "the chronic failure to see through African Union decisions has resulted in a crisis of implementation".[119] The report further noted that while the AU Assembly has adopted more than 1500 resolutions, the lack of an effective follow up on implementation undercuts the effectiveness.[120] Also, the dysfunctionality of the AU is exacerbated by the result of unclear mandates of its institutions, little or no awareness of its relevance by African citizens, lack of division of labour between the AU and its RECs, lack of accountability for performance, fragmented and chaotic focus areas of functionality and chronic underfunding.[121] As the Kagame report aptly noted, this reality can only be reversed if there is the seriousness on the part of member states to understand that "reform does not start with the Commission. It starts and ends with the leaders, who must set the right expectations and tempo".[122]

This mixed outcome is indicative of the need for a fundamental rethink and outlook regarding the enhancement of continental regionalism. While the AU's intergovernmental nature differs from what obtained under the OAU, especially in terms of its institutional set up and expansive powers allocated to such institutions, its supranational ambitions are yet to be fully attained. Table 3.2 below shows the gap between expectations and realities of AU's normative and institutional arrangements. As will be shown in the next chapter, this gap is shaped by certain politico-legal dynamics that requires skilful and deliberate counteracting strategies. Chapter 5 of this book engages in a detailed analysis of such strategies.

3.5 Conclusion

This chapter placed the AU within the discursive paradigm of the concept of supranationalism. At the core of the discussion is the need to be more contextual in the assessment of AU's supranationalism. While the chapter does not dispute the intergovernmental nature of the AU, it questions an assessment that leaves out nuances and complexities, especially as it relates to the assertive roles played by

[119] Kagame (2017), p. 4.

[120] Ibid, p. 5. See also, AU (2007), p. 29.

[121] Kagame (2017), p. 4.

[122] Ibid, p. 5.

Table 3.2 Assessment of AU supranationalism

Analytical elements of a supranational AU	Normative inputs	Expected results	Actual results
Intention	*AU Assembly*	*Assertive decision-making powers (including the power to delegate)*	*While the Assembly continues to delegate powers to the Executive Council, it has done little to transfer meaningful powers to other critical organs of the AU. This position has ensured that the organisation remains an intergovernmental entity.*
	Executive Council	*Expansive and binding coordinating powers*	*It enjoys close relations with the Assembly. It is a powerful part of AU's intergovernmental structure.*
	ACJ&HR and the African Commission	*Binding nature of the judgements and decisions of the ACJ&HR and the African Commission (based on the approval of the AU Assembly)*	*The ACJ&HR is yet to become operational. However, its Human Rights section, AfCtHPR, has been operational. It has made bold decisions against member states, thereby triggering some political backlash. However, about 75% of its decisions have not implemented by member states. The AfCtHPR remains the most gendered balance international court in the world, with women currently making up 55% of the judges on the court* *Like the AfCtHPR, member states rarely comply with the decisions of the African Commission. The AU Assembly has not shown the necessary political will to compel member states to comply with the Commission's decisions.*
	AU Commission	*Powers to initiate policies, monitor compliance and make binding, enforceable decisions*	*While the AU Commission has been able to initiate policies regarding supranational regionalism in Africa, and monitor member states' compliance, it lacks the powers to compel member states to act or penalise them for failure to act. The AU Assembly has not*

(continued)

Table 3.2 (continued)

Analytical elements of a supranational AU	Normative inputs	Expected results	Actual results
			endowed it with the requisite powers to ensure this.
Action	*Macro-normative powers (Hard law)*	*PSC's binding decision making powers regarding Article 4 (h)* *Full legislative powers of PAP* *Binding nature of the decisions of the ACJ&HR*	*The AU is yet to activate this provision despite incidents that warrant its application.* *PAP still exercises non-binding legislative powers. The amended Protocol only allows it to make "draft model laws".* *While the court is empowered to make binding decisions, enforcement remains a key concern.*
	Micro-normative powers (Soft law)	*AU Commission's "strategic reports"* *AU Agenda 2063 framework on achieving enhanced continental supranationalism* *Influential role of the epistemic community in the AU Commission* *APRM as an instrument for enhancing good governance*	*Soft law documents have played an important role in articulating AU's supranational path, and possible ways of implementation.* *Civil society has been instrumental in providing technical support in shaping both soft and hard law documents in the AU. However, civil society is still excluded from critical decision-making spheres. Similarly, structures such as PAP and ECOSOCC that are essential for civil society participation remain without any meaningful powers.* *The APRM has provided an important lens for understanding governance issues on the continent. It, however, remains a voluntary, unenforceable instrument.*
Outcomes	*Intention-driven outcomes*	*Delegation of intergovernmental and supranational powers by the AU Assembly to other AU organs; Specific attribution of enhanced powers and competences.*	*There has been little or no efforts in terms of transferring meaningful powers to AU institutions.*
	Action-driven/	*Institutional reform of the AU* *Technocratic assertiveness regarding policy articulation*	*Reform process demonstrates the recognition of AU's incapacities, and the intention to*

(continued)

Table 3.2 (continued)

Analytical elements of a supranational AU	Normative inputs	Expected results	Actual results
	processual outcomes	*and implementation Coordination and harmonisation of RECs and national policies*	*enhance its legitimacy. Reform efforts such as the reduction of the number of the commissioners of the AU Commission from eight to six, self-financing through the adoption of the 0.2% tax on eligible imports, launch of the AfCFTA, common position on negotiations with the EU post-Cotonou, and enhanced cooperation between the AU and the RECs through meetings and adoption of a protocol on relations are steps in the right direction.*
	Multi-perspectival outcomes	*Symbolic legitimacy of the AU Balancing intergovernmental and supranational powers*	*The AU remains the primary regional organisation on the continent and is recognised as the key vehicle for achieving continental supranationalism in Africa. Such recognition is, however, curtailed by its limited financial capacity, which has resulted in its heavy dependence on external donors. External donors fund over 90% of its peace and security budget, and 50-60% of its total budget. Less than 40% of AU member states pay their yearly dues. Other curtailing factors remain little or no awareness of its activities by Africans, and the inability to grant it meaningful supranational powers.*

Source: Author's construction

both state and non-state actors in the AU. In this respect, three assessment factors were considered: intention, action and outcomes. These three analytical elements show how the AU continues to navigate the fraught intergovernmental/supranational terrain, with mixed outcomes that either betrays its aspirational goals or provides a glimmer of hope and purpose. As the designated principal driver of continental integration in Africa, the AU requires both extracontinental and intracontinental legitimacy to operate efficiently and effectively. This point has been central to reform efforts since the inception of the AU, and a topical discourse on regional integration issues in Africa. Ongoing reform efforts in the form of self-financing of continental integration, establishing a continental free trade area, and enhancing the coordinating and assertive powers of the AU Commission reflect a genuine will to bring about continental supranationalism in Africa. However, nagging political, economic and legal issues persist, and raise the point of employing pragmatic strategies that are tailor made for African peculiarities. In the next chapter, attempt will be made to show the intersectional, and sometime conflictive, relationship between the law and politics of continental supranationalism in Africa.

References

Actions Pour La Protection Des Droits De L'homme (APDH) v. Republic of Cote d'Ivoire App. No. 001/2014 (2016). https://www.african-court.org/en/images/Cases/Judgment/JUDGMENT_APPLICATION%20001%202014%20_%20APDH%20V.%20THE%20REPUBLIC%20OF%20COTE%20DIVOIRE.pdf. Accessed 4 Oct 2021

African Charter on Human and Peoples' Rights (1981). https://au.int/en/treaties/african-charter-human-and-peoples-rights. Accessed 4 Oct 2021

African Civil Society Organisation (2005) Third draft of the constitution of the United Africa (UA) (The United States of Africa). African Civil Society Organisation, Yaounde

African Court on Human and Peoples' Rights website, https://www.african-court.org/cpmt/statistic. Accessed 4 Oct 2021

African Development Bank & African Union (2019) Africa Visa Openness Report 2018 (2019) https://www.visaopenness.org/fileadmin/uploads/afdb/Documents/VisaOReport2018_R15jan19.pdf. Accessed 4 Oct 2021

African Export-Import Bank (2019) African trade report: African trade in a digital world. https://s3-eu-west-1.amazonaws.com/demo2.opus.ee/afrexim/African-Trade-Report_2019.pdf. Accessed 4 Oct 2021

African Network on Debt and Development (AFRODAD), the Open Society Institute Africa Governance Monitoring and Advocacy Project (AfriMAP), and Oxfam GB (2007) Towards a people-driven African Union: Current obstacles and new opportunities https://www.opensocietyfoundations.org/publications/towards-people-driven-african-union-current-obstacles-new-opportunities. Accessed 4 Oct 2021

African Peer Review Mechanism website, https://www.aprm-au.org/map-areas/. Accessed 4 Oct 2021

African Union (1999) 'Sirte declaration. https://archives.au.int/bitstream/handle/123456789/2475/1999_Sirte%20_Decl_%20E.pdf?sequence=1&isAllowed=y. Accessed 4 Oct 2021

African Union (2002) Rules of procedure of the Assembly of the Union. https://www3.nd.edu/~ggoertz/rei/rei040/rei040.13tt1.pdf. Accessed 4 Oct 2021

African Union (2004) Strategic plan of the African Union Commission: Volume 1: Vision and mission of the African Union. https://www.iri.edu.ar/publicaciones_iri/anuario/CD%20Anuario%202005/Africa/07-au_commision-strategic%20plan%2001.pdf. Accessed 4 Oct 2021

African Union (2007) Audit of the African Union. https://www.securitycouncilreport.org/atf/cf/%7B65BFCF9B-6D27-4E9C-8CD3-CF6E4FF96FF9%7D/RO%20Audit%20of%20the%20AU.pdf. Accessed 4 Oct 2021

African Union (2009) African Union Commission, Strategic plan 2009-2012. https://reliefweb.int/sites/reliefweb.int/files/resources/08D09FE21F9917E8492575F500211460-EX%20EnglishCL%20501_XV_%20%20-%20Strategic_Plan%20Rev%209%20_b2_.pdf. Accessed 4 Oct 2021

African Union (2013) African Union Commission: Final draft strategic plan 2014-2017. http://www.iri.edu.ar/publicaciones_iri/anuario/cd_anuario_2014/Africa/22d.pdf. Accessed 4 Oct 2021

African Union (2014) Report of the twenty-fourth ordinary session of the ministerial committee on African candidatures within the international system, 27 January 2014, Addis Ababa. http://www.ip-watch.org/weblog/wp-content/uploads/2014/02/EX-CL-821-XXIV-_E_subcommittee-on-candidature.pdf. Accessed 4 Oct 2021

African Union (2018) African Union strengthens its sanction regime for non-payment of dues. https://au.int/en/pressreleases/20181127/african-union-strengthens-its-sanction-regime-non-payment-dues. Accessed 4 Oct 2021

African Union (2019, April 29) AfCFTA Agreement secures minimum threshold of 22 ratification as Sierra Leone and the Saharawi Republic deposit instruments. https://au.int/en/pressreleases/20190429/afcfta-agreement-secures-minimum-threshold-22-ratification-sierra-leone-and. Accessed 4 Oct 2021

African Union (2020a) Legal Opinion for Egypt regarding Nigeria Candidatures International System position of World Trade Organisation director, BC/OLC/24/5056.20

African Union (2020b) Newly sworn-in AfCFTA secretary general, Wamkele Mene, undertakes to serve Africa with resolute determination. https://au.int/en/pressreleases/20200418/newly-sworn-afcfta-secretary-general-wamkele-mene-undertakes-serve-africa. Accessed 4 Oct 2021

African Union. https://au.int/. Accessed 4 Oct 2021

African Union, Strategic plan of the Commission of the African Union: Volume 2: 2004-2007 Strategic framework of the African Union Commission (2004). http://www.iri.edu.ar/publicaciones_iri/anuario/CD%20Anuario%202005/Africa/08-au_commision-strategic%20plan%2002.pdf. Accessed 4 Oct 2021

Agreement establishing the African Continental Free Trade Area (2018). https://au.int/en/treaties/agreement-establishing-african-continental-free-trade-area. Accessed 4 Oct 2021

Agyemen O (1990) Pan Africanist- federalism. https://msuweb.montclair.edu/~lebelp/CERAFRM035Agyeman1991.pdf. Accessed 4 Oct 2021

Akinkugbe O (2020) Dispute settlement under the African Continental Free Trade Area Agreement: a preliminary assessment. Afr J Int Comp Law 28(Supplement):138–158

Akoth S (2007) The APRM process in Kenya: A pathway to a new state? https://www.opensocietyfoundations.org/publications/aprm-process-kenya-pathway-new-state. Accessed 4 Oct 2021

Alex Thomas v United Republic of Tanzania, App. No. 005 (2013). https://afchpr-commentary.uwazi.io/en/document/7s8x53uq1kqhbyb9?page=53. Accessed 10 Apr 2022

Ali A (2012) The admissibility of sub-regional court's decisions before the African Commission or African Court. Mizan Law Rev 6(2):241–272

Amao O (2019) African Union law: the emergence of a sui generis legal order. Routledge, London

Centre for Minority Rights Development (Kenya) and Minority Rights Group International on behalf of Endorois Welfare Council v Kenya (2009) AHRLR 75. https://www.achpr.org/public/Document/file/English/achpr46_276_03_eng.pdf. Accessed 4 Oct 2021

Chenwi I (2021, August 31) Successes of African Human Rights Court undermined by resistance from states. The Conversation. https://theconversation.com/successes-of-african-human-rights-court-undermined-by-resistance-from-states-166454. Accessed 4 Oct 2021

Connolly L (2016) Politics in place of peace: The AU's role in Burundi'. https://peaceoperationsreview.org/thematic-essays/politics-in-place-of-peace-the-aus-role-in-burundi/. Accessed 4 Oct 2021

Constitutional Rights Project and Another v Nigeria (2000) AHRLR 191. https://www.achpr.org/public/Document/file/English/achpr26_140.94_141.94_145.95_eng.pdf. Accessed 4 Oct 2021

Constitutive Act of the African Union (2000). https://au.int/sites/default/files/pages/34873-file-constitutiveact_en.pdf Accessed 4 Oct 2021

Cottier T, Hertig M (2003) The prospect of 21st century constitutionalism. Max Planck Yearb United Nations Law 7:261–328

Dagash D (2006) The OAU: Reality or fiction? Self-published.
Democratic Republic of the Congo v Burundi, Rwanda and Uganda (2004) AHRLR 19. https://www.achpr.org/sessions/descions?id=138. Accessed 4 Oct 2021
Dirar L (2014) Rethinking and theorizing regional integration in Southern Africa. Emroy Int law Rev 28(1):123–165
Ebobrah S (2009) Litigating human rights before sub-regional courts in Africa: prospects and challenges. Afr J Comp Int Law 17(1):79–101
Ernest Francis Mtingwi v Republic of Malawi App. No. 001 (2013). https://afchpr-commentary.uwazi.io/en/document/akut788k73at6gvi?page=2, Accessed 10 April 2022
Fagbayibo B (2013) In search of nuanced methods of assessing African integration. Politeia 32 (1):59–73
Fagbayibo B (2017) A normative appraisal of the African Union's membership admission rules. Verfassung und Recht in Ubersee 50(2):156–174
Finizo G (2018) Civil society involvement and ownership in the African Union integration process. In: Adar K, Finizo G, Meyer A (eds) Building regionalism from below: the role of parliaments and civil society in regional integration in Africa. Peter Lang, Bruxelles, pp 289–321
Gathii J (2009) African regional trade agreements as flexible legal regimes. North Carolina J Int Law 35(3):572–668
Gruzd S, Turiansky Y (2020) Should all African states join the APRM? https://saiia.org.za/research/should-all-africas-states-join-the-aprm/. Accessed 4 Oct 2021
Guillaume Kigbafori Soro and Others v Republic of Cote d'Ivoire App. 012/2020 https://en.african-court.org/images/Cases/Orders/GUILLAUME__KINGBAFOR.pdf. Accessed 4 Oct 2021
Helfer L (2018) Subregional courts in Africa: litigating the hybrid right to free movement of persons. Int J Const Law 16(1):235–253
Herbert R, Gruzd S (2008) The African peer review mechanism: lessons from the pioneers. South African Institute of International Affairs, Johannesburg
Hugo J (2007) Mission impossible? Colonel Ghadaffi's quest for unity. https://oldsite.issafrica.org/iss-today/missions-impossible-colonel-gadaffis-quest-for-unity. Accessed 4 Oct 2021
Huliaras A (2001) Qadhafi's comeback: Libya and sub-Saharan African in the 1990s. Afr Aff 100(398):5–25
Institute for Human Rights and Development in Africa v Angola (2008) AHRLR 43. https://africanlii.org/afu/judgment/african-commission-human-and-peoples-rights/2008/83. Accessed 4 Oct 2021
Interights & Ditshwanelo v Botswana [Communication 319/06 (2015). https://www.achpr.org/public/Document/file/English/communication_319_.06_eng.pdf. Accessed 4 Oct 2021
International PEN, Constitutional Rights Project, Civil Liberties Organisation and Interights on behalf of Ken Saro-Wiwa v. Nigeria, Communications 137/94, 139/94, 154/96 and 161/97. (1998). http://hrlibrary.umn.edu/africa/comcases/137-94_139-94_154-96_161-97.html. Accessed 4 Oct 2021
Jeng A (2012) Peacebuilding in the African Union: law, philosophy and practice. Cambridge University Press, Cambridge
Kagame P (2017) The imperative of strengthening our union: Report on the Proposed Recommendations for the Institutional Reform of the African Union. http://www.rci.uct.ac.za/sites/default/files/image_tool/images/78/News/FInal%20AU%20Reform%20Combined%20report_28012017.pdf. Accessed 4 Oct 2021
Katangese Peoples' Congress v Zaire (2000) AHRLR 72 (ACHPR 1995). https://africanlii.org/afu/judgment/african-commission-human-and-peoples-rights/1992/3. Accessed 4 Oct 2021
Kennes W (1999) African regional economic integration and the European Union. In: Bach D (ed) Regionalisation, integration and disintegration in Africa. Indiana University Press, Bloomington, pp 27–39
Maluwa T (2001) Reimagining African unity: some preliminary reflections on the Constitutive Act of the African Union. Afr Yearb Int Law 9:3–38

Maluwa T (2003) The Constitutive Act of the African Union and institutional building in postcolonial Africa. Leiden J Int law 16(1):157–170
Maluwa T (2012) Ratification of African Union treaties by member states: law, policy and practise. Melbourne J Int Law 13(2):1–49
Maluwa T (2020) Reassessing aspects of the contribution of African states to the development of international law through African regional multilateral treaties. Mich J Int Law 41(2):327–415
Mattheis F, Staeger U (2020, December 22) How member states and partners impede the African Union's quest for financial autonomy. The Conversation. https://theconversation.com/how-member-states-and-partners-impede-the-african-unions-quest-for-financial-autonomy-151115. Accessed 4 Oct 2021
Mbeki T (2002) Speech at the launch of the African Union, 9 July 2002. http://www.dirco.gov.za/docs/speeches/2002/mbek0709.htm. Accessed 4 Oct 2021
Mbeki T (2012) The African Union at ten years old: A dream deferred! Afr Insight 42(3):13–24
Media Rights Agenda and Others v Nigeria (2000) AHRLR 200 (ACHPR 1998). https://africanlii.org/afu/judgment/african-commission-human-and-peoples-rights/2000/24. Accessed 4 Oct 2021
Mgwanga Gunme and Others v Cameroon (2009) AHRLR 9. https://africanlii.org/afu/judgment/african-commission-human-and-peoples-rights/2009/99. Accessed 4 Oct 2021
Murray R (2000) The African Commission on Human and Peoples' Rights and International Law. Hart Publishers, Oxford
Mutubwa W (2020) Fragmentation of investment codes in Africa: the Pan African Investment Code (PIAC) as a centripetal continental force. J Confl Manage Sustain Dev 4(1):15–24
New Partnership for Africa's Development (2003) African Peer Review Mechanism. https://www.aprm-au.org/publications/partnership-for-africa-nepad-and-aprm/. Accessed 4 Oct 2021
Ngobeni L (2019) The African justice scoreboard: a proposal to address rule of law challenges in the resolution of investor-state disputes in the Southern African Development Community. Comp Int Law J South Afr 52(1):1–21
Olowu O (2003) Regional integration, development and the African Union agenda: challenges, gaps and opportunities. Transnatl Int Law Comp Probl 13(1):212–253
Packer C, Rukare D (2002) The new African Union and its Constitutive Act. Am J Int Law 96(2): 365–379
Protocol on Amendments to the Protocol on the Statute of the African Court of Justice and Human Rights (2014). https://au.int/en/treaties/protocol-amendments-protocol-statute-african-court-justice-and-human-rights. Accessed 4 Oct 2021
Protocol on the Statute of the African Court of Justice and Human Rights (2008). https://au.int/en/treaties/protocol-statute-african-court-justice-and-human-rights. Accessed 4 Oct 2021
Protocol relating to the establishment of the Peace and Security Council of the African Union (2002). https://au.int/en/treaties/protocol-relating-establishment-peace-and-security-council-african-union. Accessed 4 Oct 2021
Protocol to the Constitutive Act of the African Union relating to the Pan-African Parliament (2014). https://au.int/en/treaties/protocol-constitutive-act-african-union-relating-pan-african-parliament. Accessed 4 Oct 2021
Recontre Africaine pour la Défense des Droits de l'Homme v Zambia [(2000) AHRLR 321 (ACHPR 1996). https://africanlii.org/afu/judgment/african-commission-human-and-peoples-rights/1996/8. Accessed 4 Oct 2021
Schoeman M (2002) Imagining a community – the African Union as an emerging security community. Strategic Rev South Afr XXIV/1:1–26
Shaban A (2020, June 21) AU sanctions South Sudan over $9m membership debt. https://www.africanews.com/2020/06/21/au-sanctions-south-sudan-for-non-payment-of-over-9m-dues//. Accessed 4 Oct 2021
Silva K (2017) Beyond the border between the North and the South: towards a decolonization of epistemologies and fields of research on Mercosur. Revista de Direito Internacional Brasilia 14(2):413–429

Songwe V (2019) Intra-African trade: A path to economic diversification and inclusion. https://www.brookings.edu/research/intra-african-trade-a-path-to-economic-diversification-and-inclusion/. Accessed 4 Oct 2021

Statutes of the Commission of the African Union, ASS/AU/2(1) (2002). https://www.euppublishing.com/doi/abs/10.3366/ajicl.2005.13.1.74. Accessed 4 Oct 2021

Taiwo O (2019) An unhealthy and unhelpful preoccupation. https://gga.org/author/olufemi-taiwo/. Accessed 4 Oct 2021

Tangayika Law Society, The legal and Human Rights Centre v The United Republic of Tanzania App. 009/2011 and Rev. Christopher R. Mtikila v. United Republic of Tanzania App. No. 011/2011 https://www.african-court.org/en/images/Cases/Judgment/Judgment%20Application%20009-011-2011%20Rev%20Christopher%20Mtikila%20v.%20Tanzania.pdf. Accessed 4 Oct 2021

The Nubian Community in Kenya v. The Republic of Kenya, Communication 317/2006. https://www.achpr.org/public/Document/file/English/communication_317.06_eng.pdf. Accessed 4 Oct 2021

Tieku T (2017) Governing Africa: 3D analysis of the African Union's performance. Littlefield, Rowman and New York and London

Touray O (2016) The African Union: the first 10 years. Rowman & Littlefield, London

Treaty establishing the African Economic Community Treaty (1991). https://au.int/en/treaties/treaty-establishing-african-economic-community. Accessed 4 Oct 2021

Turianskyi Y (2019, March 12) African peer review: progress is being made, but there are problems. https://theconversation.com/african-peer-review-progress-is-being-made-but-there-are-problems-113048. Accessed 4 Oct 2021

Udombana J (2002) A harmony or a cacophony? The music of integration in the African Union treaty and the New Partnership for Africa's Development. Indiana Int Comp Law Rev:185–236

United Nations Economic Commission for Africa (2002) Third African Development Forum (ADF III): Defining priorities for regional integration. https://repository.uneca.org/handle/10855/30709. Accessed 4 Oct 2021

United Nations Economic Commission for Africa & African Union Commission (2018) African Continental Free Trade Area questions & answers. https://au.int/sites/default/files/documents/33984-doc-qa_cfta_en_rev15march.pdf. Accessed 4 Oct 2021

Viljoen F, Louw L (2004) The status of the findings of the African Commission: from moral persuasion to legal obligations. J Afr Law 48(1):1–22

Weiler J (1999) The constitution of Europe: do the new clothes have an emperor? And other essays on European integration. Cambridge University Press, Cambridge

Welz M (2014) A 'culture of conservatism': how and why African Union member states obstruct the deepening of integration. Strat Rev South Afr 36(1):4–24

Welz M (2020) Reconsidering lock-in effects and benefits from delegation: the African Union's relations with its member states through a principal-agent perspective. Camb Rev Int Aff 13(1):159–178

Werner W (2007) Constitutionalisation, fragmentation, politicisation, the constitutionalisation of international law as a janus-faced phenomenon. Griffen's View 8(2):17–30

Chapter 4
Understanding the Interplay of Law and Politics in the Matrix of Continental Supranationalism

The Elemental Prisms

4.1 Introduction

This chapter examines the interplay between law and politics in the operationalisation of actual and aspirational supranational arrangements in Africa. The ideas underpinning regionalism in Africa were, and are still, formulated within certain political contexts that moderate the crafting of legal norms and the implementation, or lack thereof, of those ideals. The politics of anti-colonialism; Cold War; external interference in Africa's political and economic development; dictatorship; movement for gender equality and respect for fundamental right; and globalisation and neo-liberalism have all at different periods influenced the practise and understanding of regional integration in Africa. Questions regarding the mismatch between the enthusiastic adoption of far-reaching normative documents and zero implementation or the continued disagreement on the best way forward for supranational regionalism in Africa are better understood within the intersectional prism of law and politics. As one scholar rightly pointed out, "politicization of law can render legalization of integration project irrelevant and even lead to "dissociation from law"."[1] In a similar vein, Mkandawire pointedly remarked: "We should start by getting the political story clear, before we start giving prescriptions".[2] The interplay between law and politics is thus akin to the two pedals of a bicycle, which requires the cyclic pressure and motion of both feet for advance movement.

In assessing the relationship between law and politics of continental supranationalism in Africa, three broad elemental prisms will be considered: imitation (the copying of the EU process), relational (AU-RECs, AU-member states, and AU-civil society), and the politics of reform.

[1]Dirar (2014), p. 152.

[2]Mkandawire (2014), p. 1.

B. Fagbayibo, *Transcending Member States*,
https://doi.org/10.1007/978-3-031-12451-8_4

4.2 Imitation: Copying and Pasting the EU Template

To gain a better understanding of how imitation lies at the intersection of law and politics in the African continental integration process, two issues need to be emphasised. The first is the conceptual framing of the idea of imitation or institutional mirroring, and the second is the implications of such idea for continental integration in Africa.

Imitation or institutional mirroring has been described in literature as the "diffusion model". Levi-Faur defined diffusion as the:

> process by which the adoption of a social system is communicated through certain channels overtime and triggers mechanisms that increase the probability of its adoption by other members who have not yet adopted it.[3]

As a sub-set of the diffusion model, the "policy transfer approach" best describes the similarity between the EU and the AU. As Levi-Faur puts it, the policy transfer approach is "the process by which knowledge about how policies, administrative arrangements, institution and ideas in one political setting is used in another political setting in the development of change".[4] In this regard, the success of the EU, especially in terms of its supranational features, has had a huge impact on policy-makers and architects of the integration process in Africa, both at the sub-regional and continental levels.

Elkins and Simmons, however, note that diffusion has little to do with the outcomes of policy transfers; rather it focuses on the mechanisms and processes that shape the likely outcome.[5] What this implies is that diffusion does not necessarily guarantee the successful operationalisation of a copied process, it simply points to the similarity of process and structure. In this vein, Elkins and Simmons identify the two kinds of diffusion as *adaptation to altered conditions* and *diffusion via learning*. *Adaptation to altered condition* denotes the contextualisation or adjustment of a copied process to the prevailing conditions of a particular area.[6] This is similar to what Goodin pointedly typify as "goodness of fit"[7] or what some authors have referred to as "norm localisation".[8] While *adaptation to altered condition* aims to re-shape adopted policies, *diffusion via learning* implies the adoption of policies as an instructive tool.[9] In this case, policy-makers adopt proven,

---

[3] Levi-Faur (2005), p. 23; see also Elkins and Simmons (2005), pp. 36–38.

[4] Levi-Faur (2005), p. 23.

[5] Elkins and Simmons (2005), p. 36.

[6] Ibid, pp. 39–42.

[7] This relates to how a designed objective or policy is consistent with the social order of a particular environment. See Goodin (1996), p. 37.

[8] Acharya (2004).

[9] Elkins and Simmons (2005), p. 42.

tested and successful models without engaging in an evaluation of the effectiveness of such model in a specific setting or clime.[10]

Similarly, Libman identified four ways in which Eurasian regionalism mirrors the EU.[11] The first is the "integration agenda and sequence of integration steps" (integrating trade area, establishing customs union, free movement of persons and capital, and more advanced forms of integration).[12] The second is the "structure of institutions", which essentially speaks to similarities in transnational bureaucratic set-up.[13] The third is the "formalisation and legalisation of integration" that relies on common norms and regulatory institutions. The fourth is the "explicit reference to individual EU policies and integration steps" where parallels are often drawn to show similarities of processes and policies.[14]

In situating the AU within the conceptual exposition above, two consequential issues are worth considering. The first is the extent to which AU institutions and integration processes are structured along EU lines. As shown in Table 4.1 below, AU institutions such as the Assembly, Executive Council, PAP, AU Commission, ECOSOCC, PRC, Court of Justice and financial institutions all have EU parallels. In addition to the institutional imitation, the AU has also borrowed policy structures from the EU. An example is the Common African Defence and Security Policy (CADSP) which is similar to the EU Common Security and Defence Policy (CSDP).[15] There are, however, some variations. For example, whereas the European Court of Justice (ECJ) and European Court of Human Rights (ECHR) operate as separate entities, they operate, or are expected to, as a joint entity in the AU. The AU's PSC, unlike the EU's Political and Security Committee, is modelled after the UN Security Council, with the power to take binding decisions on military interventions in AU member states.[16] This variation is what some authors have described as "norm localisation" in the AU.[17] Acharya described "norm localisation" as the process where actors "borrowed foreign ideas about authority and legitimacy and fitted them into indigenous traditions and practices".[18] The AU's shift towards a culture of accountability in terms of the rejection of unconstitutional change of government, responsibility to protect through intervention under Article 4(h) of its constitutive Act, and the adherence to good governance through the APRM are examples of how international measures, either at the UN or EU levels, have been adopted and adapted to address pressing concerns.[19] It should, however, be

[10]Ibid, pp. 42–45.

[11]Libmann (2019), p. 249.

[12]Ibid.

[13]Ibid, p. 250.

[14]Ibid.

[15]Haastrup (2013), p. 790.

[16]Ibid.

[17]Williams (2007).

[18]Acharya (2004), p. 244.

[19]Williams (2007).

Table 4.1 Comparison between the EU and the AU

Comparative lens	EU	AU
Reason for establishment	The need for continental peace and security after the devastating Second World War and economic reconstruction of Europe were the major motivation behind the formation of the EU.	The inadequacy of the OAU to address contemporary global challenges and the need to fast-track continental integration led to the creation of the AU.
Membership composition	• The EU is made up of 27 members. • Membership is not automatic. It is based on the three Copenhagen criteria: stable national institutions that are able to guarantee the adherence to the principles of democracy; administrative and institutional capacity to implement EU norms and policies; and functioning free market economy.	• The AU is composed of 55 members. • Membership is open to all African states.
Institutional architecture	• *The European Council* is composed of presidents and prime ministers of EU states • *The Council of European Union* (Council) is the primary decision-making organ of the EU. It is made up ministers from member states. • *The European Parliament* is composed of members elected directly by EU citizens. Representation is based on the population of each member state. It shares legislative powers with the Council. • *The European Commission* is the executive arm of the Union. It is responsible for initiating legislation. It is composed of a president and 27 commissioners. • *The Court of Justice* is the judicial organ of the EU. • The financial institutions: European Central Bank and European Investment Bank • The Economic and Social Committee • *The Committee of Permanent Representative* (COREPER) is made up of ambassadors of member states of the EU.	• *The Assembly of Heads of States and Government* is the supreme decision-making organ of the AU • *The Executive Council* is composed of foreign ministers or designated ministers from member states. • *The Pan-African Parliament* is the advisory and consultative legislative arm of the AU. It is expected to exercise full legislative powers in the future. Each member state has five representatives. • *The AU Commission* is the executive arm of the AU. It is headed by a Chairperson, a deputy Chairperson and six commissioners. • *The African Court of Justice and Human Rights* (ACJ&HR) is the judicial organ of the AU. It is yet to take off as a single court. However, the African Court of Human and Peoples Rights (AfCtHPR) is in existence. • The financial institutions: African Central Bank, African Monetary Fund and African Investment Bank. These are yet to be established. • The Economic, Social and Cultural Council; the Specialised Technical Committees. • *The Permanent Representative Committee* (PRC) is composed of permanent representatives of member states to the union.
	• The Council and European Parliament share decision making powers.	• The Assembly is the primary decision-making body, with the

(continued)

Table 4.1 (continued)

Comparative lens	EU	AU
Decision-making process	• Decisions are reached, depending on the matter, through consensus or Simple Majority Voting or the Qualified Majority Voting (QMV) system. • The QMV is a weighted voting system which gives each member state of the EU a certain number of votes based on its size and population.	Executive Council been responsible for the implementation of such decisions. • Decisions, in both the Assembly and Executive Council, are taken either through consensus or two-thirds majority.
Depth of regional integration	• The European single market, which encompasses free movement of persons, goods, capital and services • Economic and monetary union – the euro. • Delegation of assertive supranational powers to institutions such as the European Central Bank, European Commission, European Parliament, and the European Court of Justice.	• Continental economic integration is weak. Some of the RECs exercise more effective, supranational powers than the AU. • The African Continental Free Trade Area has been established but it is still at an early phase. However, at the REC level, FTAs (COMESA, ECCAS, ECOWAS, SADC) and Customs Union (SACU, EAC) exist in varying depths. • The continental framework on free movement is yet to become law. Supranational mobility regimes exist in RECs such as ECOWAS and the EAC. • There is no common currency. There are sub-regional monetary unions in West Africa (WAEMU), Central Africa (CEMAC) and Southern Africa (CMA).

Source: Author's construction based on the analysis in Olivier and Olivier (2004)

emphasised that adoption and adaptation have not always resulted in effective implementation. For example, the AU is yet to activate Article 4(h). In addition, its normative principles on respect for fundamental rights and good governance are yet to make significant impact on behavioural patterns as many member states continue to experience increasing anti-democratic practises. For example, while the AU has suspended regimes that have come to power through military coups, little has been done to extend this principle to incumbents who have elongated their terms of office through illegal amendments of the constitution.[20] Similarly, the AU does not extend sanctions to governments that have benefitted from widespread rigging of elections, even in cases where its election observing mission has confirmed such malpractices.[21]

[20] Abebe (2019); Fagbayibo (2017).

[21] Fagbayibo (2017), p. 166.

Similarity also extends to the AU integration process, particularly the steps towards a political and economic union. The six steps outlined in the African Economic Community Treaty (1991) mirrors the EU integrative path. According to Article 6 of the AEC treaty, the steps include: Strengthening of the RECs (5 years, 1994–1999); Removal of tariffs and duties on goods within the RECs (8 years, 1999–2007); Establishment of a free trade area and custom union within each REC (10 years, 2007–2017); Coordination and harmonisation of tariff and non-tariff systems among the RECs (2 years, 2017–2019); Establishment of an African Common Market (4 years, 2019–2023); and Consolidation of the common market, the establishment of a monetary union, central bank, parliament and single currency (5 years, 2023–2028).

Since the AU's inception, the EU has expressly encouraged this imitation through its funding of continental regionalism in Africa and capacity building programmes with AU institutions. EU's actions in this respect largely stems from the position of projecting itself as a global actor and importantly as an "opportunity to mentor Africa into deepened integration".[22] This support is further in line with the Euro-centric understanding of regionalism, which places the EU at the apex of what and how regional integration should be like. As Soderbaum rightly observed:

> from the Europe-centred viewpoint, European integration is usually considered multidimensional, sophisticated and highly institutionalized—both a descriptive and pre-scriptive contention—whereas regionalism/regional integration in the rest of the world is seen as only weakly developed, weakly institutionalized and usually reduced to either and economic or security-related phenomenon (or as an instance of 'regional cooperation').[23]

In terms of influencing the African integration drive, the EU provides strategic financial and technical support to the AU. The EU remains the biggest funder of the African integration process. It funds about 80% of the programmes budget of the AU Commission; engages the Pan African Parliament (PAP) through funding and the establishment of a joint strategy and a joint parliamentary committee; and through its principal funding structures of Pan-African Programme (PanAf) (established in 2014) and the African Peace Facility (APF) (established in 2003).[24] Both programmes have now been replaced by the European Peace Facility, which unlike the APF, is structured to bypass the AU Commission through the direct allocation of funds to sub-regional and national military operations, and allows the EU to directly procure military equipment.[25] From 2014 to 2020, the EU is expected to spend €845 million through the PanAf initiative on three key pillars: governance, migration and security (Pillar 1); investment and growth (Pillar 2); and knowledge and skills (Pillar 3). Under the pillar one, the EU intends to provide €45 million for migration management, €14.5 million on regional observatories aimed at combatting

[22] Ibid, p. 793.

[23] Soderbaum (2013) p, 2. See also Zondi (2012), p. 26.

[24] European Commission (2015); Navarro (2010), pp. 207–208; EU (2018).

[25] Hauck (2020); Fabricius (2021); ICG (2021) p. 5.

transnational crimes, €20 million towards strengthening pan-African government institutions, and another €20 million towards the implementation of continental legal instruments.[26] Under pillar two, the EU intends to support infrastructure projects (€88 million), economic integration (€40 million), and agriculture and raw materials (€40 million).[27] Under pillar three, the EU will spend €50 million on education and another €50 million on research and innovation.[28] According to the EU, between 2014 and 2020, the following were expended under the PanAf initiative: €12.5 million support for the African Continental Free Trade Area (AfCFTA) negotiations; €60 million support to health system, rural development, economic recovery and social cohesion and reconciliation in Central African countries; €50 million support for combatting the Ebola epidemic and food security crisis in the Democratic Republic of Congo; €100 million for mitigating the impact of Cyclone Idai crisis in Mozambique; €6 million support each for trade negotiations capacity development in Namibia and Botswana; €14 million support for physical and digital interconnectivity in Southern Africa; €8 million for the development of air transport network in Southern Africa; €8 million for the development of ICT sector in Eastern Africa, Southern Africa and Indian Ocean (EA-SA-IO) region; €73 million support for economic and trade integration in the Common Market for Eastern and Southern Africa (COMESA); €74 million support for job creation and investment programmes in Eastern and Southern Africa; and €20 million support for maritime and port security and safety of navigation in Eritrea, Sudan, Djibouti, Somalia, Yemen and Ethiopia.[29]

The APF is the framework through which the EU supports the AU Commission and its RECs to operationalise the African Peace and Security Architecture (APSA).[30] According to the African Peace Facility Annual Report of 2019, the EU disbursed over €2.7 billion between 2004 and 2019 to provide support under three critical rubrics: African-led peace support operations; African Peace and Security Architecture (APSA); and Early Response Mechanism (ERMs).[31] The peace support operations (PSOs) gulped 93% of the total APF contracts (€2681.2 million).[32] Other PSOs that have benefitted from APF include ECOWAS Mission to Guinea Bissau (ECOMIB), the Regional Cooperation Initiative for the Elimination of the Lord's Resistance Army (RCI-LRA), Multi-National Joint Task Force (MNJTF) of the Lake Chad Basin Commission, and the Intergovernmental Authority on Development (IGAD)-led Monitoring and Verification Mechanism (MVM)/ Ceasefire Transitional Security Arrangement Monitoring Mechanism (CTSAMM)

[26] EU (2018), p. 3.

[27] Ibid, p. 6.

[28] Ibid.

[29] European Commission (2021), pp. 123–125.

[30] EU (2017), p. 5.

[31] EU (2020), p. 10.

[32] Ibid.

in South Sudan.[33] Capacity building programmes under the APSA accounted for 6% (€171.8 million) while ERMs initiatives accounted for 1% (€28 million) of total APF contracts.[34]

As already mentioned in the foregoing, the EPF is the new framework for EU's engagement with the continent. The shift towards EPF also speaks to European policymakers' perception of Africa's security issues as a threat to European peace and stability.[35] The EU has budgeted €5 billion, from 2021 to 2027, to achieve EPF objectives.[36] However, non-military funding for African security will continue under the APF until 2024.[37] Unlike the APF, the EPF has a global scope, with support for institutional capacity building and ERMs placed under the new Neighbourhood, Development and International Cooperation Instrument.[38] This change is in line with EU's approach of harmonising its member states' defence and military cooperation under a coherent foreign policy umbrella.[39] In addition, the EU's experience in funding security initiatives across the continent shaped its position on moving towards a flexible, EU controlled approach. For example, the financial support to the AU Mission in Somalia (AMISOM), where costs ballooned beyond initial expectations, thereby prompting the EU to cut contributions in 2016, much to AU's chagrin, was an experience that the EU would not want to repeat.[40] The experience with funding ad-hoc security arrangements, such as MNJTF and the G5 Sahel Joint Force, where, unlike AMISOM, the EU's financial commitment was limited and less bureaucratic, reinforced the benefits of a flexible option.[41]

EU's influence, particularly its financing of continental integration and ideological purview, negatively impacts the politico-legal legitimacy of continental integration in two key ways. One is how it curtails the objective legitimacy of the AU. Objective legitimacy in this respect denotes the way in which the AU exercises full control over its programmes and projects, sustainability of such programmes, and the ability to assert itself over its member states and regional economic communities (RECs). Central to these three factors is the question of the extent to which the AU owns the regional integration process, which further speaks to the limitation of external interference. The EU has on occasions used its funding as a manipulative political tool to further its agenda. For example, the EU bypassed the AU by funding ad-hoc security arrangements such as the MJTF and G5 in the Sahel.[42] This act undercuts the AU's normative role in ensuring that peace and security matters are

---

[33] EU (2017), pp. 16–18.

[34] EU (2020), p. 10.

[35] ICG (2021), p. 4.

[36] Ibid.

[37] Ibid, p. 5.

[38] Ibid.

[39] Ibid.

[40] Ibid, p. 6.

[41] Ibid, pp. 6–7.

[42] ICG (2017), pp. 12–13.

done within the APSA framework. Relatedly, the EU's selective approach to funding peace and security measures has in certain cases led to rivalry and competition between AU and its RECs, an action that weakens relational engagement.[43] Furthermore, the EU has shown how its actions can affect the sustainability of AU projects. In 2016, the EU unilaterally reduced its funding of the AU Mission in Somalia (AMISOM) by 20%, and subsequently suspended payments to AMISOM troops, based on the AU's failure to meet its Pillar Assessment on the management of EU funding.[44] Although the funding was later resumed, the disruption of the AU mission served as a hard lesson on dangers of excessive reliance on external funding.[45] Similarly, the EU has also used its funding to ensure that Africa negotiate its Economic Partnership Agreement (EPA) with sub-regional groupings rather than a continental collective.[46] In 2018, the AU Executive Council adopted the AU African common position on negotiating a post-Cotonou trade agreement, which proposed that Africa should negotiate as a group, to be represented by the AU, separately from the African Caribbean and Pacific (ACP) group of states.[47]

In terms of the subjective legitimacy of the AU, the EU influence manifests through the inability of the AU to envision a continental regionalism outside of Eurocentric, neo-liberal paradigms. Beyond institutional similarities, the AU has anchored its socio-economic integrative agenda to the objectives of a free market economy, with growth linked to increased foreign investment and integration into the global economy. As Staeger observed, the EU helps sustain this agenda by explicitly promoting economic liberalisation schemes and providing technical and financial support to African regional trade agreements.[48] The AEC Treaty, NEPAD, Agenda 2063, and AfCFTA all speak to this singular objective, with little or no indication of exploring relevance, suitability and context.[49] This approach limits the possibility of a decolonial, Afrocentric conception of continental regionalism. While the EU might appear appealing as a referential framework on a theoretical plane, the reality is that Africa will have to fashion its own approach. Africa's search for lessons must transcend the adoption of EU's institutional architecture and policies. As Olivier & Olivier pointed out, "authentic integration in Africa seems possible, but according to architecture still to be discovered and designed".[50] Such "architecture" should be autochthonous and sensitive to local specificities. Nevertheless, it should also include elements that have been responsible for the success of other integration initiatives. These include variables like peace and security, good governance and human rights. Furthermore, the Afrocentric idea of regionalism should speak to

---

[43] Ibid, pp. 14–15.

[44] Ibid, p. 19.

[45] Ibid.

[46] Sicurelli (2010), p. 183.

[47] AU (2018d).

[48] Staeger (2016), p. 992.

[49] AU (2001), pp. 8–9; AU (2013), p. 6.

[50] Olivier and Olivier (2004), p. 362.

broadening the ideational foundations of African regionalism in a way that critically interrogates the assumed supremacy of Eurocentric norms by centring pan-African epistemic notion of plurality and equality of thoughts and worldview.

The table above shows that despite AU's imitation of the EU process, there still exists some fundamental differences. The EU's institutional and normative processes are deeper than that of the AU. It also shows that there is deeper integration at the sub-regional level in Africa.

4.3 Complex Relational Dynamics

Relational issues within the African continental integration ecosystem is governed by a mix of binding and non-binding instruments. These instruments are aimed at finding some balance and unity in regional integration landscape that is defined by multiple politico-legal systems, divergent understanding of the expected shape of regional integration, and the unwillingness to commit to integrative agendas and projects. Complex relational dynamics under regional integration is not necessarily a negative thing; such is expected in a situation where different actors, with different national and regional interests, must interact. It, however, becomes problematic in a situation where there exists no pragmatic approach to manage and channel it into a feasible agenda. The complex relational issues within the continental integration process has often resulted in paralysis and remains one of the key focus of reform efforts. This section will show how these issues continue to hinder meaningful progress.

4.3.1 AU-REC Relations

Underlining AU-REC relations is the principle of subsidiarity. As Nathan noted, the principle of subsidiarity "means that a central authority should play a secondary role; performing only those functions that cannot be performed at a more local level".[51] In this respect, RECs are expected to be the first line of action on addressing integrative issues and only when they are not able to efficiently and effectively fulfil this will the AU step in. Article 3(l) of the AU Constitutive Act mandates the AU to coordinate and harmonise the policies of existing and future RECs.[52] Although there are

[51] Nathan (2016), p. 1.

[52] This derives from Article. 4(1)(d) of the AEC Treaty (1991).

Table 4.2 Member states of major sub-regional organisations in Africa[a]

COUNTRIES	AMU	CEMAC	COMESA	CENSAD	EAC	ECCAS	CEPGL	ECOWAS	IOC	IGAD	MRU	SACU	SADC	WAEMU	ICGRL
ALGERIA	*														
ANGOLA						*							*		*
BENIN				*				*						*	
BOTSWANA												*	*		
BURKINA FASO				*				*						*	*
BURUNDI			*		*	*	*								
CAMEROON		*				*									
CAPE VERDE				*				*							
CENTRAL AFRICAN REPUBLIC		*		*		*									*
CHAD		*		*		*									
CONGO		*				*									*
COMOROS			*	*					*				*		
COTE D'IVOIRE				*				*			*			*	
DEMOCRATIC REPUBLIC OF CONGO			*			*	*						*		*
DJIBOUTI			*	*						*					
EGYPT			*	*											
ESWATINI			*									*	*		
ERITREA			*	*						*					
ETHIOPIA			*							*					
GABON		*				*									
GAMBIA				*				*							
GHANA				*				*							
GUINEA				*				*			*				
GUINEA BISSAU				*				*						*	

(continued)

Table 4.2 (continued)

COUNTRIES	AMU	CEMAC	COMESA	CENSAD	EAC	ECCAS	CEPGL	ECOWAS	IOC	IGAD	MRU	SACU	SADC	WAEMU	ICGRL
EQUATORIAL GUINEA		*				*									
KENYA			*	*	*					*					*
LESOTHO												*	*		
LIBERIA				*				*			*				
LIBYA	*		*	*											
MADAGASCAR			*						*				*		
MALAWI			*										*		
MALI				*				*						*	
MAURITANIA	*			*											
MAURITIUS			*						*				*		
MOROCCO	*			*											
MOZAMBIQUE													*		
NAMIBIA												*	*		
NIGER				*				*						*	
NIGERIA				*				*							
UGANDA			*		*					*					*
RWANDA			*		*	*	*								*
SAO TOME				*		*									
SENEGAL				*				*						*	
SEYCHELLES			*						*				*		
SIERRA LEONE				*				*			*				
SOMALIA				*						*					
SOUTH AFRICA												*	*		
SOUTH SUDAN			*		*					*					*
SUDAN			*	*						*					*

TANZANIA					*								*		*
TOGO				*				*						*	
TUNISIA	*			*											
ZAMBIA			*										*		*
ZIMBABWE			*										*		

Author's construction based on information on the AU and RECs' websites

[a]There are many other regional cooperation arrangements on the continent dealing with security, harmonisation of laws, monetary union, and economic integration. This includes, but not limited to, the Multinational Joint Task Force (MJTF) (Composed of Benin, Cameroon, Chad Niger and Nigeria); the Common Market Area (CMA) (Composed of South Africa, Eswatini, Lesotho and Namibia); the Organisation for the Harmonisation of Business Laws in Africa (OHADA) (Composed of Benin, Burkina Faso, Cameroon, Central African Republic, Chad, Comoros, Congo, Cote d'Ivoire, Equatorial Guinea, Gabon, Guinea, Guinea-Bissau, Mali, Niger, Senegal and Togo); and the G5 Sahel (Composed of Burkina Faso, Chad, Mali, Mauritania, and Niger)

numerous sub-regional organisations in Africa (see Table 4.2 below), the AU only recognises 8 of these as the building blocks of continental integration in Africa.[53]

In achieving the objective of harmonising the frameworks of RECs, a Protocol on the Relations between the AU and RECs was drafted in 2008, to replace the 1998 protocol that was adopted under aegis of the Organisation of African Unity (OAU).[54] This Protocol never came into force. A major problem of the protocol is that it only provides vague articulation of roles and functions of the AU and RECs. There are no specific guidelines on how the AU and RECs are supposed to align their policies, the functions of the AU liaison offices within the RECs headquarters, and how REC-established national integration structures should interface with the AU liaison office.[55]

However, there is a new Protocol amending the 2008 Protocol. The Protocol came into force in November 2021 upon the signatures of the AUC Chairperson and three RECs.[56] Unlike the 2008 protocol, the "Protocol Amending the 2008 Protocol on Relations between the AU and RECs" covers a wider scope of activities such as gender equality, good governance, human rights, peace and security, and further stipulates the nature of the mid-year coordinating meeting between the AU and RECs.[57] It prioritises the principles of subsidiarity and complementarity, by allowing RECs to deal with issues that are primarily within their area of competence.[58] The new protocol established the following interactive structures: the Bureau of the Assembly and Chairpersons of the RECs;[59] the Committee on Coordination (composed of the chairperson and chief executives of financial institutions of the AU and the AUDA-NEPAD);[60] and the Coordination Secretariat (composed of the representatives of the AU, RECs and other AU organs).[61] The protocol encourages horizontal cooperation among RECs for undertaking joint programmes.[62] Furthermore, RECs are encouraged to share information and invite each other to meetings where issues of mutual interest are discussed.[63] The AU can

---

[53]The recognised RECs are: Arab Maghreb Union (UMA), Common Market for Eastern and Southern Africa (COMESA), Community of Sahel–Saharan States (CEN–SAD), East African Community (EAC), Economic Community of Central African States (ECCAS), Economic Community of West African States (ECOWAS), Intergovernmental Authority on Development (IGAD), and Southern African Development Community (SADC).

[54]See Protocol on Relations between the (AU) and the RECs (2008).

[55]Fagbayibo (2019b), p. 450.

[56]Erasmus and Hartzenberg (2022).

[57]Article 7 of the Protocol Amending the 2008 Protocol on Relations Between the AU and the RECs (2019).

[58]Ibid, Articles 3 and 12(2).

[59]Ibid, Article 7.

[60]Ibid, Article 8.

[61]Ibid, Article 10.

[62]Ibid, Article 16.

[63]Ibid, Article 17.

also attend, without voting rights, the meetings of RECs.[64] In addition, the AU will open permanent liaison offices within the headquarters of the RECs.[65] In order to promote the principle of common position, RECs are allowed to negotiate with external parties to the extent that this does not conflict with the objectives of the Constitutive Act and the AEC Treaty.[66] The protocol is binding on the parties, and any unjustifiable derogation will be dealt with in accordance with the sanctioning principles of the AU Constitutive Act.[67]

In line with the objective of achieving AU-RECs cooperation, the AU held its first mid-year AU-REC coordinating meeting on the 8th of July 2019 in Niamey, Niger.[68] The meeting made declarations regarding the report on the status of regional integration in Africa; the division of labour among member states, RECs and the AU; mobilisation of resources by member states, RECs, AU Commission and AUDA-NEPAD towards the strengthening of regional integration; and mandated the AU Commission, RECs and other stakeholders to finalise the draft protocol on AU-REC relations, which has now now come into effect, for consideration by the Executive Council.[69]

Another normative instrument that speaks to AU-REC relations is the "Memorandum of Understanding on Cooperation in the Area of Peace and Security Between the African Union, the Regional Economic Communities", which was adopted in 2008.[70] This MoU is legally binding between the AU and its RECs. It is, however, curtailed by the fact that it fails to specify or clarify the roles, functions and powers of the AU and RECs. For example, the MOU stipulates that the arrangement for cooperation will include exchange of information, meetings and joint activities but provides no specifics on division of labour or thresholds of intervention between the AU and RECs.[71]

One other attempt at ensuring coordination and harmonisation of the frameworks of the RECs is the COMESA-EAC-SADC Tripartite Free Trade Area (TFTA), which was launched in June 2015. Comprising 29-member states, with a combined population of 800 million people, the idea of the TFTA is not to create a new regional institution but to "start working towards a merger into a single REC with the objective of fast tracking the attainment of the African Economic Community".[72] Positioned as a building block of the AfCFTA, the TFTA Agreement commits to championing and expediting the continental integration process under the Treaty establishing the African Economic Community and the Constitutive Act of the

[64] Ibid, article 20.

[65] Ibid, Article 22.

[66] Ibid, Article 29.

[67] Ibid, Article 23.

[68] AU (2019b).

[69] Ibid.

[70] MoU between AU and RECs (2008).

[71] Ibid, Article 15.

[72] COMESA, EAC, & SADC (2008).

African Union through regional initiatives; resolve the issue of overlapping membership of its member states to RECs; and deepen regional integration and trade amongst its member states.[73] In ensuring that there is no overlapping and conflictive issues, the TFTA Agreement stipulates that no new tariff and non-tariff barriers will be imposed on member states, and that the Agreement will build on existing frameworks for harmonisation purposes.[74] The TFTA Agreement is yet to come into force as it needs at least 14 ratifications, and only eight have ratified thus far.[75] The question on how the TFTA will contribute to the harmonisation objectives of the AU, and also as a complementary element of the AfCFTA,[76] will depend on the political willingness of its member states to commit to its trade liberalisation agenda.

The lack of a binding normative framework, which has now been remedied by the new protocol, including the ambiguities in existent documents, fosters an incoherent and conflictive relationship between the AU and RECs. The 2019 AU Report on the state of regional integration aptly captured this point:

> African integration is a goal that no one institution or body can achieve on its own. It involves several national, regional and continental entities, and with inefficient and ineffective coordination, the process can take a beating. Coordinating the activities of the different stakeholders in implementing the integration agenda thus poses a major challenge to the success of African integration.[77]

Another challenge is that RECs are at different stages of development and are encumbered by nagging issues of underfunding, lack of capacity, physical infrastructure challenges, and little or no assertive powers over their member states.[78] As noted in the foregoing, the AU and RECs have in some cases found themselves in competition for accessing EU funding for trade negotiations and peace and security issues. The lack of effective harmonisation of laws within RECs is another critical drawback. RECs are expected to be the springboard for eventual continental harmonisation of laws, however, the fragmentation of legal systems remain a hindering factor. Due to the colonial enterprise, African nations subscribe to different Eurocentric legal traditions—common law, civil law and in some cases hybrid legal systems (e.g. South Africa). Other factors responsible for the diversity of laws in Africa include the existence of various indigenous laws within a particular country and the introduction of the system of federalism, which has resulted in the different

[73] TFTA Agreement (2015).

[74] Ibid, Articles 9 & 10.

[75] This includes Namibia, Burundi, Egypt, Uganda, Kenya, South Africa, Botswana and Rwanda.

[76] The TFTA is in line with the variable geometry stipulation of Article 19 of the AfCFTA Agreement: "State Parties that are members of other regional economic communities, regional trading arrangements and custom unions, which have attained among themselves higher levels of regional integration than under this Agreement, shall maintain such higher levels among themselves".

[77] AU Commission (2019), p. 14.

[78] See NEPAD (2015), pp. 26–29.

application of laws within a particular state.[79] This reality has resulted in a situation where countries find it convenient to harmonise around a shared legal system (e.g. the OHADA, CEMAC and WAEMU) or sub-regional (e.g. SADC and ECOWAS).

The Organisation of the Harmonisation of Business Laws in Africa (OHADA) is the most successful harmonisation of law project on the continent. The character of the OHADA Treaty, which was adopted on 17 October 1993, is essentially pro-development and business inclined.[80] Built around the existing economic and political relations among francophone African countries,[81] the Treaty aims to accelerate economic development and foreign investments in member states through the provision of a secure judicial environment. The Treaty regulates—through the Uniform Acts—the following areas: company law, general commercial law, securities, enforcement measures, insolvency law, arbitration, accounting law and transport.[82] At present, there are seventeen member states spread across west and central Africa.[83] Since the majority of member states are francophone countries, the OHADA laws are largely based on the French legal system.[84] In pursuant of the goal of continental integration, the Treaty provides that membership is open to all member states of the AU.[85] Despite OHADA's appeal as a possible nucleus or framework for continental harmonisation, its prioritisation of the French language and civil law for the interpretation and application of norms remain an impediment as it will have to accommodate other legal traditions.[86] However, this does not prevent other RECs from adopting and adapting its best practises, especially in terms of political willingness to create an environment where transnational laws become binding and directly applicable in member states.[87]

[79] Bamodu (1994), pp. 125–130.

[80] See generally, Dickerson (2005).

[81] Each of the OHADA member states belong to the two major French based economic and monetary zones: West Africa—*Union Economique et Monetaire Ouest Africaine* (UEMOA) and Central Africa—*Communaute Economique et Monetaire l'Afrique Centrale* (CEMAC).

[82] OHADA website.

[83] They include Benin, Burkina Faso, Cameroon, Central African Republic, Chad, Comoros, Congo, Cote d'Ivoire, Democratic Republic of Congo, Gabon, Equatorial Guinea, Guinea, Guinea -Bissau, Mali, Niger, Senegal and Togo. Most of the OHADA members are francophone countries with few exceptions: Equatorial Guinea (Spanish), Guinea -Bissau (Portuguese) and the English-speaking parts of Cameroon.

[84] The laws of Guinea Bissau (which was colonised by Portugal) and Equatorial Guinea (colonised by Spain) are similar to the French legal system. This was due to the influence of the French Commercial Code on the Spanish and Portuguese laws. These laws belong to the civil law tradition. See La Porta et al. (1998), p. 1118.

[85] OHADA Treaty – General Clause Title 1, art. 53.

[86] Fagbayibo (2009), pp. 317–318.

[87] Oppong (2011), p. 111.

4.3.2 AU-Member States Relations

The state-centric nature of continental regionalism makes AU member states primary and privileged players in the regional integration matrix. Unlike the RECs, member states have direct representations in structures, like the AU Assembly and Executive Council, where binding decisions on continental integration are taken. As members of RECs, member states also play a key role in issues that directly and indirectly shape the politico-legal direction of the AU. AU—member states relations are typically discussed within certain paradigms of engagement. This includes inter-state negotiations and compromises within the AU, member states' compliance with AU norms, roles of regional hegemons in shaping continental regionalism, and the extent to which certain member states obstruct or aid the enhancement of the powers of the AU. Through these broad arenas of engagement, law and politics converge and diverge in continental integration process. In the context of this chapter, some specific interactive dynamics are worth exploring. This is discussed below.

In what is described in literature as the "spaghetti bowl" effect, the landscape of regional integration in Africa is defined by multiple RECs with overlapping and replicated membership.[88] As shown in Table 4.2 below, only two AU member state, Algeria (AMU) and Mozambique (SADC), belong to one REC. Despite AU's position on the rationalisation of membership of RECs, Morocco, Democratic Republic of Congo, and Burundi have in recent years applied to be members of ECOWAS, EAC and SADC respectively. However, in 2019, SADC rejected Burundi's application, stating that it has failed to meet its requirement for adherence to democratic norms.[89] Several reasons have been identified for the multiple membership of RECs by African countries. These range from strategic and political reasons (a case of not putting all of one's eggs inside the same basket); economic reasons (possibility of reaping higher economic growth rates and geo-strategic calculations to access bigger markets and gain influence); complementarity (possibility of integrating on various fronts); historical reasons (shared colonial inheritance of regional structures); geographical proximity (contiguous boundaries and resources); need for additional external resources; political pressure; and cultural vision.[90] The negative implications of multiple membership for continental integration far outweighs the positives. Some of the adverse implications of multiple and overlapping memberships of RECs include inadequate payment of financial contributions to the various RECs (including to the AU), low implementation of programmes, low attendance to meetings, and the implementation of conflicting programmes.[91] Byiers et al. showed how Rwanda, due to its overstretched financial commitments to different regional organisations, have had to renegotiate its levy

[88]Byiers et al. (2019); AU & UNECA (2006), p. 50.

[89]EIU (2019).

[90]AU & UNECA (2006), pp. 52–54; Byiers et al. (2019), pp. 2–3, 5–6; Welz (2014), pp. 17–18; Gathii (2009), pp. 642–656.

[91]AU & UNECA (2006), pp. 54–58; Gathii (2009), pp. 656–666.

commitments to the EAC, and also its 0.2% import levy contribution to the AU.[92] Where RECs have similar programmes and objectives, member states find themselves in a position of replicating obligations and commitments. For example, countries such as the Democratic Republic of Congo, Malawi, Mauritius, Seychelles, Zambia, and Zimbabwe that have concurrent memberships of COMESA and SADC must make duplicated free trade area commitments to both organisations.[93] In a situation where the RECs are at varying levels of developments or have different objectives, member states are caught in the conflicting situation of having to conform and breach commitments at the same time. For example, member states that belong to a far more advanced customs union regional integration arrangement under EAC (Kenya and Uganda) and SACU (e.g. Eswatini) are also expected to conform to COMESA's embryonic free trade arrangement.[94] Another problem is that external partners such as the UN and the EU often struggle to identify the line of cooperation when faced with overlapping regional frameworks.[95]

Another element of AU—member states relational dynamics is the problem of compliance. Compliance with AU norms is far from been the expected organisational default mechanism as member states routinely flout stipulated political, legal and economic objectives of the organisation. Similar position exists in the RECs.[96] The AU compliance crisis is best understood within two interrelated perspectival frames: demand and supply sides.[97] The demand side perspective denotes the normative stipulations regarding compliance with organisational norms.[98] Articles 23 and 30 of the AU Constitutive Act stipulate the consequences of non-compliance. This includes suspension from AU activities, denial of the right to speak or vote or present candidates for AU positions when a member has defaulted payment of dues, and the imposition of sanction.[99] These provisions are central to ensuring that AU decisions stemming from the AU Assembly—either based on its own initiative or coming from other AU organs such as the Executive Council, the AU Commission, the African Commission on Human and Peoples' Rights

---

[92] Byiers et al. (2019), p. 13.

[93] AU & UNECA (2006), p. 54.

[94] Ibid.

[95] Ibid, p. 7.

[96] For example, Himbara (2020) shows how member states in the East African Community (EAC) continue to routinely flout organisational norms and procedures. This includes actions such as bordure closure between Rwanda and Uganda since February 2019; Tanzania's ban on Uganda's timber, sugar and maize; Kenya's reluctance to open its market to Uganda's manufactured products; and Tanzania's decision to bar Kenyan Airways from flying into the country in retaliation to Kenya's refusal to allow Tanzania's truck drivers from entering the country due to the COVID-19 pandemic. Similarly, the Nigerians government, in violation of ECOWAS norms, closed its land borders (for the movement of goods) with Benin, Cameroon, Chad and Niger from August 2019 until December 2020. See Kwarkye and Matongbada (2021).

[97] Fagbayibo (2019b), p. 453.

[98] Ibid.

[99] See Articles 23 & 30 of the AU Constitutive Act.

(AfCHPR), and the African Court on Human and Peoples' Rights (AfCtHPR)—are complied with.

There are, however, reasons why demand-oriented provisions such as this may not engender full compliance. One reason is the ambiguity or vagueness of such provisions. According to the legitimacy theory of compliance, the indeterminacy of norms or provisions could provide member states with the ammunition to either disregard or struggle to comply.[100] In the context of the AU, Elvy pointed out that the inability to provide clear time frames from when the AU Assembly issues directives on non-compliance to when such directives are communicated to the relevant member state provides a loophole for inaction.[101] In addressing this issue of ambiguity regarding sanctions against defaulting states under Article 23(2) of the Constitutive Act, the AU in 2018 released clear guidelines on thresholds of implementation. It includes the following thresholds:[102]

- Cautionary (which applies to member states that have not paid 50% of their assessed dues in six months and deprives such member states the right to contribute to AU meetings);
- Intermediate (which applies to member states in arrears for 1 year and suspends the member states from nominating their nationals for appointment or participation in AU activities and employment); and
- Comprehensive (which applies to member states that have defaulted payments for 2 years and are liable for a combination of cautionary and intermediary sanctions plus suspension from participating in AU meetings).

Another problem is the deliberate political strategy of the AU Assembly to refuse to impose sanctions or redefine the demand provisions against errant member states. For example, the AU Assembly has never activated Article 4(h), even when responsible AU structures such as the PSC has recommended intervention. According to Tieku, one reason why this provision is yet to be invoked is due

> to the informal understanding in African diplomatic circles that African governments will vehemently oppose any attempt to label conflicts in their states as genocide ... instead ... the AU leadership came to an informal agreement that they will intervene in any AU member state where a major violent conflict is occurring without invoking the intervention clause.[103]

Kuwali also argued that the lack of a common definition on what constitutes genocide, war crimes and crimes against humanity under Article 4(h) may cause paralysis and politicisation of intervention.[104] This position has, however, been addressed by the, yet to be ratified, Malabo Protocol, which provided specific

[100] Franck (1988), pp. 713–714.
[101] Elvy (2012), pp. 90–91.
[102] AU (2018a).
[103] Tieku (2019), p. 235.
[104] Kuwali (2008), p. 107.

definitions of genocide, war crimes and crimes against humanity.[105] The fact that the Burundi case came after this protocol was drafted, and yet the AU Assembly refused to act despite the PSC's recommendation of Article 4(h) intervention, further lends credence to the prioritisation of politics.[106]

The supply side of compliance speaks to both transnational and national dimensions that accentuate the possibility of non-compliance.[107] The transnational aspect focuses on the extent to which member states have endowed regional institutions with the requisite competence to monitor and enforce compliance. One major drawback in this respect is that regional institutions lack the technocratic capacity to ensure effective supervision.[108] The 2014 African Capacity Report highlighted that many of African regional organisations remain hampered by the inability to recruit competent staff, and importantly, do not have advanced research units to anticipate or counteract compliance issues.[109] Similarly, the 2007 AU Audit Report highlighted the inefficient recruitment process at the AU, which is often based on a quota system, and thus restricts the possibility of employing competent persons and also understaffing issues.[110] Secondly, transnational institutions such as PAP and AU Commission lack the normative powers to prescribe or enforce directives to member states, and have to rely on the AU Assembly to help carry out enforcements.[111] The AU Assembly often defaults to placing premium over member states' solidarity by resorting to either a tepid response or completely ignoring the recommendations to act. At the national level, the supply-side constraints range from a dysfunctional public service that is incapable of implementing transnational programmes,[112] deliberate strategies by the executive to weaken and/or side-line the relevant national structures such as the legislature and judiciary,[113] political instability and conflicts,[114] and weak economic structures. Either occurring separately or jointly, these factors are serious impediments to member states' realising the salient goals of continental integration. This then calls for a strategic approach that sees national and AU reforms as conjoined rather than isolated measures. These issues are further explored in the next chapter.

---

[105] See Articles 28B – 28D of the Protocol on Amendments to the Protocol on the Statute of the African Court of Justice and Human Rights (2014).

[106] Connolly (2016).

[107] Fagbayibo (2019b), p. 454.

[108] Ibid.

[109] ACBF (2014), pp. 58–59, 74–75.

[110] AU (2007b), pp. 50–51.

[111] Fagbayibo (2019b), p. 454.

[112] Mkandawire (2002), pp. 15–16; Ayee (2005), pp. 21–23; Igbokwe-Ibeto (2019), pp. 7–9.

[113] Aniwa (2008) p. 74. Ellett (2015), p. 7.

[114] ACBF (2014), p. 58; Viljoen and Louw (2007), p. 27; IMF (2001), p. 4; UNECA et al. (2012), p. 72.

4.3.3 AU-Civil Society Relations

Civil society is involved in the continental integration process through a range of normative and non-normative activities. The ECOSOCC is established as the primary platform through which civil society is expected to participate in the continental integration process. According to Article 22(1) of the AU Constitutive Act, the ECOSOCC serves as an advisory organ composed of different social and professional bodies from member states. As a means of facilitating this involvement, the AU renamed the OAU Secretariat supporting the Conference for Security, Stability, Development and Cooperation in Africa (CSSDCA) as the African Citizens' Directorate (CIDO) in 2005.[115] CIDO is a unit under the AU Commission and has three responsibilities: liaison with civil society organisations on the continent; outreach to the diaspora outside Africa; and coordinates the secretariat functions of ECOSOCC.[116]

Article 22(2) of the AU Constitutive Act grants the AU Assembly the powers to determine ECOSOCC's governing framework. In line with this, the AU Assembly adopted the ECOSOCC Statute, which was a culmination of work done by the AU and CSOs, in 2004.[117] According to the statute, the objectives of ECOSOCC include the promotion of dialogue between all segments of the African people, promote the participation of civil society in the implementation of policies and programmes of the AU, and support the policies and programmes of the AU.[118] It is composed of 150 CSOs from within Africa and the diaspora, with the stipulation that the election of members must ensure 50% gender equality and that 50% of representatives must be between ages of 18 and 35.[119] The organs of ECOSOCC include the General Assembly (which is the highest decision making body); a Standing Committee (which coordinates the works of the organ); Sectoral Cluster Committees (which works on different thematic issues); and the Credentials Committee (which examines the credentials of members of the organ).[120] In terms of the eligibility of membership of ECOSOCC, CSOs seeking membership have to be registered for at least 3 years in any of the AU member states, and show that in terms of their membership and funding, there are at least 50% Africans or African diaspora and that 50% of their funding must come from the members of the organisation.[121] This provision is aimed at excluding foreign CSOs from ECOSOCC.

---

[115] AFRODAD et al. (2007), p. 29.

[116] Ibid, p. 30.

[117] Ibid, p. 33; ECOSOCC Statute.

[118] Article 2 of the ECOSOCC Statute.

[119] The 150 members include two CSOs from each AU member state, 10 CSOs operating at regional level, eight CSOs operating at continental level, 20 CSOs from the African diaspora, and six ex-officio members nominated by the AU Commission after consultation with member states. See Ibid, Article 4.

[120] Ibid, Article 8.

[121] Ibid, Article 6.

Despite the state-centric nature of continental integration, CSOs play several roles in shaping the AU process. Finizo conceptualised CSOs participation in the continental integration process under four broad functions.[122] The first is the articulation of political demands at the continental level. Under this rubric, civil society engage in networking activities with officials aimed at making their political demands heard.[123] One major example here is how civil society continue to push for democratisation and adherence to human rights in the AU through cases before the AfCtHPR, and the demand that member states implement the decisions emanating from these organs.[124] The second is promoting the change and strengthening of the AU. In this respect, CSOs have been able to push for the adoption on protocols on women; made strategic inputs to the 2007 "Grand Debate on Union Government"; drafted a constitution for an envisaged "United States of Africa" in 2005; participated in shaping the AU Agenda 2063 document; set up online platforms in popularising and curating AU activities; and have played central role in providing consultancy functions to the AU in drafting policies and programmes.[125] The third is the constituent function of civil society. This speaks to the active role of civil society in the creation of new institutions under the AU.[126] Examples include the influence of civil society in the institutional design of the AfCtHPR and its merger with the African Court of Justice, and the establishment of special human rights rapporteurs by the African Commission.[127] Lastly, is the way CSOs provide support to the functional activities of the AU. Civil society continue to play an influential role in the promotion and protection of fundamental rights and democratic governance in the AU.[128] In this regard, CSOs engage in initiatives that promotes awareness of the activities of the AU human rights system, the submission of cases to the Commission and Court, ensuring that the periodic reports of member states to the African Commission are accurate and factual, and norm and agenda setting activities through organising seminars and conferences on specific aspects of the ACHPR.[129]

Despite these involvements, several issues continue to undermine the effectiveness of civil society in the matrix of continental integration. First is the lack of coherent and consistent approach on how civil society is expected to access the AU and contribute to the development of continental integration. While ECOSOCC is supposed to be the primary platform for such engagement, there is no articulate mechanism that systematically streamlines the activities of other CSOs that interact

---

[122] Finizo (2018), pp. 307–313.

[123] Ibid, p. 307.

[124] Ibid, p. 308.

[125] Ibid, pp. 308–309; ACSO (2005); Tieku (2017), pp. 48–50.

[126] Finizo (2018), p. 310.

[127] Ibid, pp. 310–311.

[128] Ibid, p. 311.

[129] Ibid, pp. 311–312.

with the AU outside the ECOSOCC framework.[130] Furthermore, CIDO has been criticised for lack of transparency in the way it regulates CSOs' access, and invitation, to the AU.[131]

The second point is ECOSOCC's legitimacy question. In this respect, the process of electing ECOSOCC members at the national and continental levels remain opaque, with little or no knowledge of the emergence of such representatives and the agenda they aim to pursue at ECOSOCC.[132] This is why ECOSOCC has been referred to as a "club of friends" that are connected to government rather than the grassroot.[133] This perception is further enhanced by the limited awareness of the existence and activities of ECOSOCC by the African populace.[134] Furthermore, the eligibility requirements of ECOSOCC is exclusionary. For example, the requirement that a CSO must be registered in an AU member states ignores the reality that some CSOs cannot afford to seek registration, or are even deregistered, in oppressive and authoritarian member states.[135] According to Musila, over the last 15 years, 11 African countries have adopted legislation and policies aimed at curtailing the activities of CSOs.[136] Constraining measures include stringent registration requirements, restrictions of foreign funding and hiring of foreigners, and mandating state officials to interfere in the day-to-day running of CSOs.[137]

Third is the role of member states in curtailing the influence of civil society in the operational milieu of continental integration. Some national governments delegitimise CSOs that are critical of government as neo-colonial and western agents who have no credibility to represent the citizens.[138] National governments also try to influence CSOs by either establishing rival, government backed CSOs and push for those CSOs to be national representatives.[139] In addition, some member states have refused to invite CSOs to AU summits hosted by them.[140]

Lastly is the lack of funding for ECOSOCC. Like the entire AU, ECOSOCC is hampered by insufficient funding by member states. As Finizo observed, in 2014, the AU allocated a paltry sum of US$993.10 to ECOSOCC operations.[141] This shows the little or no relevance attached to civil society participation in the AU. Beyond the rhetoric of civil society involvement in AU activities, there must be a more concerted

[130]Ibid, p. 314.

[131]Ibid. See also AU (2007b), p. 76.

[132]AFRODAD et al. (2007), p. 6.

[133]Ibid, p. 37.

[134]Ibid, p. 6.

[135]Finizo (2018), p. 315.

[136]Musila (2019).

[137]Ibid.

[138]Finizo (2018), p. 314.

[139]Ibid, p. 315.

[140]Ibid, p. 314.

[141]Ibid, p. 315.

effort geared towards enhancing the physical and material infrastructures of such participation.

4.4 The Politics of Reforms

The theme of reform has been a recurring component of the AU since its formation. As the AU is a product of a major overhaul process,[142] it is of little surprise that political elites, technocrats and scholars alike have consistently engaged in the discursive business of refining its institutional praxis. To put differently, the aspiration to move the AU from an intergovernmental structure to a supranational entity remains an underlying factor, and thus the linchpin of reform efforts. Since the formation of the AU, reform efforts have either been comprehensive (dealing with a general institutional overhaul) or thematic (dealing with specific issues such as finance, peace and security, or specific AU organs etc.). Before going into the details of these reforms and how they form the site for politico-legal engagements and disengagements, it is important to first understand the philosophical underpinning of AU reforms.

The issue of African agency is at the core of reform efforts. In this respect, agency denotes the quest for owning the narrative and charting a course that is driven by African actors and context. Zondi described African agency as "the capacity and will of Africa to become an agent of its own transformation, development and relocation from the periphery to the centre".[143] According to Mazrui, the concept of *Pax Africana* underpins African agency as it speaks to an Africa "that is protected and maintained by Africa herself".[144] The mantra "African solution to African problems" is the key descriptive language for conveying this point. It is what Ani described as "the "who" question" in the quest of addressing challenges facing the continent.[145] In this respect, African countries are expected to take the lead in terms of initiating and implementing integration ideas and policies for continental development. In addition to the "who" are the "what" and "how" questions. "What" speaks to the content and scope of the initiatives while "how" refers to the methodological process of achieving such programmes. The "who", "what" and "how" all form the basis of many of the reform efforts. Issues of peace and security, democratic governance, self-financing of continental integration, and the strengthening the powers of transnational institutions are some of the themes covered by both comprehensive and thematic reform documents and programmes.

[142] For a detailed analysis of reform efforts that led to the eventual conception of the AU, see Tieku (2017) pp. 76–90.

[143] Zondi (2012), p. 26.

[144] Mazrui (1967), p. 203.

[145] Ani (2018), p. 141.

Having considered the philosophical underpinning of reform efforts, the next step is to understand the scope and breadth of reform efforts. In doing this, it is important to understand reform efforts in epochal terms. This chronological focus helps place things in context, as it explains the ideational mood that informed the strategic drive towards reforms. There are two broad epochs that define attempts at reforms in the AU. The first is from 2005 to 2011, which were the early years of the organisation, and were aimed at resolving the thorny issues between those that wanted an immediate establishment of a Union Government and those that preferred an incremental approach to achieving continental supranationalism. The second phase is from 2015—present, mainly marked by a pragmatic incremental approach. It must be emphasised that this second epochal phase is a post-Ghaddafi era,[146] with the absence of any significant power bloc pushing for the immediate establishment of a United States of Africa. In this respect, this section will discuss the two epochs, and provide further analysis on the problematics of AU reforms.

4.4.1 Powerplay Between the Maximalists and the Minimalists (2005–2011)

This phase was mainly defined by the attempt to find some form of compromise between the maximalist camp, headed by Muammar Ghaddafi (Libya), and the minimalist camp, driven by Olusegun Obasanjo (Nigeria) and Thabo Mbeki (South Africa). Ghaddafi's role as one of the major financiers of the AU further helped to bolster his position as an ardent advocate of the immediate establishment of a federal union of African states. Seeing that the establishment of the AU in 2002 was essentially a triumph of the minimalist camp, the Ghaddafi camp embarked on a series of efforts to redefine and push for amendments that speak to the immediate establishment of supranational structures. At the 4th Ordinary Session of the Assembly of Heads of State and Government, held in Abuja, Nigeria on 30 and 31 January 2005, Ghaddafi again tabled the proposal on the unification of the continent under a federal structure.[147] The AU Assembly then put together a committee of Heads of State and Government to explore the feasibility of this objective. The Committee was chaired by the President of the Republic of Uganda and composed of Botswana, Chad, Ethiopia, Niger, Senegal, and Tunisia, and was tasked with liaising with the Chairperson of the AU Commission and submit a report by the next Summit in July 2005.[148] The Committee convened a conference, which included a variety of governmental and non-governmental stakeholders, in November 2005, where it

[146] For a discussion on the implications of the demise of Muammar Ghaddafi in 2011 on the state of continental integration in Africa, see the following: Fagbayibo (2011); Ikome (2012).

[147] Assembly/AU/Dec.69 (IV).

[148] Wapmuk (2009), pp. 658–659.

was agreed that although a Union Government was imperative, it has to be achieved incrementally.[149]

To achieve this objective, the AU Assembly established a Committee of Seven—chaired by President Olusegun Obasanjo (Nigeria), and the Heads of State and Government of Algeria, Kenya, Senegal, Gabon, Lesotho, and Uganda—to consider and submit a report on the modalities of establishing a Union Government, and measures aimed at strengthening the AU Commission.[150] The Committee of Seven presented its report in July 2006, detailing the imperative of shared values and common interests and strategic focus areas as key ingredients of achieving a Union Government.[151] Shared values spoke to issues of adherence to the rule of law, democratic governance, transparency in public policy making and prioritisation of indigenous knowledge systems.[152] The report considered 16 strategic focus areas: continental integration (assist member states in building national constituencies for the Union Government/United States of Africa); education, training, skills development, science and technology (promote the exchange of students and academic staff among universities, harmonise the curricula of primary and secondary schools, and promotion of scientific research); energy (a consolidate inventory of hydropower resources in member states and the harmonisation of energy policies); environment (exchange experiences regarding environmental issues and build consensus on emerging environmental issues); external relations (build consensus among member states regarding international issues); food, agriculture and water resources (formulate a continental food policy and self-sufficiency and water resources development strategies); gender and youth (promote gender mainstreaming and participation of youths in Union Government activities); governance and human rights (strengthen existing legal and regulatory regimes in member states); health (harmonisation of health policies and combatting trans-border diseases); industry and mineral resources (harmonisation of member states' industrial policies); finance (manage finance of the Union and the establishment of Union financial institutions); peace and security (establishment and operationalisation of an African Standby Force); social affairs and solidarity (establishment of social security in member states, and research on African traditional solidarity); sport and culture (promotion of research and culture research and participation of African teams in sporting events); trade and customs union (free movement and African common position at international fora); and infrastructure, information technology and biotechnology (harmonisation of transportation and communication policies).[153]

As member states could not agree on these modalities, the 9th Ordinary Summit in Accra, Ghana, in July 2007 was dedicated to holding the "Grand Debate" on the proposed continental government. As expected, the "Grand Debate" was between

[149] Ibid, p. 659.

[150] Assembly/AU/Dec.90 (V).

[151] AU (2006).

[152] Ibid, pp. 6–7.

[153] Ibid, pp. 8–13.

those that preferred an immediate continental government (led by Libya and Senegal) and those that favoured integration in phases and stages (led by Nigeria and South Africa).[154] Rather than providing concrete steps on establishing the Union Government, the AU Assembly decided to provide a compromise document, titled the Accra Declaration. The Accra Declaration essentially affirmed the position of the gradualists and more importantly, paved the way for the first comprehensive audit of the AU.[155]

Based on the terms of the Accra Declaration, an independent High-Level Panel of the Audit of the AU, headed by Adebayo Adedeji, was set up the AU Assembly in 2007.[156] The panel was tasked with extensively reviewing all the organs of the AU, the decisions and agreements of the AU, the state of political and economic integration, and the review of the financial management of the organisation.[157] The report provide incisive and critical comments on the dysfunctionality of the AU as an organisation, and how this can be remedied. It noted that the AU Assembly has not provided the requisite leadership needed for accelerating regional integration.[158] It recommended that its sessions should be more focused, devoted to reviewing the implementation of past decisions, and devoted to themes on regional integration.[159] It further recommended that for continuity and effective leadership, the Chairperson of the AU Assembly should hold office for two, instead of one, years.[160]

In terms of the AU Commission, the report indicated that the vaguely articulated delineation of powers and functions within the organisation has resulted in lack of supervision, failure to delegate functions to Directors and mid-level staff, non-existent internal communication, low morale among staff and consequently, a dysfunctional system.[161] The Report further noted that an inefficient recruitment process (based on the application of a quota system and inadequate publicity of vacancies) restricts the employment of competent persons and leads to understaffing issues in some of the departments of the Commission.[162] The Report then recommended the following measures: bequeathing the Chairperson with powers to exercise full authority, which includes the power to assign portfolios to Commissioners; compulsory induction for all members and staff of the Commission; four-year tenure for elected posts, with the elections of the Chairperson and his or Deputy

[154]Wapmuk (2009), pp. 660–661.

[155]AU (2007a).

[156]However, Cilliers (2008, p. 103) noted that the audit came about as a result of an attempt by Southern African states to checkmate the then Chairperson of the AU Commission, Alpha Konare, who was viewed as belonging to the maximalist ideological camp.

[157]AU (2007b), pp. xvi–xix.

[158]Ibid, p. xxiii.

[159]Ibid.

[160]Ibid.

[161]Ibid, pp. 47–48.

[162]Ibid, pp. 50–51.

taking place a year before those of the Commissioners; assigning the coordination of staff matters and inter-departmental issues to the Secretary to the Commission; mandatory regular meetings of the Commissioners and the Directors; and the establishment of the AU Service Commission (AUSC) to be responsible for recruitment, appointments, promotions and enforcing discipline.[163]

The report also provided some important recommendations on other AU organs. It noted that the composition of the Executive Council as an all-purpose body, which prioritises foreign affairs ministers, is impractical as many of the issues it has to deal with require specialised competences of other ministries.[164] As such, it recommended that the Executive Council of Foreign Ministers be renamed Council of Ministers, with the Specialised Technical Committees (STCs) becoming the sectoral Council of Ministers.[165] The report highlighted that the imperative of reviewing the powers of PAP and how its members are elected.[166] It noted that the legitimacy of PAP is hinged to its ability to exercise meaningful legislative powers and the direct elections of its members.[167] In terms of the AfCtHPR, the report noted that the stipulation that requires the prior consent of member states before individuals can approach the court limits access to the administration of justice.[168] It also identified the dependence of the court on foreign donors, the lack of clarity in terms of the relationship between the court and the African Commission, and the shortage of human resources.[169] It then recommended the accelerated merger of the court with the African Court of Justice (ACJ), allocation of more resources to the court, strict adherence to the decisions of the court, and the mandatory recognition of the competence of the court by member states.[170]

In 2009, Ghaddafi used the opportunity of his chairmanship of the AU Assembly to push for the reform of the AU Commission. This then led to the AU Assembly, at its 12th Ordinary Session in January 2009, adopting the decision to transform the AU Commission into an AU Authority.[171] Under the AU Authority, the positions of the Chairperson, Deputy Chairperson and Commissioner would be re-designated as President, Vice President and Union Secretary respectively.[172] The Union Secretaries will be assigned twelve reconfigured portfolios.[173] The Authority's

[163] Ibid, pp. 46–77.

[164] Ibid, p. 36.

[165] Ibid.

[166] Ibid, p. 84.

[167] Ibid.

[168] Ibid, p. 90.

[169] Ibid.

[170] Ibid, p. 91.

[171] AU (2009).

[172] Ibid.

[173] These include Defence, Peace and Security; Political Affairs and External Relations; International Trade and Co-operation; Continental and Regional Integration; Development, Finance and Economic Planning; Youth, Culture & Social Development; Education, Science and Technology; Agriculture & Water; Environment and Natural Resources; Continental Justice and Legal Affairs; Labour & Migration; and Health & Population. See Ibid.

responsibilities or areas of jurisdiction can be classified, depending on the political sensitivity of the issues concerned, under two rubrics.[174] The first rubric deals with issues that have little impact on national sovereignty: Continent-wide poverty reduction; Inter-regional and continental infrastructure; Global warming, desertification and coastal erosion; Epidemics and pandemics; Research/university centres of excellence; Food security. The second rubric is matters which will have direct impact on state sovereignty: Free movement of persons; Foreign and Defence policy; International trade and negotiations; Transnational crime; and Peace and security. According to Anyangafac & Mpyisi, the proposed AU Authority is more in line with the gradualist ideology since it only emphasises a change in structure rather than a change in the decision-making or implementation process of the AU.[175] However, the decision to transform the AU Commission was reversed by the AU Assembly in 2012, with the AU Commission remaining an intergovernmental body.[176]

The last reform effort in this epochal phase was the financial reform of the AU. In 2011, the AU Assembly inaugurated the "High Level Panel on Alternative Sources of Financing the African Union", chaired by the former Nigerian president, Olusegun Obasanjo, with the mandate of reviewing the eight financing options that were initially recommended by the AU Commission, and then come up with a more feasible plan of action.[177] Out of the eight options proposed by the AU Commission, the Panel chose three, basing its decision on the ease of collection, little strain on government, sustainability and equity.[178] The following recommendations were made by the Panel: US$2.00 hospitality levy per stay in a hotel, US5 cents levy per text message sent, and US$5.00 travel levy on flight tickets originating from or coming to Africa from outside Africa.[179] This proposal was opposed by member states whose economy depended on tourism. The argument was that the hospitality levy would make the tourism sector uncompetitive and put a strain on the their already struggling airline industry.[180] Another concern was that such levy would ensure that tourism-based economies, who are mainly composed of small and medium-sized AU member states, would end up becoming the largest contributors to the AU budget.[181] Due to these concerns, the AU decided to shelve the report.[182]

[174] Ayangafac and Mpyisi (2009), p. 4.

[175] Ibid, p. 3.

[176] Ikome (2012), p. 75; Welz (2014), p. 12.

[177] AU (2012).

[178] Ibid, p. 5.

[179] Ibid, p. 6.

[180] Apiko and Aggad (2018), p. 2.

[181] Ibid.

[182] AU (2016b).

4.4.2 *Pragmatic Incrementalism (2015: Present)*

The death of Muammar Ghaddafi in 2011, and the end of the presidencies of Olusegun Obasanjo (in 2007) and Thabo Mbeki (in 2008) repositioned the ideological paradigm of advancing AU reform efforts. These political actors principally defined the ideological positions of the maximalist and minimalist groups by providing funds and driving ideational agendas in the AU. Libya has been marred by violent conflicts since the death of Ghaddafi, and as such retreated from making any significant contribution to the continental integration agenda. The administrations that succeeded Obasanjo and Mbeki in Nigeria and South Africa respectively have shown little or no appetite for ideational pursuits around continental integration. In addition, the succeeding administrations in both countries have had to deal with encumbering challenges such as sluggish economic growth and the fight against terrorism and insurgency (in Nigeria). The implication of this is the opening of space for other member states to shape the reform efforts. The emergence of the Rwandan president, Paul Kagame, as the arrow head of the AU reform agenda should be understood in this context. Despite his poor human rights record,[183] Kagame's supposedly effective and efficient management of the Rwandan economy, coupled with an astute public relations machinery, positioned him as someone that has the requisite skills to turn things around at the AU.[184] Although some member states, and observers, have expressed strong objections to Kagame's approach on AU reforms,[185] this has not stalled developments around the implementation of some reform priorities. As Louw-Vaudran observed, there are two camps opposed to Kagame's reform drive: member states that do not want a strong, supranational AU Commission; and those that agree that the AU needs a major overhaul but that it should be more consultative and bottom-up.[186]

The position from 2012 shifted from the immediate establishment of a Union Government or the United States of Africa to one defined by a pragmatic incremental approach. This approach does not reject the imperative of establishing a Union Government or the need to quicken the pace of achieving continental supranationalism. However, it prioritises the importance of achieving bold reforms in phases by carefully navigating the fraught intergovernmental/supranational dynamics of the AU. The AU Agenda 2063 document captures this by deferring the discussion on the agreement on the nature and establishment of a continental government to 2030, and

[183] See e.g. Human Rights Watch (2020); Amnesty International (2020).

[184] Turianskyi (2019b). For an analysis on allegations about how the Rwandan government manipulates economic data to reflect positive economic performance see the following sources: Wilson and Blood (2019); ROAPE (2019).

[185] For example, member states of SADC noted that many of the focus subjects of the AU reforms lacked substance and were not subjected to proper consultation. See Turianskyi (2019b). Similarly, Adebajo (2017) noted that the Kagame report was "rushed, lacks substance, and its fluffy recommendations are on a level of vacuity as to be of no real utility. These are physicians who are proposing half-baked cures to ills that have not been properly diagnosed".

[186] Louw-Vaudran (2018).

segmenting progression into short, medium and long terms, to be achieved over 50 years. In addition, unlike the first epochal phase, the current reform effort has been institutionalised through the establishment of three implementation structures within the AU: reform implementation at the head of state level; reform implementation unit at the office of the AU Commission Chair; and mechanisms to ensure that AU decisions are legally binding.[187] Similarly, this epochal phase has enjoyed more visibility and public relations management than the previous epochal phase. One of the key reasons behind this is technological advancements, which has provided multiple multimedia platforms for promoting the cause of AU reforms.[188]

The AU Agenda 2063 is the flagship document of the AU transformation process. Adopted in 2015, the AU Agenda 2063 is a general outline of seven aspirational goals that are necessary for the attainment of an integrated Africa. It includes a prosperous Africa based on inclusive growth and sustainable development; an integrated continent, politically united, based on the ideals of Pan-Africanism and the vision of Africa's renaissance; an Africa of good governance, democracy, respect for human rights, justice, and the rule of law; a peaceful and secure Africa; an Africa with strong cultural identity, common heritage, values and ethics; an Africa whose development is people-driven, relying on the potential of African people, especially its women and youth, caring for children; and an Africa as a strong, united, and influential global player and partner.[189] It is segmented into three phases, which will be achieved over a period of 50 years: short-term (first 10 years); medium-term (10–25 years); and long-term (25–50 years).[190] In the first 10 years (2014–2023), twelve flagship programmes are expected to be implemented. These are: an African virtual and E-University, formulation of a commodities strategy, establishment of an annual African stakeholders' forum, silencing the guns by 2020, the immediate implementation of programmes such as the Continental Free Trade Area, African passport and free movement protocol, strengthen Africa's use of outer space, establishment of African financial institutions, integrated high speed train network, unification of African air space, implementation of the Grand Inga Dam project, and the Pan-African E-Network.[191] At the 30th AU Summit in January 2018, the AU Assembly officially established and launched the Single African Air Transport Market, with the aim of creating "a single unified air transport market in Africa to advance the liberalization of civil aviation in Africa and act as an impetus to the continent's economic integration agenda".[192] Similarly, the AU has adopted the AfCFTA Agreement and free movement protocol in 2018. In addition, the AU

[187] AU (2017b), pp. 2, 9–10.

[188] The AU is very visible on social media platforms such as *Twitter*, *Facebook* and *Instagram*, where issues around reforms and continental integration activities are presented and aimed at a much broader and youthful audience.

[189] AU (2015a), pp. 6–7.

[190] AU Commission (2015), p. 5.

[191] Ibid, pp. 4–5.

[192] AU (2018b).

Table 4.3 Contributions to the total budget of the African Union (Operational, Programme and Peace Support budgets)[a] (in %)

Year	Member states	External donors
2014	42	57
2015	33	66
2016	40	59
2017	26	73
2018	41	58
2019	46	54
2020	38	61

Source: Author's compilation from the following sources: AU (2018c); Apiko and Aggad (2018), p. 1; AU (2021)

[a]The operational budget finances the cost of running the administration of the AU. It is financed exclusively by member states. The programmes budget covers the execution of programmes approved by the AU Assembly. It is mainly financed by external donors. The peace support budget finances peace and security operations across the continent. This is also mainly financed by external donors, especially the EU. See generally the AU website

Agenda 2063 document has spurred other activities around the institutional transformation of the AU. This is discussed below.

A pronounced component of the AU reforms is the issue of self-financing the continental integration process. This has been approached through two main, interrelated activities: domestic resource mobilisation and the adoption of financial management strategies. The first intervention under domestic resource mobilisation was the decision to review the scale of assessment of member states' contributions to the AU. At the 2015 AU Summit, the AU Assembly adopted a new scale of assessment that is targeted at ensuring that member states fund 100% of the operation budget, 75% of the programme budget, and 25% of the peace and security budget.[193] However, at the 2019 AU Summit, African leaders adopted a revised scale of assessment (2020–2022), and committed to reviewing the assessment every 3 years.[194] The new scale of assessment has three tiers: Tier 1 is assessed at 45.151% percent of the Union's assessed budget (member states with GDP over 4%); Tier 2 is assessed at 32.749% of the Union's assessed budget (member states with GDP between 1-4%); and Tier 3 is assessed at 22.100% of the Union's assessed budget (member states with GDP less than 1%).[195]

The second intervention in respect of domestic resource mobilisation was the 2016 AU Assembly adoption of the report of the High Representative on the Peace Fund, Donald Kabureka, on the proposed 0.2% import levy on all "eligible imports" to finance the AU.[196] As shown in Table 4.3 below, the AU depends on external

[193] AU (2015b).

[194] AU (2019a).

[195] Ibid.

[196] AU (2016a). The Obasanjo Report of 2012 had also considered the option of an 0.2% import levy, but later discarded this. AU (2012), p. 5.

partners for financing the bulk of its total budget. According to Pharatlhatlhe & Vanheukelom, the decision to implement the 0.2% import levy was triggered by two major issues.[197] The first was the inability of member states to commit to the 2015 scale of assessment and the second was the EU's sudden decision to alter its funding of peace support to Somalia, thereby putting the AU in an embarrassing cash-strapped situation.[198] It is anticipated that the import levy will raise about US $1.2 billion per year for the AU.[199] Member states are expected to pay the import levy into a special AU account in their respective Central Bank, which will then remit the money to the AU.[200] In addition, member states are increasingly putting in place a mechanism to collect the import levy. As of June 2020, only 17 AU member states (31% of member states) are at various stages of implementing this decision.[201]

The second component on self-financing is the adoption of rules on accountable and prudent financial management of AU budget and resources. In this respect, the AU mandated the F15, a group of 15 AU finance ministers, to recommend an equitable scale of assessment, a more robust sanctions regime for failure to pay financial dues and an effective budget process.[202] In 2018, the AU Assembly formally adopted the nine golden rules of financial management that was recommended by the F15 and mandated the F15 to sit jointly with the Permanent Representatives Committee (PRC) and the Executive Council in scrutinising the AU budget.[203] An impact of the works of the F15 was the decision to cut the AU budget for 2019 by 12%.[204]

The table above shows the extent of financial dependence on external donations by the AU. From 2014 to 2020, the average of external donations to the AU is at 61% compared to member states' 38% contribution. This position is further complicated by the fact that fewer than 40% of member states pay their annual financial dues to the organisation.[205]

The last discussion under this epochal phase is the "Report on the Proposed Recommendations for the Institutional Reform of the African Union" (Kagame Report). At the 2016 AU Summit, the AU Assembly mandated the Rwandan president, Paul Kagame, to oversee the preparation and submission of a report on

---

[197] Pharatlhatlhe and Vanheukelom (2019), p. 9.

[198] Ibid. ICG (2017), pp. 12–13.

[199] Sow (2016).

[200] AU (2019a).

[201] AU (2020a).

[202] See AU (2019c), p. 2.

[203] The nine golden rules include: (i) Member States' contributions should cover a minimum threshold of the budget; (ii) Revenue must be predictable; (iii) Budgets must be credible; (iv) Expenditure ceilings should be set; (v) All expenditure must be authorised; (vi) Resource flows and transactions must be reliable and efficient. (vii) Institutional accountability; (viii) Reporting should be an integral part of the financial management process; (ix) There should be a centralized process for engaging partners. See Ibid, 15.

[204] AU (2018c).

[205] PSC Report (2021).

the proposed institutional reforms of the AU as envisaged by Agenda 2063.[206] In this respect, Kagame appointed a team of nine pan-African advisory team, composed of the public and private sector actors, to assist with the review process.[207] The report was submitted to the AU Assembly, and was adopted at its January 2017 summit as a framework for reforming the AU.[208] Similar to, but not as detailed, the Adedeji Report of 2007, the Kagame Report provided critical observations about the dysfunctionality of the AU. It highlighted the crisis of implementation of AU decisions, limited relevance of the organisation to African citizens, overdependence on external funders, fragmented organisation and lack of focus, lack of accountability, and unclear division of labour between the AU and its RECs.[209] In summing up AU's incapacity, the Report noted: "we have a dysfunctional organisation in which member states see limited value, global partners find little credibility, and our citizens have no trust".[210] The Report then recommended four focus areas: Focus on key priorities with continental scope (focus on priorities that will make real difference in the lives of Africans and establish clear divisions between the AU and RECs); Realign African Union institutions to deliver against those priorities (realign the African Union Commission structures, organs, and specialised technical agencies to focus on the agreed priorities); Manage the African Union efficiently at both political and operational levels (create an efficient AU Commission, get real value and impact from AU organs, improve the quality and impact of AU's decision-making methods, and ensure timely implementation of AU Assembly decisions); and Sustainably self-finance the African Union (ensure financial autonomy and strengthen financial management and accountability).[211] It highlighted the need for the AU to focus on key priorities with continental scope such as political affairs; peace and security; economic integration; and Africa's global representation and voice.[212]

The implementation of the Kagame Report has been incorporated into AU's organisational structure. In this respect, three implementation structures have been

[206] AU (2016b).

[207] This included Cristina Duarte (former Minister of Finance of Cabo Verde), Donald Kaberuka (former President of the African Development Bank), Acha Leke (Senior Partner, McKinsey & Co.), Carlos Lopes (former Executive Secretary of the U.N. Economic Commission for Africa), Strive Masiyiwa (Executive Chairman, Econet Wireless), Tito Mboweni (former Governor of the South African Reserve Bank and former South African finance minister), Amina J. Mohammed (former Minister of Environment of Nigeria and current deputy Secretary-General of the United Nations), Mariam Mahamat Nour (Minister of Economy and International Cooperation of Chad), and Vera Songwe (former Regional Director for West and Central Africa, International Finance Corporation and currently the Executive Secretary of the U.N. Economic Commission for Africa). See Kagame (2017), p. 3.

[208] AU (2017a).

[209] Kagame (2017), p. 4.

[210] Ibid, p. 5.

[211] Ibid, p. 5–6.

[212] Ibid., p. 7.

established: reform implementation at the head of state level; reform implementation unit at the office of the AU Commission Chair; and mechanisms to ensure that AU decisions are legally binding.[213] The Report has impacted the AU reform process in several ways. In terms of its recommendation on having a lean and performance-oriented AU Commission senior leadership team, the AU Assembly adopted the decision to reduce the number of AU Commission commissioners from eight to six.[214] Similarly, the recommendation on a streamlined and better coordinated interaction between the AU and RECs resulted in the first mid-year coordination meeting between the AU and RECs on 8 July 2019 in Niamey, Niger.[215] Furthermore, it has led to the drafting of an amended Protocol on the relations between the AU and RECs. The transformation of the NEPAD Planning and Coordinating Agency (NPCA) into African Union Development Agency - NEPAD (AUDA), granting it legal personality and serving as the technical body of the AU, flows from one of the recommendations of the report.[216] Similarly, the APRM is now officially recognised as a specialised agency of the AU, and has further been mandated to track member states' progress regarding the AU Agenda 2063 and the UN Sustainable Development Goals (SDGs).[217] In addition, activities around financial reforms, which are discussed in the preceding paragraphs, are integral aspects of the recommendations of the report.[218]

4.4.3 The Problematics of Reform Efforts

The discussion above has shown the chronological and ideational trajectories of reforms in the AU. The current phase of reform efforts in the AU is a consequential one, which has the potential of changing the narrative of lethargic approach to continental integration. However, some concerns remain. This pertains to the way in which political elites see reform efforts as a turf for contestation, and how this results in the tension between law and politics of continental regionalism. While contestation is not necessarily a negative phenomenon, as it provides space for critical reflection, it becomes problematic when it is not anchored to serious pragmatic and ideational pursuits. Such delink manifests in various problematic ways. In no order of importance, below are some of the hindering issues.

The first is the à la carte disposition towards reform efforts. What this implies is that some member states refuse to accept that the elements of the reform process are conjoined rather than disjointed and dispensable parts. In this respect, some member

[213] AU (2017b), pp. 2, 9–10.

[214] Louw-Vaudran (2019).

[215] Ibid.

[216] See Kagame (2017), p. 8.

[217] Turianskyi (2019a).

[218] AU (2017b), pp. 4–6.

states tend to pick and choose the aspects of the reform process that is politically (and personally) convenient and discard the rest. For example, while member states rushed to adopt and ratify the AfCFTA Agreement, there has been a more noticeable reluctance to do the same with the free movement protocol that was also adopted on the same day as the agreement. The inability to see the relational contexts of both documents, and how one without the other can slow down the entire process, and betrays the essence of pan-Africanism, is indicative of such "pick and choose" mentality of advancing and deepening continental integration. Similarly, member states have shown very little interest towards transforming the AU beyond the technocratic efficiency of the AU Commission. While the technocratic efficiency and autonomy of the AU Commission is crucial, there are other aspects of the AU that are of equal importance, and central to making the works of the AU Commission meaningful. This includes the granting meaningful legislative powers to PAP and ensuring strict compliance with the decisions of judicial and quasi-judicial organs.

The growing tendency of member states to engage in anti-democratic practises despite signing up to reform measures that advance fundamental rights objectives is another element of this à la carte disposition. As many internal and external reports on assessment of democracy in Africa show, there are increasing authoritarian tendencies in many member states.[219] The same national institutions that are expected to implement key reform measures are deliberately weakened and turned into rubber stamp machineries for the executive, and the supposed recipients of the benefits of reforms are subjected to cruel treatment by the state. Reports consistently show that the leading figure in the AU institutional transformation process, Paul Kagame, runs a tyrannical government that stifles the fundamental human rights of citizens.[220]

The second problem is the personality driven nature of reform efforts. As shown in the preceding discussion, AU reform efforts have mostly been shaped by personalities. The problem with this is that once those leaders leave office or step down as drivers of the process, the ideas and institutional measures often become abandoned projects. To circumvent this, the AU has made attempts to institutionalise the current reform process by establishing official monitoring and implementation structures within the organisation. Despite this, the sustainability of the momentum remains questionable as reforms are not anchored to durable, autonomous institutions. The expected engine room of implementation, the AU Commission, currently has no enforcing powers and beyond rhetoric, the actual commitment to transferring such competence to the organ remains missing. The same applies to other critical organs such as PAP, AUDA-NEPAD, and APRM. Similar to this is the normative gap. What this implies is that some of the key reform priorities exist outside the binding normative purview of the AU. Although issues such as tightening the sanctions regime for non-payment of dues have become the normative rules, important reform measures such as the payment of the 0.2% import levy, free movement norms

[219] Cheeseman (2019), p. 5; AU (2020b), p. 16, Musila (2019).

[220] See e.g. Human Rights Watch (2020); Amnesty International (2020); Turianskyi (2019b).

(including the African passport), common position on issues on the global stage, and adherence to trade rules are issues that are yet to acquire the force of law.

Lastly is the absence of civil society in the reforms matrix. While it is true that CSOs have played important roles in articulating the paradigms of reforms, and even providing critical support to AU organs in this respect, they remain largely excluded from the implementation of the agenda. The discussions around implementation and choices on which part of the reform agenda to keep or discard is still heavily state-centric. Government and civil society are at cross purposes on how to shape and scale the priorities of the reform agenda. There is little effort to seriously consider the views of civil society on issues such as self-financing the AU,[221] strengthening key AU organs, and measurable opinion on the state of continental integration.[222]

4.5 Conclusion

At the heart of the success or failure of continental regionalism in Africa is the nature of its relational dynamics. Both intra and extra African relational dynamics are thus important arenas for assessing the progress and pitfalls of regional integration. In addition, these arenas of engagement provide the platform through which law and politics either converge or diverge, with serious implications for the development of transnational objectives. This chapter discussed the three broad prisms through which the interplay of law and politics determine the progression, or the lack thereof, of the AU's supranational ambitions. The first is the imitation conundrum, where the AU has essentially "copied and pasted" the EU regionalism format. This has resulted in the inability of the AU to engage in more contextual integrative path and encourages the EU to continue to see itself as a financial and ideological "mentor" of the AU. The second is the complex intra-African relational dynamics. Under this, the three relation issues were discussed: AU—RECs, AU—Member states, and AU—Civil society. These three relationship dynamics show how stakeholders engage in activities that often contradict integrative objectives, and thus undercut AU's ability to assert itself as a relevant dispenser of supranational norms. The last prism is the politics of reforms in the AU. Here, the chapter looked at the two epochal phases of AU reforms and some of the issues that undercut effective realisation of envisaged reform priorities. The next chapter of this book builds on the many problems identified in the preceding chapters by engaging in a prescriptive politico-legal policy analysis of the way forward for continental supranationalism in Africa.

---

221 Fagbayibo (2019a).

222 Fagbayibo (2016).

References

Abebe A (2019, July 8) It's time for the African Union to put a stop to 'third-termism'. Al-Jazeera. https://www.aljazeera.com/opinions/2019/7/8/its-time-for-the-african-union-to-put-a-stop-to-third-termism. Accessed 4 Oct 2021

Acharya A (2004) How ideas spread: whose norms matter? Norm localization and institutional change in Asian regionalism. Int Organ 58(2):239–275

Adebajo A (2017, September 4) Why alchemical ideas for healing AU could kill the patient. Business Day. https://www.businesslive.co.za/bd/opinion/columnists/2017-09-04-adekeye-adebajo-why-alchemical-ideas-for-healing-au-could-kill-the-patient/. Accessed 4 Oct 2021

African Civil Society Organisation (2005) Third draft of the constitution of the United Africa (UA) (The United States of Africa). African Civil Society Organisation, Yaounde

African Network on Debt and Development (AFRODAD), the Open Society Institute Africa Governance Monitoring and Advocacy Project (AfriMAP), and Oxfam GB. (2007). Towards a people-driven African Union: Current obstacles and new opportunities https://www.opensocietyfoundations.org/publications/towards-people-driven-african-union-current-obstacles-new-opportunities. Accessed 4 Oct 2021

African Union (2001) New Partnership for Africa's Development (NEPAD). http://www.dirco.gov.za/au.nepad/nepad.pdf. Accessed 4 Oct 2021

African Union (2006) Study on an African Union government: Towards the United States of Africa. https://archives.au.int/bitstream/handle/123456789/2656/Study%20on%20%20an%20African%20union%20government%20towards%20the%20united%20statesof%20Africa_E.pdf?sequence=1&isAllowed=y. Accessed 4 Oct 2021.

African Union (2007a) Accra Declaration, Assembly/AU/Decl.2(IX). https://archives.au.int/bitstream/handle/123456789/249/Assembly%20AU%20Decl%202%20%28IX%29%20_E.PDF?sequence=1&isAllowed=y. Accessed 4 Oct 2021

African Union (2007b) Audit of the African Union. https://www.securitycouncilreport.org/atf/cf/%7B65BFCF9B-6D27-4E9C-8CD3-CF6E4FF96FF9%7D/RO%20Audit%20of%20the%20AU.pdf. Accessed 04 October 2021

African Union (2009) Decision of the special session of the Assembly of the Union Government, AU/Dec.233(XII). https://au.int/sites/default/files/decisions/9559-assembly_cn_1_3_february_2009_auc_twelfth_ordinary_session_decisions_declarations_message_congratulations_motion.pdf. Accessed 4 Oct 2021

African Union (2012) Progress report on the high level panel on alternative sources of financing the African Union chaired by H.E Olusegun Obasanjo, former president of Nigeria consultations with member states, Assembly/AU/18(XIX), Nineteenth Ordinary Session, 15–16 July 2012, Addis Ababa, Ethiopia. Accessed 4 Oct 2021

African Union (2013) African Union Agenda 2063: A shared strategic framework for inclusive growth and sustainable development: Background note. https://www.au.int/web/sites/default/files/newsevents/workingdocuments/29732-wd-27_08_agenda_2063_background_note_en_0.pdf. Accessed 11 January 2020

African Union (2015a) Agenda 2063: The Africa we want. https://au.int/sites/default/files/documents/36204-doc-agenda2063_popular_version_en.pdf. Accessed 4 Oct 2021

African Union (2015b) Twenty-fifth ordinary session of the Assembly of the Union, 14 – 15 June 2015 Johannesburg, South Africa. https://au.int/sites/default/files/decisions/9664-assembly_au_dec_569_-_587_xxiv_e.pdf. Accessed 4 Oct 2021

African Union (2016a) Frequently asked questions about financing the Union. https://au.int/sites/default/files/pages/31953-file-faq.pdf. Accessed 4 Oct 2021

African Union (2016b, July 25) Summary of the 27th AU summit decisions. Press Release No 25. https://www.au.int/web/sites/default/files/pressreleases/31218-pr-pr_25_-_summary_of_27th_au_summit_decisions_-_tax_imports_to_finance_au_establish_protocol_to_issue_african_passports_to_citizens_and_mandate_of_chairperson_and_commiss.pdf. Accessed 4 Oct 2021

African Union (2017a) Decision on the outcome of the retreat of the Assembly of the African Union on the institutional reform of the African Union. Assembly/AU/Dec.635(XXVIII). https://au.int/sites/default/files/decisions/32520-sc19553_e_original_-_assembly_decisions_621-641_-_xxviii.pdf. Accessed 4 Oct 2021

African Union (2017b) Report on the implementation of the decision on the institutional reform of the African Union. https://au.int/sites/default/files/documents/33272-doc-au_reform_implementation_report_july_2017_final_v2.pdf. Accessed 4 Oct 2021

African Union (2018a, November 27) African Union strengthens its sanction regime for non-payment of dues. https://au.int/en/pressreleases/20181127/african-union-strengthens-its-sanction-regime-non-payment-dues. Accessed 4 Oct 2021

African Union (2018b, January 28) Establishment and launching of a Single African Air Transport Market (SAATM). https://au.int/en/newsevents/20180128/establishment-and-launching-single-african-air-transport-market-saatm. Accessed 4 Oct 2021

African Union (2018c, July 6) Financial reforms at the African Union lead to massive cuts of the Union's Budget. https://au.int/en/pressreleases/20180706/financial-reforms-african-union-lead-massive-cuts-unions-budget. Accessed 4 Oct 2021

African Union (2018d) The African Union Executive Council adopts the African common position for negotiations of a new cooperation agreement with the European Union. https://au.int/en/pressreleases/20180327/african-union-executive-council-adopts-african-common-position-negotiations. Accessed 4 Oct 2021

African Union (2019a) Africa is financing its development agenda through domestic resource mobilization. https://au.int/en/articles/africa-financing-its-development-agenda-through-domestic-resource-mobilization. Accessed 4 Oct 2021

African Union (2019b) African Union first mid-year coordination meeting between the African Union, the Regional Economic Communities and the regional mechanisms, 8 July 2019 Niamey, Niger. https://www.tralac.org/documents/resources/african-union/2968-first-mid-year-coordination-meeting-between-the-au-recs-and-the-regional-mechanisms-declaration-july-2019/file.html. Accessed 4 Oct 2021

African Union (2019c) Financing the African Union: Towards the financial autonomy of the African Union. https://au.int/sites/default/files/pages/35739-file-financing_the_union_6.pdf. Accessed 4 Oct 2021

African Union (2020a) Financing the African Union: Towards the financial autonomy of the African Union. https://au.int/sites/default/files/documents/38739-doc-report_on_financing_of_the_union_jun_2020_002.pdf. Accessed 10 Apr 2022

African Union (2020b) First continental report on the implementation of Agenda 2063. https://au.int/sites/default/files/documents/38060-doc-agenda_2063_implementation_report_en_web_version.pdf. Accessed 4 Oct 2021

African Union (2021) African Union sustainable funding strategy gains momentum. https://au.int/ar/node/37145. Accessed 4 Oct 2021

African Union (n.d.) Member States. https://au.int/en/member_states/countryprofiles2, Accessed 08 April 2022

African Union and the United Nations Economic Commission for Africa (2006) Assessing regional integration in Africa II: Rationalising regional economic communities. https://repository.uneca.org/bitstream/handle/10855/5611/bib-42496_I.pdf?sequence=1&isAllowed=y. Accessed 4 Oct 2021

African Union Commission (2015) African Union Agenda 2063: First ten year implementation plan. https://www.au.int/web/sites/default/files/newsevents/workingdocuments/29732-wd-27_08_agenda_2063_background_note_en_0.pdf. Accessed 4 Oct 2021

African Union Commission (2019) African regional integration report: Towards an integrated and prosperous and peaceful Africa. https://au.int/sites/default/files/documents/38176-doc-african_integration_report-eng_final.pdf. Accessed 4 Oct 2021

Agreement Establishing a Tripartite Free Trade Area Among the Common Market for Eastern And Southern Africa, the East African Community and the Southern African Development

Community (2015). https://www.tralac.org/documents/resources/tfta/1083-tfta-agreement-june-2015-english/file.html. Accessed 4 Oct 2021
Amnesty International (2020) Rwanda 2019. https://www.amnesty.org/en/countries/africa/rwanda/report-rwanda/. Accessed 4 Oct 2021
Ani M (2018) Three schools of thought on "African solutions to African problems". J Black Stud 50(2):135–155
Aniwa M (2008) Rationalising regional economic communities and implementing the Treaty Establishing the African Economic Community: the role of parliaments. In: Murithi T (ed) Towards a union government for Africa: challenges and opportunities. Institute for Security Studies, Pretoria, pp 69–78
Apiko P, Aggad F (2018) Analysis of the implementation of the African Union's 0.2% levy: progress and challenges. http://ecdpm.org/wp-content/uploads/BN98-Apiko-Aggad-November-2017.pdf. Accessed 4 Oct 2021
Ayangafac C, Mpyisi K (2009) The proposed AU authority: hybridisation, balancing, intergovermentalism and supranationalism. https://issafrica.s3.amazonaws.com/site/uploads/AUAUTHORITY19JUN09.PDF. Accessed 4 Oct 2021
Ayee J (2005) Public sector management in Africa. https://www.afdb.org/fileadmin/uploads/afdb/Documents/Publications/00457499-EN-ERWP-82.PDF. Accessed 4 Oct 2021
Bamodu G (1994) Transnational law, unification and harmonisation of international commercial law in Africa. J Afr Law 38(2):125–130
Byiers B, Woolfrey S, Medinilla A, Vanheukelom J (2019) The political economy of Africa's regional 'spaghetti bowl". Synthesis report. European Centre for Development Policy Management (ECDPM). https://ecdpm.org/publications/political-economy-africas-regional-spaghetti-bowl-synthesis-report/. Accessed 4 Oct 2021
Cheeseman N (2019) A divided continent – BTI 2018 regional report Africa. https://www.bertelsmannstiftung.de/fileadmin/files/BSt/Bibliothek/Doi_Publikatio en/Regional-Report_NW_BTI-2018_Africa-A-Divided-Continent_2019.pdf. Accessed 4 Oct 2021
Cilliers J (2008) Africa in the new world: How global and domestic developments will impact by 2025. Institute of Security Studies, Pretoria
COMESA, EAC and SADC (2008) Final communique of the joint COMESA-EAC-SADC heads of state and government tripartite summit. http://repository.eac.int/bitstream/handle/11671/558/Final%20Communique Nairobi%20-%2020%2010%2008%20_2_.pdf?sequence=1&isAllowed=y. Accessed 4 Oct 2021
Connolly L (2016) Politics in place of peace: The AU's role in Burundi' https://peaceoperationsreview.org/thematic-essays/politics-in-place-of-peace-the-aus-role-in-burundi/. Accessed 4 Oct 2021
Constitutive Act of the African Union (2000). https://au.int/sites/default/files/pages/34873-file-constitutiveact_en.pdf. Accessed 4 Oct 2021
Decision on the proposals of the Great Socialist People's Libyan Arab Jamahiriya, Assembly/AU/Dec.69 (IV) https://au.int/sites/default/files/decisions/9551-assembly_en_30_31_january_2005_auc_fourth_ordinary_session.pdf. Accessed 4 Oct 2021
Decision on the report of the committee of seven heads of state and government chaired by the president of the Republic of Uganda on the proposals of the Great Socialist People's Libyan Arab Jamahiriya, Assembly/AU/Dec.90 (V), https://au.int/sites/default/files/decisions/9552-assembly_en_4_5_july_2005_auc_fifth_ordinary_session_decisions_declarations_and_resolution.pdf. Accessed 4 Oct 2021
Dickerson C (2005) Harmonising business law in Africa: OHADA calls the tune. Columbia J Transnatl Law 44(17):17–73
Dirar L (2014) Rethinking and theorizing regional integration in Southern Africa. Emroy Int Law Rev 28(1):123–165
Economic Intelligence Unit (2019, June 13) SADC rejects Burundi's membership application. https://country.eiu.com/article.aspx?articleid=338104417&Country=Burundi&topic=Politics&subtopic=Forecast&subsubtopic=International+relations. Accessed 4 Oct 2021

Elkins K, Simmons B (2005) On waves, clusters and diffusions: a conceptual framework. Am Acad Polit Soc Sci 598(1):33–51

Ellett R (2015) Judicial independence under the APRM: From rhetoric to reality. Occasional paper 212. South African Institute for International Affairs (SAIIA). https://media.africaportal.org/documents/saia_sop_212_ellett_20150402.pdf. Accessed 4 Oct 2021

Elvy S (2012) Theories of State Compliance with International Law: Assessing the African Union's ability to ensure state compliance with the African Charter and Constitutive Act. Georgian J Int Comp Law 41(1):75–155

Erasmus G, Hartzenberg T (2022) How relevant is the Protocol on Relations between the RECs and the AU? https://www.tralac.org/blog/article/15548-how-relevant-is-the-protocol-on-relations-between-the-recs-and-the-au.html. Accessed 8 Apr 2022

European Commission (2015) African Union Commission and European Commission meet to bring new impetus to the EU-Africa partnership. http://europa.eu/rapid/press-release_IP-15-4810_en.htm. Accessed 4 Oct 2021

European Commission (2021) 2020 annual report on the implementation of the European Union's instruments for financing external actions in 2019. https://ec.europa.eu/international-partnerships/system/files/intpa-annual-report-2020-swd_en.pdf. Accessed 10 April 2022

European Union (2017) African Peace Facility: Annual report 2016. https://www.africa-eu-partnership.org//sites/default/files/documents/apf_ar2016_en_v1_web.pdf. Accessed 4 Oct 2021

European Union (2018) Africa as one: Pan-African Programme: 2014–2017. https://eeas.europa.eu/sites/default/files/panaf_brochure_2014-2017-en.pdf. Accessed 4 Oct 2021

European Union (2020) African Peace Facility: Annual report 2019. https://op.europa.eu/en/publication-detail/-/publication/4ce12dc7-d5f9-11ea-adf7-01aa75ed71a1. Accessed 10 April 2022

Fabricius, P. (2021) EU peace and security funds can now bypass the African Union. https://issafrica.org/iss-today/eu-peace-and-security-funds-can-now-bypass-the-african-union. Accessed 30 Mar 2021

Fagbayibo B (2009) Towards the harmonisation of laws in Africa: is OHADA the way to go? Comp Int Law J South Afr 42(3):309–3222

Fagbayibo B (2011) The Libyan revolution: Thoughts on a post-Gaddafi era of African integration. Discussion paper. Consultancy African Intelligence. https://www.polity.org.za/article/the-libyan-revolution-thoughts-on-a-post-gaddafi-era-of-african-integration-2011-09-16. Accessed 4 Oct 2021

Fagbayibo B (2016) 'I am an African': a critical examination of the politics of transnational identity within the context of African integration. Afr Dev 41(2):185–202

Fagbayibo B (2017) A normative appraisal of the African Union's membership admission rules. Verfassung und Recht in Ubersee 50(2):156–174

Fagbayibo B (2019a) The African Union's self-financing agenda: 3 ideational measures that should guide it. https://www.africaportal.org/features/african-unions-self-financing-agenda-3-ideational-measures-should-guide-it/. Accessed 4 Oct 2021

Fagbayibo B (2019b) The legal regime of compliance with regional norms in Africa: reframing the paradigms of engagement. Afr J Int Comp Law 27(3):446–465

Final Communique of the COMESA-EAC-SADC Tripartite Summit on their Vision Towards a Single Market and Deepening COMESA-EAC-SADC Integration (2008, October 22). https://www.tralac.org/blog/article/14248-the-institutional-arrangements-of-the-tripartite-free-trade-area.html. Accessed 4 Oct 2021

Finizo G (2018) Civil society involvement and ownership in the African Union integration process. In: Adar K, Finizo G, Meyer A (eds) Building regionalism from below: the role of parliaments and civil society in regional integration in Africa. Peter Lang, Bruxelles, pp 289–321

Franck T (1988) Legitimacy in the international system. Am J Int Law 82(4):704–759

Gathii J (2009) African regional trade agreements as flexible legal regimes. North Carolina J Int Law 35(3):572–668

Goodin R (1996) Institutions and their design. In: Goodin R (ed) The theory of institutional design. Cambridge University Press, Cambridge, pp 1–53

Haastrup T (2013) EU as mentor? Promoting regionalism as external relations practice in EU-AU relations. J Eur Integr 35(7):785–800

Hauck V (2020) The latest on the European Peace Facility and what's in it for the African Union. https://ecdpm.org/wp-content/uploads/Latest-European-Peace-Facility-What-African-Union-Briefing-Note-120-ECDPM-September-2020.pdf. Accessed 30 Mar 2021

Himbara D (2020) East African Community integration: One step forward, two steps back. https://www.theafricareport.com/39264/east-african-community-integration-one-step-forward-two-steps-back/. Accessed 4 Oct 2021

Human Rights Watch (2020) Rwanda: Events of 2019. https://www.hrw.org/world-report/2020/country-chapters/rwanda. Accessed 04 October 2021

Igbokwe-Ibeto C (2019) African bureaucracy and public administration: analysing the normative impediments and prospect. Afr Public Serv Deliv Perform Rev 7(1):1–11

Ikome F (2012) After Ghaddafi and Mubarak: a new North African role in the African Union. Africa Insight 42(3):68–90

International Crisis Group (2017) Time to reset African Union – European Union Relations. https://www.crisisgroup.org/africa/255-time-reset-african-union-european-union-relations. Accessed 4 Oct 2021

International Crisis Group (2021) How to spend it: new EU funding for African peace and security. https://d2071andvip0wj.cloudfront.net/297-eu-au-funding-2021.pdf. Accessed 4 Oct 2021

International Monetary Fund (2001) West Africa Economic and Monetary Union: Recent economic developments and regional policy issues in 2000. https://www.imf.org/external/pubs/ft/scr/2001/cr01193.pdf. Accessed 4 Oct 2021

Kagame P (2017) The imperative of strengthening our union: Report on the Proposed Recommendations for the Institutional Reform of the African Union. http://www.rci.uct.ac.za/sites/default/files/image_tool/images/78/News/FInal%20AU%20Reform%20Combined%20report_28012017.pdf. Accessed 4 Oct 2021

Kuwali D (2008) The conundrum of conditions for intervention under article 4(h) of the African Union Act. Afr Secur Rev 17(4):89–111

Kwarkye S, Matongbada M (2021, March 22) Nigeria's border closures haven't served their purpose. https://issafrica.org/iss-today/nigerias-border-closures-havent-served-their-purpose. Accessed 4 Oct 2021

La Porta R, Lopes-de-Silanes F, Shleifer A, Vishy R (1998) Law and finance. J Polit Econ 106(6):1113–1155

Levi-Faur D (2005) The global diffusion of regulatory capitalism. Ann Am Acad Polit Soc Sci 598(1):12–32

Libmann A (2019) Learning from the European Union? Eurasian regionalism and the "global script". Outlines Global Transformation: Polit Econ Law 12(2):247–268

Louw-Vaudran L (2018, July 19). Kagame to push for sign-off of reforms in fourth African Union summit. Daily Maverick. https://www.dailymaverick.co.za/article/2018-07-19-kagame-to-push-for-sign-off-of-reforms-in-fourth-african-union-summit/. Accessed 4 Oct 2021

Louw-Vaudran L (2019) Is the AU becoming more efficient? https://issafrica.org/iss-today/is-the-au-becoming-more-efficient. Accessed 4 Oct 2021

Mazrui A (1967) Towards a Pax Africana: a study of ideology and ambition. University of Chicago Press, Chicago

Memorandum of Understanding on Cooperation in the Area of Peace and Security Between the African Union, the Regional Economic Communities (2008). https://www.peaceau.org/uploads/mou-au-rec-eng.pdf. Accessed 4 Oct 2021

Mkandawire T (2002) Incentives, governance and capacity development in Africa. Afr Iss 30(1):15–20

Mkandawire T (2014) On the politics of regional integration. Keynote address at the TRALAC annual conference, Cape Town, 15–16 May. http://www.mandelaschool.uct.ac.za/sites/default/files/image_tool/images/78/News/MKANDAWIRE_Regional_Integration_Transcript.pdf

Musila G (2019) The spread of anti-NGO measures in Africa: Freedoms under threat. https://freedomhouse.org/report/special-report/2019/spread-anti-ngo-measures-africa-freedoms-under-threat. Accessed 4 Oct 2021
Nathan L (2016) Will the Lowest Be First? Subsidiarity in Peacekeeping in Africa. http://www.up.ac.za/media/shared/237/PDFs/Publications/competition-and-subsidiarity-in-peacemaking-in-africa.zp84164.pdf. Accessed 4 Oct 2021
Navarro J (2010) The creation and transformation of regional parliamentary assemblies: lesson from the Pan-African Parliament. J Legislat Stud 16(2):195–214
NEPAD Planning and Coordinating Agency (2015) Capacity development implementation plan for Africa's regional economic communities. https://www.nepad.org/publication/capacity-development-implementation-plan-africas-regional-economic-communities. Accessed 4 Oct 2021
Olivier G, Olivier M (2004) Models of regional integration: the European Union and the African Union. South Afr Public Law 19(1):351–364
Oppong R (2011) Legal aspects of economic integration in Africa. Cambridge University Press
Peace and Security Council Report (2021) AU financial independence: still a long way to go. https://issafrica.org/pscreport/psc-insights/au-financial-independence-still-a-long-way-to-go. Accessed 4 Oct 2021
Pharatlhatlhe K, Vanheukelom J (2019) Financing the African Union: On mindset and money. Discussion paper. European Centre for Development Policy Management (ECDPM). https://ecdpm.org/wp-content/uploads/DP240-Financing-the-African-Union-on-mindsets-and-money.pdf. Accessed 4 Oct 2021
Protocol Amending the 2008 Protocol on Relations Between the African Union and the Regional Economic Communities, MYCM/AU/5(I) (2019). https://archives.au.int/bitstream/handle/123456789/8441/MYCM_AU_5%20%28I%29_E.pdf?sequence=6&isAllowed=y. Accessed 4 Oct 2021
Protocol on Amendments to the Protocol on the Statute of the African Court of Justice and Human Rights (2014). https://au.int/en/treaties/protocol-amendments-protocol-statute-african-court-justice-and-human-rights. Accessed 4 Oct 2021
Protocol on Relations between the African Union (AU) and the Regional Economic Communities (RECs) (2008). http://archive.au.int/collect/auacalan/import/English/Protocol_Relations_AU_RECs_E.pdf. Accessed 4 Oct 2021
Review of African Political Economy (ROAPE) (2019) A straightforward case of fake statistics. http://roape.net/2019/04/18/a-straightforward-case-of-fake-statistics/. Accessed 4 Oct 2021
Sicurelli D (2010) Regional partners? Perceptions and criticisms at the African Union. In: Lucarelli S, Fioramonti L (eds) External perceptions of the European Union as a global actor. Routledge, Abingdon and New York, pp 180–194
Soderbaum, F. (2013) What's wrong with regional integration? The problem of Eurocentrism. Working paper RSCAS 2013/64. European University Institute (EUI) https://papers.ssrn.com/sol3/papers.cfm?abstract_id=2399858. Accessed 4 Oct 2021
Sow M (2016) Figure of the week: The African Union introduces a new funding structure https://www.brookings.edu/blog/africa-in-focus/2016/07/27/figure-of-the-week-the-african-union-introduces-a-new-funding-structure/#:~:text=The%20new%20import%20tax%20excludes,of%20its%20peace%20support%20operations. Accessed 4 Oct 2021
Staeger U (2016) Africa–EU relations and normative power Europe: a decolonial pan-African critique. J Common Mark Stud 54(4):981–998
Statutes of the Economic, Social and Cultural Council of the African Union (2004). https://au.int/sites/default/files/documents/30971-doc-ecosocc_statutes-english_1.pdf. Accessed 4 Oct 2021
The African Capacity Building Foundation (2014) Africa Capacity Report 2014: Capacity imperatives for regional integration in Africa. https://www.acbf-pact.org/africa-capacity-report-2014-capacity-imperatives-regional-integration-africa. Accessed 4 Oct 2021
The Common Market for Eastern and Southern Africa (COMESA) (n.d.) Member States. https://www.comesa.int/members/. Accessed 4 Oct 2021
The Community of Sahel-Saharan States (CENSAD) (n.d.). https://au.int/en/recs/censad. Accessed 4 Oct 2021

The East African Community (EAC) (n.d.) EAC Partner States. https://www.eac.int/eac-partner-states. Accessed 8 Apr 2022
The Economic and Monetary Community of Central Africa (CEMAC) (n.d.). https://www.cemac.int/node/34. Accessed 4 Oct 2021
The Economic Community of Central African States (ECCAS) (n.d.) Member Countries. https://ceeac-eccas.org/en/#structure. Accessed 4 Oct 2021
The Economic Community of the Great Lakes Countries (CEPGL) (n.d.). https://www.minaffet.gov.rw/eac-2-1#:~:text=The%20Economic%20Community%20of%20the,in%20Gisenyi%2FRubavu%20in%20Rwanda. Accessed 4 Oct 2021
The Economic Community of West African States (ECOWAS) (n.d.) Member States. https://ecowas.int/member-states/. Accessed 4 Oct 2021
The Indian Ocean Commission (IOC) (n.d.) IOC Member States. https://www.commissionoceanindien.org/presentation-coi/etats-membres-coi/. Accessed 4 Oct 2021
The Intergovernmental Authority on Development (IGAD). (n.d.). The IGAD Region. https://igad.int/about-us/the-igad-region. Accessed 4 Oct 2021
The International Conference on the Great Lakes Region (ICGLR). (n.d.) ICGLR Overview. https://www.icglr.org/index.php/en/site-map/icglr-overview. Accessed 4 Oct 2021
The Mano River Union (MRU) (n.d.). https://ecfr.eu/special/african-cooperation/mano-river-union/ . Accessed 4 Oct 2021
The Southern African Customs Union (SACU) (n.d.) What is SACU? https://www.sacu.int/about/what_is.html. Accessed 4 Oct 2021
The Southern African Development Community (SADC) (n.d.) Member States. https://www.sadc.int/member-states. Accessed 4 Oct 2021
The West African Economic and Monetary Union (WAEMU) (n.d.) About WAEMU. http://www.uemoa.int/en/about-uemoa. Accessed 4 Oct 2021
Tieku T (2017) Governing Africa: 3D analysis of the African Union's performance. Littlefield, Rowman and New York and London
Tieku T (2019) Ruling from the shadows: The nature and function of informal international rules in world politics. Int Stud Rev 21(2):225–243
Treaty establishing the African Economic Community Treaty (1991). https://au.int/en/treaties/treaty-establishing-african-economic-community. Accessed 4 Oct 2021
Treaty on the Harmonisation of the Business Law in Africa (OHADA). https://www.ohada.org/en/treaty-on-the-harmonization-of-the-business-law-in-africa/. Accessed 4 Oct 2021
Turianskyi Y (2019a) African peer review: progress is being made, but there are problems. https://theconversation.com/african-peer-review-progress-is-being-made-but-there-are-problems-113048. Accessed 4 Oct 2021
Turianskyi Y (2019b) Kagame's AU reforms will struggle to survive without him. https://mg.co.za/article/2019-02-23-00-kagames-au-reforms-will-struggle-to-survive-without-him/. Accessed 4 Oct 2021
United Nations Economic Commission for Africa, African Union & the African Development Bank (2012) Assessing regional integration in Africa V: Towards an African Continental Free Trade Area. https://www.uneca.org/sites/default/files/PublicationFiles/aria5_print_uneca_fin_20_july_1.pdf. Accessed 4 Oct 2021
Viljoen F, Louw L (2007) State compliance with recommendations of the African Commission on Human and Peoples' Rights, 1994-2004. Am J Int Law 101(1):1–34
Wapmuk S (2009) In search of greater unity: African states and the quest for an African Union Government. J Altern Perspect Soc Sci 1(3):645–671
Welz M (2014) A 'culture of conservatism': how and why African Union member states obstruct the deepening of integration. Strateg Rev S Afr 36(1):4–24
Williams P (2007) From non-intervention to non-indifference: the origins and development of the African Union's security culture. Afr Aff 106(423):253 279
Wilson T, Blood D (2019) Rwanda: where even poverty data must toe Kagame's line. https://www.ft.com/content/683047ac-b857-11e9-96bd-8e884d3ea203. Accessed 4 Oct 2021
Zondi S (2012) The African Union audit and the state of continental integration: an analysis. Afr Insight 42(3):25–41

Chapter 5
Transcending Member States

Pathways to Building Continental Supranationalism in Africa

5.1 Introduction

This chapter explores the feasible pathways to achieving a meaningful continental supranationalism in Africa. It contends that such a development should be understood through a triptych analytical frame. These are internal dynamics (issues such as enhancing the AU's technocratic efficiency, self-restraint mechanisms and bottom-up supranational regionalism); external dynamics (the role of global actors on current and future issues that affect supranational regionalism in Africa, including domestic uncertainties determining the global projection of these powers); and the syncretic dynamics (which speaks to a practical policy position on balancing both internal and external dynamics and determining the suitability of application). As already indicated in the previous chapters, the ideas and strategies around achieving continental supranationalism in Africa are essentially woven around rejigging internal measures as a means of enhancing Africa's global stature. At the heart of this triptych analysis is the syncretic dynamics. Before discussing these three interrelated ideas, this chapter starts with a discussion of the imperative of a repurposed worldview, a factor that forms the ideational basis of the triptych dynamics. It then discusses the three dynamics, with the intention of distilling the feasible pathways for enhancing continental supranationalism in Africa

B. Fagbayibo, *Transcending Member States*,
https://doi.org/10.1007/978-3-031-12451-8_5

5.2 A Repurposed African Worldview

Over the years, African intellectuals, politicians and transnational documents have expressed what an African worldview should be like. Nnamdi Azikiwe's "Renascent Africa",[1] Ali Mazrui's "*Pax Africana*",[2] Kwame Nkrumah's "Philosophical Consciencism",[3] Thabo Mbeki's "African Renaissance",[4] the Lagos Plan of Action's idea of self-sufficiency,[5] and the AU Agenda 2063 "The Africa We Want" document, are some of the ideas that have animated the pan-African unity discourse. However, there remains a disconnect between these articulations and the practises of African national and regional actors in the global milieu.[6] Beyond the oft-repeated, and well intentioned, objective of moving Africa from the peripheral of global *realpolitik*, the question that has not so much been prioritised is the expected shape or the definitive guideline that should underline such objective. This missing link has deprived the lofty goals of continental supranationalism the benefits of realistic and feasible attainments. To put this differently, it is not enough to merely understand that internal and external factors influencing the development of regionalism in Africa but mainly to see how such understanding can shape the way Africa relates with itself and with the rest of the world through a strategic and beneficial prism. How the rest of the world relates to Africa, and how Africa sees itself within the matrix of global dynamics essentially stem from different worldviews. External parties, such as the EU, China, the U.S., and Russia, relations with Africa stem from

---

[1]Azikiwe identified the five bases of the idea of "Renascent Africa" or "New Africa" as: spiritual balance (respect of the view of others); social regeneration (equitable and democratic African society); economic determinism (equal and fair distribution of wealth); mental emancipation (eliminating all traces of inferiority complex among Africans); and national *risorgimento* (the feeling of national greatness which results from the combination of the previous four factors). Azikiwe (1968), pp. 8–10.

[2]The idea of *Pax Africana* is one that is centred on the imperative of Africans taking the primary responsibility of maintaining peace and security on the continent. As Mazrui (1967, p. 203) noted, *Pax Africana* speaks to an Africa "that is protected and maintained by Africa herself".

[3]Nkrumah observed that there are three broad features of the African society: the indigenous traditional way of life; the presence of Islam; and the Christian tradition and culture of Western Europe. He argued that the synthesis of these three is necessary for forging a new ideology that has the original African humanist principles at its core. Nkrumah (2001), pp. 68–70.

[4]Mbeki's idea of African renaissance' is one built on the exigencies of restoring Africa's dignity, and using such power and restoration to push for the economic and political development of the continent. Mbeki (1998).

[5]The Lagos plan of action was adopted by African leaders in 1980, with the central aim of reducing Africa's reliance on the western world and utilising the continent's immense natural resources for achieving self-sufficient economic development. OAU (1980).

[6]As Achebe (2011) retorted: "This is how I see the chaos in Africa today and the absence of logic in what we're doing. Africa's postcolonial disposition is the result of a people who have lost the habit of ruling themselves, forgotten their tradition way of thing, embracing and engaging the world without sufficient preparation. . .We are like the man in the Igbo proverb who does not know where the rain began to beat him and so cannot say where he dried his body".

geopolitical and geostrategic viewpoints shaped by their specific aspirations to be global superpowers.

According to Moghalu, a worldview "is a reflection of the inner world of an individual or group, which he or she or they project in their outward actions, and which influences the world around them by creating certain realities".[7] Aerts et al. provided seven basic elements that should inform individual or organisational worldview:

> 1. What is the nature of our world? How is it structured and how does it function? 2. Why is our world the way it is, and not different? Why are we the way we are, and not different? What kind of global explanatory principles can we put forward? 3. Why do we feel the way we feel in this world, and how do we assess global reality, and the role of our species in it? 4. How are we to act and to create in this world? How, in what different ways, can we influence the world and transform it? What are the general principles by which we should organise our actions? 5. What future is open to us and our species in this world? By what criteria are we to select these possible futures? 6. How are we to construct our image of this world in such a way that we can come up with answers to (1), (2), and (3)? 7. What are some of the partial answers that we can propose to these questions?[8]

These seven elements speak to core issues of knowledge of oneself and the world, agency and how such informs geo-strategic calculations and designs, and how the understanding of the present informs the future *vice versa*. As Moghalu observed, four issues should shape the worldview of Africa's approach to development: framework, values, strategy and organisation.[9] In this respect, he proposed the need for a strong value system (that eliminates corruption and bad governance), leadership (that is built on transparency and accountability), strategy (engagement of serious review of options and scenario, and how this should shape policy outcomes), and the embrace of an organising principle (discipline to organise effective outcomes for the continent).[10]

Halloran argued that the Chinese worldview can be pinned down to three interrelated timeless truths:

> a) a fatalistic, cyclical view of time and space characterized by meticulous interconnectivity of things big and small, b) a morally-relativistic universe in which the only absolute evil is chaos and the only good is stability, a platform on which progress is built, and c) the clan, not the individual, as the basic productive unit of society.[11]

In reinforcing its internal and external strength, China highlights the importance of Confucianism as a societal blueprint for stability, prioritisation of the group above the individual, and the emphasis on its 5000 years of civilisation (in particular the

[7] Moghalu (2013), p. 13.

[8] Aerts et al. (1994), p. 25.

[9] Moghalu (2013), p. 13.

[10] Ibid, pp. 18–20.

[11] Halloran (2011).

continued reference to its "civilisation state"[12] status).[13] It is through this carefully curated cultural and historical prism that China has been able to build and assert itself as a global force to reckon with.

In terms of the European worldview, Vennesson observed that European Union (EU) policy-makers are deliberate in engaging in strategic and purposeful foreign policy calculations that will result in positive and desirable outcomes for the EU.[14] As he further observed, such worldview has two significant roles: shapes the identity of the EU as an international actor and (in)directly shape the European integration project.[15] The EU's identity as an international actor is what has been described as "EU actorness". Sjöstedt defines EU actorness as "the capacity to behave actively and deliberately in relation to other actors in the international system".[16] Bretherton and Volger identify three features of EU actorness as presence, opportunity and capability. Presence signifies the ability of the EU "to exert influence; to shape the perceptions and expectations of others".[17] In spite of its external character, presence is ultimately a result of internal policies and processes.[18] Opportunity is described as the extent to which external dynamics shape EU's action or inaction.[19] As they further explained, the ideological environment of post-Cold war, which prioritised globalisation and neo-liberal orientations, played an important role in shaping the external policies and processes of the EU.[20] Capability speaks to EU's ability to formulate and implement policies.[21] At the heart of this is the nature of the institutional development and interaction within the EU, particularly how this affects operational efficiency and internal coherence.[22] In essence, EU's worldview is largely shaped by a neo-liberal perspective of global *realpolitik,* which then plays a key role in the way the EU relates with other international actors and also as an organising platform for persuading EU citizens regarding the rationality of its actions.

This linkage between intra-continental identity formation and the projection of geo-strategic influence in relation to external parties lie at the heart of repurposing

---

[12]The term "civilisation state" has also been ascribed to countries such as India, Turkey, Russia, and the U.S. According to Rachman (2019), "a civilisation state is a country that claims to represent not just a historic territory or a particular language or ethnic-group, but a distinctive civilisation". Rachman further noted that the idea has illiberal undertones as many of the countries that claim to a civilisation state tend to stifle individual freedoms and exclude minority groups. For a critical perspective of the concept of civilizational state, see e.g. Acharya (2020).

[13]Halloran (2011).

[14]Vennesson (2007), p. 1.

[15]Ibid, p. 9.

[16]Sjöstedt (1977), p. 16.

[17]Bretherton and Volger (1999), p. 5.

[18]Ibid, pp. 5–6.

[19]Ibid, p. 7.

[20]Ibid, pp. 7–8.

[21]Ibid, p. 9.

[22]Ibid, pp. 9–12.

Africa's worldview. As Chinweizu pointed out, without having meaningful power, Africa is unable to guarantee its autonomy and implement bold reforms.[23] In the context of building an effective continental supranational regime, several organising questions are worth reflecting on. These are: to what extent are supranational objectives central to Africa's developmental quest? Are regional institutions and normative instruments fit for purpose? Should Africa's relation with external parties alter the ideational agenda of building effective continental supranationalism? These questions revolve around the imperatives of a coherent and common African approach to both internal and external exigencies, innovative means of strengthening AU institutions, adopting a rational and carefully considered strategy to policy choices and outcomes, and having a fundamental and pragmatic position on the issue of agency. These questions are considered in the following section.

5.3 A Triptych Analysis

The ability of continental supranationalism to project meaningful power and autonomy within and outside Africa is predicated on numerous fundamentals. However, this chapter adopts a triptych lens, one that views external and internal strands as continuous, contiguous and as such, strategic for the development of continental supranationalism in Africa.

5.3.1 Internal Dynamics: Repositioning the Centre

The politics of the internal management of the continental integration process has in recent years become more focal. At the core of this is the question of agency, particularly the extent to which this informs the ownership and quality of decisions on the direction of continental regionalism. The lack of such agency is often linked to the excessive influence of external parties, including uncertainties around the parties' national political and economic processes, and how these negatively alter the calculus of continental integration. This point will be further explored in the next subsection. Of significant importance in this subsection is an understanding of the critical internal pillars that will determine the shape of continental supranationalism in Africa. These pillars are: broader institutional realignment and reforms; self-restraining measures; bottom-up supranational regionalism, and enhanced state capacity.

[23] Chinweizu (2011), p. 95.

5.3.1.1 Pillar 1: Broader Institutional Realignment and Reforms

Technocratic Competence of the AU Commission

The imperative of technocratic competence in the calculus of continental supranationalism cannot be overstated. As already shown in the previous chapter, the ongoing institutional reforms of the AU has at its core the strengthening of the AU Commission, which is seen as the "engine room" of continental integration in Africa. As discussed in Chap. 4, prior to the Kagame report, the 2007 AU Audit Report painted a disturbing picture of the dysfunctional internal administration of the Commission. Similarly, the AU Commission Strategic Plan 2004–2007, a document prepared by the AU Commission, made the following observation:

> The Commission of the African Union, which is supposed to be the engine of the Union and of the integration process, does not yet possess the necessary capacities to achieve the stated objectives. The institutional heritage of the OAU is characterized by numerical and qualitative staff shortage, ineffective structures resulting in compartmentalisation of the Departments, a highly hierarchical and bureaucratic organisational structure, and systems and procedure that do not enhance modern transparent and results oriented management.[24]

These critical deficiencies detract from AU Commission's ideational and practical capacity to meaningfully drive supranational regionalism on the continent. The politics of state-centric regionalism predetermines the parameters of the kind of powers member states are willing to transfer to the Commission. The unenthusiastic posture of member states thus feeds into the organisational culture of the Commission to the extent that it provides no incentive or motivation for competence and ideational capacity. The ongoing AU reforms has unfortunately been cosmetic at best in addressing the fundamental problems that undercut technocratic competence at the AU Commission. The mere reduction of AUC Commissioners from eight to six is not the necessary panacea for an organisation that requires a radical reorganisation.

Addressing the technocratic competence of the AU Commission is one that must be underlined by the fundamental question of how it should deliver its functions. The question is whether its functions should be delivered along corporate lines (like a private sector organisation), or facilitatory ones (where the AU's role is only to facilitate the correct application of norms at sub-regional and national levels), or a blend of intergovernmental and supranational elements (where roles are strategically assigned and shared between national and transnational agencies, between AU and RECs, and between AU organs)? Each of these elements has measures that could be useful for sharpening the AU. The corporate model brings to the table the prioritisation of lean, efficient and performance management-driven organisational

[24] AU (2004), p. 7. This position is further reiterated in the AU Strategic Plan 2009–2012 document. It highlighted the following problems: inadequate and inflexible structural arrangements; unsupportive organisational culture; administrative and leadership challenges; weak reputation, presence and reach in the continent; and inadequate finances. See AU (2009), p. 17.

processes. Together with the facilitatory model, it highlights the need to carefully identify feasible governance, security and capacity-building measures, and, therefore, deploy resources towards achieving such objectives. Lastly, the blend of supranational and intergovernmental elements brings together the corporate and facilitatory models by identifying issues of low and high politics, and then strategically mainstreaming continental integration goals into sub-regional and national processes.

The above-noted objectives can only be achieved through a strategic outlook that considers several issues. One is the capacity of the AUC Chair. This speaks to the eligibility of the individual, an inclusive election process, and the kinds of powers to be exercised by the Chair.[25] According to Rule 38(2) of the Rules of Procedure of the Assembly (Rules), the election of the Chairperson and Deputy Chairperson of the Commission shall be determined by "competent women or men with proven experience in the relevant field, commensurate leadership qualities and a good track record in government, parliament, international organizations or other relevant sectors of society".[26] This requirement is too general as it provides no specific content or context that determines the identification of such criteria. In order to remedy this, the AU Assembly in 2018 adopted five criteria for the election of the leadership of the AU Commission. These are: equitable regional representation and gender parity; predictable inter and intra-regional rotation, attracting and retaining top talents, accountable and effective leadership and management, and transparent and merit-based selection.[27] In this respect, the Assembly mandated the amendment of Rule 38 of the Rules of Procedure of the Assembly to include the following:

> The selection process should ensure the appointment of the best possible candidate who embodies the highest standards of efficiency, competence and integrity as well as demonstrating a firm commitment to Pan-Africanism and the objectives, principles and values of the AU, proven managerial abilities, extensive experience in international relations and strong diplomatic and communications skills.[28]

Furthermore, the Assembly established a panel of five eminent persons, one from each of Africa's five regions, to oversee the pre-selection of candidates for the AU Commission's leadership positions.[29] However, there is still the need to be more specific about these criteria. For example, there must be a deliberate indication of gender balance: one that speaks to a rotational policy that stipulates that where the Chair is a man, the Deputy Chair should be a woman, and a rolling arrangement that prescribes that a male Chairperson should be followed a female Chairperson *vice versa*.[30] Table 5.1 below shows that since its establishment, the AU Commission has

---

[25] See Fagbayibo (2012), pp. 20–27.

[26] Rules of Procedure of the Assembly.

[27] AU (2018c), p. 3.

[28] Ibid, p. 5.

[29] Ibid, p. 4.

[30] Fagbayibo (2012), p. 23. In terms of gender parity within the AU, as at 2019, the number of women in representational offices was 32%, 40% of professional staff members (P1–P5), 58% in general services. See AU (2020a), p. 6.

Table 5.1 Chairpersons and deputy Chairpersons of the AU since its formation

Name	Duration	Nationality	Gender
Chair: Amara Essy (Acting)	2003	Cote d'Ivoire	Male
Deputy Chair: Patrick Kayumba Mazimhaka	2003	Rwanda	Male
Chair: Alpha Oumar Konaré	2003–2008	Mali	Male
Deputy Chair: Patrick Kayumba Mazimhaka	2003–2008	Rwanda	Male
Chair: Jean Ping	2008–2012	Gabon	Male
Deputy Chair: Erastus Mwencha	2008–2012	Kenya	Male
Chair: Nkosazana Dlamini-Zuma	2012–2017	South Africa	Female
Deputy Chair: Erastus Mwencha	2012–2017	Kenya	Male
Chair: Moussa Faki	2017-Current	Chad	Male
Deputy Chair: Thomas Kwesi Quartey	2017–2021	Ghana	Male
Deputy Chair: Monique Nsanzabaganwa	2021-Current	Rwanda	Female

Source: Author's compilation from information provided on the AU website

only had one female Chairperson, and one female deputy Chairperson. However, in the current dispensation (2021–2024), there is an equal gender representation, three each, of commissioners in the AU Commission.[31] On the question of competence and track record, the question should be centred around such individual's ideational understanding of the exigencies of continental regionalism, and the extent to which their previous record reinforces this understanding. How for example has such individual, either in public or private sector capacity, achieved certain objectives that are central to deepening regionalism in Africa? How is such individual able to provide a rigorous intellectual basis of their ideological position on the way forward for African regionalism? These are some of the questions that can give proper content and context to the criteria for selection.

Regarding the election process of the Chairperson and the Deputy Chairperson of the AU Commission, there should be a more inclusive mechanism that starts with the composition of a recruitment committee that is made up of governmental and non-governmental actors. In this respect, the committee could include governmental actors nominated by the AU Assembly (possibly the Executive Council), representatives of PAP, a reputable Africa-based and owned recruitment agency (or team of agencies), and representatives of civil society organisations. Such inclusive composition should then be tasked with finding and shortlisting competent and capable candidates. The names could then be forwarded to the AU Assembly, where a final decision can be made as to the right candidate. This process will require an amendment of Rule 38 of the Rules of Procedure of the Assembly. The idea of this outlined process is to ensure a careful balancing of intergovernmental and

[31] Josefa Sacko (Female: Agriculture, Rural Development, Blue Economy and Sustainable Environment); Albert Muchanga (Male: Economic Development, Trade, Industry and Mining); Amani Abou-Zeid (Female: Infrastructure and Energy); Bankole Adeoye (Male: Political Affairs, Peace and Security); Minata Samate (Female: Health, Humanitarian Affairs and Social Development); and Mohamed Belhocine (Male: Education, Science, Technology and Innovation).

supranational dynamics of continental integration, and more fundamentally, to include a much broader perspective in the appointment of the individual that is expected to drive the technocratic process of continental regionalism in Africa.

On the powers to be exercised by the Chair of the AU Commission, it is important to consider how the Chair shares his or her powers with other AU organs and member states.[32] With respect to the Chair's control of the Commission, there should be a concerted effort in exploring ways in which the Chair is in the position to assign portfolio to the Commissioners. This position was recommended by the Kagame led AU reforms process but was rejected by the AU Assembly. It was also recommended by the 2007 AU Audit Report. However, there are more innovative and strategic ways of achieving this. The ability to assign portfolio is an important process in the matrix of having the motivation and power to shape policies and achieve the stated objectives of continental regionalism. In order to ensure that the AU Assembly accepts any proposal on transferring their powers to assign portfolios to the Chairperson, it has to be clearly stated that the former still retains the role of making the final appointments (similar to the suggested process of electing the Chair and Deputy Chair of the AU Commission) and the powers to ratify the decision of the Chair on the assignment of portfolios to Commissioners. This will require that the Chair to submit his or her plans regarding suitability for specific positions to the AU Assembly as a means of guiding the latter on the nomination and appointment process. Once the candidates have been identified, the Chair could then provide a motivation as to why each of the candidate has been assigned specific portfolio for the final consideration of the AU Assembly.[33] This process will require an amendment of Rule 39 the Rules of Procedure of the Assembly. In addition, the Chair should be the tasked with the responsibility of heading the AU committee on implementation of common policies objectives, which should also include the powers to delegate his or functions to transnational or national representatives. Lastly, the relationship between the Chair and member states is of critical importance. This will also require a more strategic balancing of the state-centric DNA of African regionalism with a carefully crafted incremental supranational drive. One way to achieve this is to consider ways in which specific member states can choose to enter into binding agreements with the AU Commission on the development and implementation of integration objectives. In this regard, the Chair could then assign representatives to be involved in national processes focused on economic development, political reforms, and the implementation of trade and migration policies. Such involvement should have two objectives. One is to ensure that the AU Commission is abreast of national issues and how they impact regionalism, and secondly, be in the vantage position of ensuring compliance with integration objectives.

The second leg of the strategic outlook on technocratic competence is the nature of the AU Commission itself. This point speaks to the internal bureaucratic and administrative efficiency of the Commission. The Kagame Report recommended

[32] Fagbayibo (2012), p. 25.

[33] Ibid, p. 27.

that the functions and priorities of the AU should be streamlined and limited to issues such as political affairs, peace and security, economic integration, and Africa's global representation. This, however, requires an organisation that fully understands the philosophical exigencies of pan-Africanism and can deliver on the technical mandates of regionalism. Issues such as rigorous recruitment process;[34] transparency and accountability of processes and measures; targeted capacity building programmes; the feeding of the activities of the African Union Youth Volunteer Corps (AU-YVC)[35] into the Commission's recruitment and development agenda; and a more proactive and engaged interface with governmental and non-governmental stakeholders are essential ingredients of strengthening the AU Commission. The AU Commission's relations with RECs is critical as it further opens the avenue to adopt and adapt useful operational methods of organisations such as the Economic Community of West African States (ECOWAS) and the East African Community (EAC) in the implementation of its protocols on free movement, free trade and private sector involvement in regionalism. As shown in a 2019 AU report on the progress of regional integration, RECs such as the Southern African development Community (SADC), Common Market for Eastern and Southern Africa (COMESA) and the Inter-governmental Authority on Development (IGAD), have lessons for the AU on diversified models of regional integration, infrastructure development, peace and security, and social matters.[36] Such learning process is what Cabral had described as "constructive emulation".[37]

Reforming PAP and ACJ&HR

The enhanced technocratic competence of the AU Commission cannot exist outside the broader politico-legal realignment and reforms of AU institutions. This position is one that speaks to the crucial point of reassessing the politico-legal strategies of transferring supranational powers to key AU institutions. Despite the overwhelming state-centric framework of the AU, there are ways in which critical organs can exercise effective binding powers on member states. In achieving this, it is imperative to consider the organising principles that such realignment and reforms should be anchored to. These are legitimacy, rationalisation, and flexibility.

Legitimacy denotes the perception of the recipients of binding norms regarding the transparency and quality of the norm making body. As Franck puts it, legitimacy

[34] For a detailed analysis of the politics of staffing and recruitment at the AU Commission, see Tieku et al. (2020), pp. 461–481.

[35] The AU-YVC is an AU programme that trains and deploy young Africans to all AU member states in order to share their skills and learn more about the imperatives of development and Africa's position in the global environment. The areas of focus include Education; Health and HIV/AIDS; Peace and Security; Information and Communications Technology; Business and Youth Entrepreneurship; and Agriculture and Environment. See the AU website.

[36] See generally, AU Commission (2019).

[37] Cabral (2007), p. 146.

is "the quality of a rule which derives from a perception on the part of those to whom it has come into being in accordance with right process".[38] In the case of transnational courts, legitimacy is further determined by the extent to which states are willing to submit and consent to the jurisdiction and decisions of the court.[39] Rationalisation is a term that is often used to describe the importance of AU relations with its RECs, particularly in terms of division of labour, which allows the RECs to take charge of issues under their political jurisdiction.[40] This understanding should also be factored into how AU organs operate within the continental supranationalism matrix. Flexibility relates to how willing and able member states can proceed with integration objectives at a much deeper and faster pace.[41] This pragmatic approach considers the reality that not all the 55 AU member states are willing and/or able to proceed with supranational regionalism at the same pace and depth. These three issues are interwoven as will be shown in the discussion below.

The legitimacy of AU institutions such as the AU Commission, PAP and the ACJ&HR will rest on the ability to achieve rationalisation and flexibility, especially as it impacts on the ability of these institutions to effectively navigate the politico-legal exigencies of supranational continental integration. In other words, the key question is whether the exercise of supranational powers by these institutions reflect the legitimacy of their existence. This is predicated on issues such as the awareness of their operational measures, transparent appointment process, powers to determine the parameters of the initiation and implementation of their decisions, and the realistic adherence to their decisions. Another important factor that stems from legitimacy is the issue of accountability. In recent times, there have been allegations of corruption, wasteful expenditure, nepotism, and sexual harassment levelled against the PAP and AU Commission, further exposing these institutions to serious questions about their existence.[42]

The realisation of the aforementioned objectives will require a deliberate strategy that outlines how the AU Assembly is able to transfer its decision-making powers and as such endow these institutions with realistic supranational powers. The AU Commission has already been considered under pillar 1, and as such only the other two, PAP and ACJ&HR will be discussed here.

The legitimacy of PAP rests on its competence to make binding, not model, laws. Despite the suggestions of some writers about the pragmatism of model laws,[43] there is enough evidence to show that AU member states rarely comply with binding norms let alone mere recommendations. In addition, national legislatures are often too preoccupied with national politics, coupled with needless interference from the executives, to see the political benefits or rationale behind complying with

---

[38] Franck (1988), p. 706.

[39] Oppong (2014), p. 64.

[40] See generally, AU & UNECA (2006).

[41] See generally, Fagbayibo (2016).

[42] See e.g. Fagbayibo (2018b); Allison (2020).

[43] Musila (2007), p. 9.

regulations that are not binding. What we are then left with is to find strategic ways that balances endowing PAP with legislative powers (especially in phases) with the necessity of state-centric legislative authority.

The unwillingness of member states to take any meaningful step towards achieving this is a major diminishing factor. In correcting this, there is a need to explore ways in which willing member states can start transferring some legislative powers to PAP. This flexibility approach will require strategic partnerships between the PAP on the one hand and willing member states and sub-regional parliaments on the other hand.[44] Such arrangement should include, but not limited to, areas such as the direct elections of PAP representatives coming from such member state(s), allowing participating national parliaments to first send any bill that has direct implication for regionalism to PAP for consideration and/or guidance, and granting PAP the power to initiate bills on areas that fall within its exclusive competence.[45] This will have a number of legal implications.

The first is the need to amend the existing PAP Protocol by inserting a clause that allows willing member states and RECs to enter into arrangements with PAP for it to exercise partial or full legislative powers in specific areas. For example, Musila proposed that the PAP could start exercising powers over issues that have assumed a transnational character.[46] These include human rights, trade, immigration and free movement of people.[47] He further noted that the exercise of full legislative powers by the PAP should be underpinned by the well-known principle of subsidiarity, one that allows national and sub-regional legislative organs to retain powers over local issues.[48] Mpanyane averred that PAP's transformation, particularly as it relates to transferring meaningful legislative powers to the organ, should start from the activation of a framework that ensures "practical cooperation and regular interaction with other AU institutions".[49] This includes activities such as joint briefings and submission of reports with relevant AU institutions and the continuous engagement with national and regional legislative bodies.[50]

The second point relates to establishing close working relations between PAP and national and sub-regional parliaments in terms of identifying laws that have direct impact on deepening regional integration and exploring ways of getting advisory and facilitatory opinions from PAP on bills that impact continental regionalism. In this context, PAP representatives or relevant committee members could also visit national or sub-regional parliaments and further interact with civil society during the consideration of the bill. The advantage here is that while PAP can exercise meaningful legislative powers, relevant national or sub-regional parliaments will still

[44] Fagbayibo (2018a), p. 638.

[45] Ibid.

[46] Musila (2007), p. 9.

[47] Ibid.

[48] Ibid.

[49] Mpanyane (2009), p. 10.

[50] Ibid.

reserve the right to pass laws within their jurisdictions.[51] The general idea is to enhance the complementary, rather than a conflictive, role of transnational institutions in the matrix of continental integration.

The third point relates to the need to adopt the code that allows for the direct election of parliamentarians, as envisaged under Article 5(3) of the amended PAP protocol. Similar to the discussion above, one way of achieving this is the signing of a Memorandum of Understanding (MoU) between AU and willing member states on the modalities of organising direct elections of national legislators to PAP. Such MoU should further stipulate that such elections will be monitored and verified by the AU in accordance with its rules and norms on democracy and governance.

The envisaged ACJ&HR thus has the potential of fast-tracking closer integration through its jurisprudence. Based on its exclusive competence, the court will be expected to adjudicate on pertinent issues such as member states' ratification of and adherence to key principles and instruments, multi-level governance within the AU, human rights violations, the role of sub-regional institutions within the multi-layered integration framework, legitimacy of national regimes and appropriate sanctions for non-compliance with the AU rules and regulations. For the ACJ&HR to effectively undertake these functions, certain points need to be given utmost priority. The effective realisation of this task rests on four critical points. These four points rest on the political willingness of member states to ratify the ACJ&HR protocol to quicken the establishment of the merged court.

The first is the appointment and quality of judges. The appointment of judges to the Court should be merit driven. In this regard, such judges should be dynamic, progressive and have a good grasp of international law and politics. The practise of appointing judges from national courts to transnational courts is another problematic issue. As Oppong rightly observed, governments could use such appointment to manipulate the appointed judges and/or even use the activism of the judge while serving on the transnational court as a pretext for terminating his or her national employment.[52] This was the case in East Africa when Kenya, in reaction to the *Nyong'o* case threatened, albeit unsuccessfully, to remove the two EACJ Kenyan judges, claiming that there were allegations of corruption against them in Kenya.[53] Furthermore, the issue of gender balance in appointment has to be sacrosanct as this keys into the ambitions of the AU, in particular the AU Agenda 2063 goal of achieving gender balance in all structures of governance in Africa by 2023. The African Court on Human and Peoples' Rights (ACtHPR) is currently the most gender balanced international court in the world, as six out of its 11 judges are women.[54] This important development should serve as an instructive guide for other regional courts and the soon to be established ACJ&HR. As Dawuni argued, the sustainability of gender parity goal in African regional courts must be rooted in

[51] Fagbayibo (2018a), p. 639.

[52] Oppong (2014), p. 66.

[53] Alter et al. (2016), p. 303.

[54] Dawuni (2018).

quality-oriented standards.[55] This includes the revision of the selection methods in African regional goals; the need to move beyond the descriptive representation of women towards the substantive analyses of what women representation means; the imperative of mainstreaming gender parity into all AU structures; the importance of women judges mentoring young girls and other women; continued vigilance to ensure that the progress made becomes institutionalised; and the need for sustained advocacy by gender activist in order to ensure that the progress recorded by the AfCtHPR is replicated across the continent.[56]

The delicate nature of the task before the Court, especially in relation to the entrenchment of democratic norms and values, deepening of African integration and a jurisprudence rooted in African context require a pragmatic and nuanced method of adjudication. Africa's different legal traditions (common, civil and customary) should be used as a platform for enriching the jurisprudence of the court.

Secondly, it is important to provide the Court with a sound support framework. In order to ensure efficiency and maximum output, the ACJ&HR should be provided with adequate research support, skilled personnel and a working environment conducive to productivity. Serious effort should be devoted to attracting efficient and knowledgeable researchers and administrators that will assist the judges. Another aspect is the need to ensure the financial viability of the court particularly as it relates to the salaries of the judges, staff and investment in virtual and physical research materials that would enable to the courts function efficiently. Furthermore, there has to a deliberate investment in platforms that help to popularise the works of the court and awareness of its activities by Africans.[57] This includes a well-functioning and up-to-date website; wide distribution of judgements and information of the court's processes to law libraries in African universities; translation of the activities of the court into local languages; engagement with civil society and traditional authorities; and sustained internship programmes.

Thirdly, to prevent the Court from being subdued by an avalanche of cases, it is pertinent that national and sub-regional judicial organs are granted the powers to act as Court of first instance in some cases that fall within the exclusive competence of the ACJ&HR. The Court's reliance on national structures, either as judicial partners or as an instrument of ensuring compliance, implies that national institutions conform to the minimum democratic standards set down by the AU. The idea of using national courts to enforce regional judgements is already the practise in the EAC, Organisation of the Harmonisation of Business Laws in Africa (OHADA), ECOWAS and COMESA, and it will be beneficial to learn from the successes and challenges of these courts in this regard. In addition, national and sub-regional courts could also be used as courts of first of instance in interpreting transnational rules, and only refer cases to the ACJ&HR for final interpretation. As Kufuor suggested in the case of ECOWAS Community Court of Justice (ECCJ), ACJ&HR could also explore the possibility of on-site participation in the adjudication of certain issues

[55] Ibid.

[56] Ibid.

[57] Oppong (2011), pp. 185–186.

that have implications for continental trade and human rights objectives.[58] This would allow transnational judges the opportunity to apply their knowledge of the law in a domestic setting.[59] In addition, it would also enhance the legitimacy of the ACJ&HR mainly because it grants local civil society the opportunity to directly participate in transnational processes.[60] This will also help in addressing the nagging issue of physical accessibility.

The fourth point is the imperative of ensuring individual access to the ACJ&HR. The 2007 AU Audit Report emphasised that individual access is central to effectiveness of the ACJ&HR, especially its ability to administer justice.[61] Article 29 of the ACJ&HR Protocol does not allow for individual access to the General Affairs section of the court while Article 30(f) only allows for individual access to the Human Rights section subject to "a declaration (by the concerned member state) accepting the competence of the Court to receive cases".[62] The declaration is to be made in terms of Article 34(6) of the Protocol to the African Charter on Human and Peoples' Rights on the Establishment of the African Court on Human and Peoples' Rights. Out of the court's 30 member states, only 10 (Benin, Burkina Faso, Côte d'Ivoire, Gambia, Ghana, Malawi, Mali, Rwanda, Tanzania, and Tunisia) have ever made the declaration. Four of these 10 (Rwanda, Benin, Tanzania and Cote d'Ivoire) have thus far withdrawn the declaration to allow individual and NGO access.[63] In *Femi Falana v. African Union*, the applicant challenged the legality of Article 34(6), claiming that it violates the right of individuals from member states that are yet to make the declaration to access the court for effective remedy.[64] The court ruled against the applicant noting that it is the sovereign right of member states to make a declaration at the time of the ratification of the Protocol under international law.[65]

Individual access to regional courts enhances their legitimacy by ensuring consistency of support from national courts.[66] Individual access to regional courts in Africa already exists in some of the RECs. Regional courts such as the East African Court of Justice (EACJ), the Common Market for Eastern and Southern Africa (COMESA) Court of Justice, and the ECCJ all provide for varying degrees of individual access.[67] Both EACJ and ECCJ allow for individual access without the need for the exhaustion of local remedies.[68]

[58] Kufuor (1996), p. 11.

[59] Ibid.

[60] Fagbayibo (2019b), p. 458.

[61] AU (2007), p. 90.

[62] Article 8 of the ACJ&HR Protocol.

[63] de Silva (2019); Windridge (2020).

[64] Application no. 001/2011.

[65] Ibid, para. 49.

[66] Oppong (2014), p. 73.

[67] Art. 30 of the EAC Treaty (2006), Article 26 of the COMESA Treaty (1993), ECOWAS Supplementary Protocol A/SP.1/01/05, Art. 4.

[68] Oppong (2014), p. 73.

The reform of AU institutions can only be effective if it is accompanied by a feasible implementation mechanism. The high incidences of non-compliance continue to curtail effective regionalism at sub-regional and continental levels. As noted in the previous chapters, the majority of the 1500 decisions by the AU has either not been implemented or there are no available mechanisms to track their implementation. Similarly, about 75% of the decisions of the AfCtHPR have been ignored by member states. The way out of this quagmire rests on pragmatic politico-legal measures. One such method is the utilisation of the AU's stringent guidelines on sanctions relating to non-payment of financial dues.[69] In this respect, the focus should be expanded to include non-compliance with AU regulations, with deviant member states subjected to the cautionary, intermediate and comprehensive punitive thresholds. However, this could be adapted to include an in-built monitoring mechanism. In this regard, there is the need to establish an inter-institutional implementation body - headed by the AU Commission Chairperson, the REC to which such member state(s) belong, representative of civil society, an appointee of the AU Assembly (possibly a designated AU high representative for implementation of decisions), and the head of African Union Development Agency (AUDA)—NEPAD—tasked with assessing compliance issues and making binding recommendations on punitive measures. The idea here is to explore series of persuasive and diplomatic measures before arriving at stringent disciplinary actions. As will be shown in the discussion below, beyond the wilful disregard of regional rules, other factors such as weak state capacity, political instability, and weak economies could also be responsible for non-compliance. Therefore, it is essential to be contextual, and engage issues on a case-by-case basis.

5.3.1.2 Pillar 2: Self-restraining Measures

The second pillar deals with the need to strengthen self-restraining institutional and normative measures. Mazrui used the term "self-pacification" to denote the imperative of devising political methods of preventing the escalation of competition to conflicts or large-scale civil wars in Africa.[70] Building on Mazrui's thesis, the AU has developed governance and security platforms such as the Peace and Security Council (and its early warning systems mechanism), the African Standby Force (ASF), the African Peer Review Mechanism (APRM) and the African Governance Architecture (AGA) to stem the spate of conflicts. Furthermore, the AU Agenda 2063 envisaged the resolution of conflicts, "silencing the guns", by 2020. However, the AU has been postponed this to 2030 due to the Covid-19 pandemic and the enormity of the security issues that continue to bedevil the continent.[71]

[69] AU (2018a).

[70] Mazrui (1994), p. 39.

[71] Du Plessis (2020).

According to a 2007 Oxfam report, over a period of 15 years, 1990–2005, Africa lost USD284 billion to conflicts and wars.[72] It is also estimated that about 24 African countries have spent around USD300 billion on conflicts since 1990.[73] Furthermore, within the same period, the continent's economy shrunk by an average of 15% yearly.[74] In terms of the impact of instability on regional integration, the International Monetary Fund (IMF) showed how the political conflict in Cote d'Ivoire led to serious decline in output and invariably weakened the general economic performance of the West African Economic Monetary Union (WAEMU) in 2000.[75] In a 2014 report, the African Capacity Building Foundation (ACBF) noted that some of Africa's RECs were so immersed in conflict resolution that issues of trade negotiations had to be relegated to the bottom of the priority list.[76] Viljoen and Louw observed the nexus between political stability and compliance with the decisions of the African Commission on Human and Peoples' Rights (AfCHPR):

> If political situation is characterized as 'stable', 'relatively stable', or 'civil war'. Compliant states are more likely to fall into the categories of 'stable' or 'relatively stable'. Cases of clear noncompliance, such as that involving Angola, Burundi, the DRC, and Sudan, are more likely in the context of civil war and relative instability.[77]

Security issues due to political instability has also been identified as one of the reasons why some member states have been reluctant to comply with regional protocols on free movement.[78]

While the number of conflicts has increased over the years,[79] the AU continues to struggle to effectively curb excesses that have the potential of snowballing into conflict and other humanitarian disasters in member states. These include the manipulation of elections, growing autocratic tendencies and the brutal suppression of dissenting voices. Several reports continue to show the worrying decline of democratic practises in member states. In 2019, Cheeseman observed that "half of all African states are autocracies (36% hardline, 14% moderate), while the other half are democracies (5% consolidating, 34% defective, 11% highly defective)".[80] According to the 2021 Freedom House report, only 9 African countries qualify as

---

[72] IANSA et al. (2007), p. 9.

[73] Ibid.

[74] Ibid.

[75] IMF (2001), p. 4.

[76] ACBF (2014), p. 58.

[77] Viljoen and Louw (2007), p. 27.

[78] UNECA et al. (2012), p. 72.

[79] According to a 2021 report, out of the 34 armed conflicts around the world in 2020, Africa accounted for 15 of those conflicts. This includes serious armed conflicts in Cameroon (Ambazonia/North West and South West), Ethiopia (Tigray), Libya, Mali, Mozambique (north), Lake Chad Region (Boko Haram), Western Sahel Region, DRC (East), DRC (east-ADF), Somalia, and South Sudan. Similarly, out of the 16 socio-political crises with maximum intensity globally, Africa accounted for eight: Chad; Mali; Nigeria; Ethiopia; Ethiopia (Oromiya); Kenya; Rwanda-Burundi; and Morocco-Western Sahara. See Escola de Cultura de Pau (2021).

[80] Cheeseman (2019), p. 5.

Table 5.2 The state of freedom in Africa

Countries	Status
Algeria, Angola, Burundi, Cameroon, Djibouti Central African Republic, Chad, Democratic Republic of Congo, Egypt, Equatorial Guinea, Eritrea, Eswatini, Ethiopia, Gabon, Libya, Mali, Congo, Rwanda, Somalia, South Sudan, Sudan, Uganda, Western Sahara	Not Free
Benin, Burkina Faso, Comoros, Cote d'Ivoire, Guinea, Guinea Bissau, Kenya Lesotho, Liberia, Madagascar, Malawi, Mauritania, Morocco, Mozambique, Niger Nigeria, Senegal, Sierra Leone, Gambia, Togo, Zambia, Somaliland (not recognised as a state by the AU)	Partially Free
Botswana, Cabo Verde, Ghana, Mauritius, Namibia, Seychelles, South Africa, São Tomé and Príncipe, Tunisia	Free

Source: Author's adaptation from Freedom House (2021)

free in terms of the guarantee of political rights and civil liberties (see Table 5.2 below).[81]

The table above paints a worrying picture of the state of freedom on the continent. It shows that the majority of Africa's estimated 1.3 billion people live under conditions that are either partially free or not free. South Africa is the only regional hegemon that falls under the free status. Nigeria and Kenya are partially free, and Egypt is not free. This places a big question mark on the legitimacy of these regional hegemons to champion the advancement of democracy on the continent. Similarly, Tella argued that democratic deficit undercuts the ability of regional hegemons to project soft power across the continent.[82] The index further confirms the nexus between political stability and freedom, as all the countries under the free status, and many of the countries under the partly free status enjoy some degree of political stability.

Similar to the Freedom House report is the 2020 AU report. This report assessed the extent of member states' compliance with regional norms of democracy and good governance in 2019. The report noted that:

> The continent fell significantly short of realising its targets on ensuring that democratic values and practices are the norm, realising 27% of her 2019 target. The only significant progress that was recorded was on operationalising the African Charter on Democracy – with a score based on countries that have signed and ratified the Charter achieving 98% and 87% of the 2019 target respectively. However, progress on integrating the Charter into national planning and development instruments has been slow – exhibited by the weak performance of 22% against the 2019 target. Similarly, the percentage of the African population who believe that elections are free, fair and transparent; and the proportion of the population on the continent that perceives that there is press freedom and associated freedom of speech – pitched at 26% and 13% respectively of the 2019 targets. This reflects a weak performance of the continent. Furthermore, the continent fell short by 86% of its 2019 target regarding the proportion of people who believe that there are effective mechanisms and oversight institutions to hold their leaders accountable.[83]

[81] Freedom House (2021).

[82] Tella (2021).

[83] AU (2020b), p. 16.

The AU's supposed promotion of democratic values is further undercut by its inability to prevent leaders with questionable democratic credentials from either heading the AU Assembly or driving programmes aimed at improving integrative objectives. Essentially, the AU has only marginally moved away from its predecessor's regime-boosting and club-diplomacy approach, which emphasises solidarity among heads of state over and above affirming democratic tenets. As Mkandawire pointedly noted,

> [T]wo factors have worked against the pan-African dream. One has been authoritarian rule. There has never been a federation of dictators. The second is the shallowness of our individual national visions has not permitted us to see that regional integration is an important ingredient in any meaningful transformation of our countries and continent.[84]

Self-restraint measures require a change of mindset and mental models on the part of national politicians and policy makers. It demands the imperative of seeing the strong link between effective national policies/institutions and attainment of effective continental regionalism.[85] As Adedeji rightly asserted, a state that cannot provide social amenities within its jurisdiction cannot be expected to provide meaningful support for the same objective at the regional level.[86] Similarly, an autocratic regime cannot genuinely support regional objectives on democratisation and the protection of fundamental human rights.

5.3.1.3 Pillar 3: Bottom-up Supranational Regionalism

The third pillar speaks to investing in bottom-up continental regional integration initiatives. One of the essential features of Africa's integration process is its elite driven, top-down approach, with very little room for civil society to make effective contributions. Beyond the nominal recognition of civil society platforms in the AU, there remains little or no consideration of citizen participation in the articulation and implementation of integrative goals.[87] Some relevant issues remain peripheral concerns. This includes issues such as referenda on continental integration measures; coordination and mainstreaming of various private sector activities into a well-articulated continental agenda; utilisation of traditional authorities in enhancing awareness; promotion of the use of African languages in driving continental integration;[88] incorporation of informal cross-border trades into the architecture of continental free trade arrangements;[89] and exploring realistic ways through which citizens can fund and benefit from continental programmes. Similarly, the place of women in the discourse and processes of continental supranationalism must extend

---

[84] Mkandawire (2015), p. 220.

[85] Ibid.

[86] Africa Renewal (2002).

[87] Tieku (2017), pp. 48–50. See also Finizo (2018) pp. 307–313.

[88] Diop (1987), pp. 11–14. See also Ndhlovu (2017), pp. 89–109.

[89] Sommer and Nshimbi (2018), pp. 7–10.

beyond the rhetorical plane. As Nyabola pointed out, pan-African integration drive remains steeped in a patriarchal, "Man-Africanism" paradigm:

> Man-Africanists never attacked the patriarchal colonial state. At its most idealistic, Pan-Africanism was still a project driven by elite men. And so, Man-Africanism has never seen the liberation of women as a priority; the oppression of women has never seemed as grave or as urgent as the suffering of powerful men. Focused on *formal* power and the public sphere, it will never seek to overturn private hierarchies of exploitation if the primary beneficiaries will be women. It will never remake the African Union into a grassroots movement, because the grassroots are not powerful men. It will never reject external interventions that strengthen the central state, because the central state is powerful men. It will never defend the women of South Sudan from violent sexual assault, because the war has been started and perpetuated by powerful men. Its principle of solidarity is powerful men.[90]

The role of young people in the African integration process is another issue. Africa is regarded as the youngest continent in the world with about 60% of its population under the age of 25.[91] However, this important segment of the African population remains marginalised in the political and economic spheres. According to the International Labour Organisation (ILO), out of the over 226 million youth on the continent, 13.4 million are unemployed, 52.5 million are not in employment, education or training, and 54.4 million are working but poor.[92] The African Youth Charter (AYC) is the primary AU instrument for youth development and empowerment. It makes provisions for the participation of young people in national governance structures and the socio-economic upliftment of the youth.[93] Other AU documents that deal with youth are the Youth Decade Plan of Action and the Malabo Decision on Youth Empowerment. The Youth Decade Plan of Action encompasses five priority areas: education and skills development; youth employment and entrepreneurship; governance, peace and security; youth health and sexual reproductive health rights; and agriculture, climate change and the environment.[94] The Malabo Decision on Youth Empowerment enjoined member states reduce youth and women unemployment by at least 2% annually over the next 5 years; maintain, extend and harmonise labour market information systems in support of youth employment; improve and increase responsiveness of the education and training systems to current and future labour market needs; and accelerate appropriate social protection coverage expansion for the youth, women, informal economy and rural workers.[95]

These objectives remain largely unfulfilled. Through gerontocratic practises, young people continue to be excluded from political participation, making the political space an exclusive preserve of old men. As such, a continent that is

[90] Nyabola (2016).

[91] Mo Ibrahim Foundation (2019).

[92] ILO (2019).

[93] See Articles 9-19 of the African Youth Charter (2006).

[94] AU website (Youth development).

[95] AU (2011).

described as the "youngest continent in the world" is ruled by leaders with an average age of 62.[96]

The absence of these explain the disconnection between regionalism and regionalisation in Africa. The former refers to official programmes and policies aimed at consolidating regional institutions, while the latter describes interactive engagements among non-state actors in processes that do not necessarily involve regional organisations or state actors.[97] The issue of devising bottom-up effective processes for regional integration in Africa is discussed under the syncretic dynamic.

5.3.1.4 Pillar 4: Enhanced State Capacity

The capacity of national institutions to implement regional integration policies and laws remain an integral and crucial aspect of regionalism. Strong national institutions not only ensure the meaningful translation of transnational objectives into national norms but could also serve as instructive institutional lessons for regional institutions. In terms of the latter, some scholars have noted how the European Economic Commission (now EU Commission) and European Central Bank (ECB) were modelled on the French public administration and the German Bundesbank respectively.[98] According to the managerial theory of compliance, it is observed that non-compliance to international norms and regulations are not necessarily due to outright disregard on the part of member states but is in some cases the result of lack of financial and administrative capacity in public service.[99] The public service sector in many African countries have come under serious scrutiny over the years. The fiscal crisis created by structural adjustment policies in the 1980s played a major part in undercutting the technical and administrative capacity of national institutions.[100] This significant cut in public investment ensured the diminished state capacity and invariably led to a demoralised and ill-equipped public service sector.[101] Subsequently, other detracting factors set in. This includes the fall in real wages, patronage system of employment, overwhelming negative citizen perception of public administration, insufficient training and capacity development strategies for public servants, and the transplantation of ill-suited Eurocentric policies and programmes.[102] These are factors that are antithetical to the effective and efficient implementation of regional integration programmes.

In addressing the issue of public administration, the AU in 2011 adopted the African Charter on Values and Principles of Public Service and Administration. Its

---

[96] Yahya (2017).

[97] Acharya (2012) 12. See also Bach (2017), pp. 5–6.

[98] Cini (2002), p. 47. See also Heisenberg & Richmond (2002), p. 208.

[99] Chayes and Chayes (1993), pp. 193–195.

[100] Mkandawire (2002), p. 15.

[101] Ibid, pp. 15–16.

[102] Ayee (2005) pp. 21–23. See also Igbokwe-Ibeto (2019), pp. 7–9.

objectives include the commitment of member states to providing quality and innovative service delivery; modernising and strengthening the capacity of public service; encouraging the participation of citizens in public administration processes; improving the working conditions of public servants; encouraging the harmonisation of public service and administration among member states for the purpose of regional and continental integration; promotion of gender equality in public service; strengthen cooperation among member states, RECs and the international community on improving public service; and encourage the sharing of experiences and best practises among member states.[103] While these points are laudable, they are yet to form the core principles of public service administration, and also shape the nexus between regional integration programmes and public service in member states. Enhancing the technocratic capacity of the state to fulfil regional integration objectives will have to revolve around three-pronged strategies. The first is the establishment of a continental technical assistance programme, that is tasked with identifying the critical problems of public administration and then deploying the requisite human and financial resources for addressing them. This platform should include institutions such as the African Peer Review Mechanism (APRM), African Development Bank (AfDB), United Nations Economic Commission for Africa (UNECA), the African Capacity Building Foundation (ACBF), designated RECs and willing member states.[104] The effectiveness of this platform would have to revolve around peer-review measures (APRM), intervention capacity building programmes (ACBF and AfDB), funding strategies (AfDB and UNECA), and monitoring and evaluation interventions (RECs, APRM and AfDB).

The second is the need to prioritise a flexible approach. There are different cultural, political and economic contexts that inform public service administrations in African countries, a factor that should feed into AU's ambition to harmonise public administration structures. One of the criticisms levelled against foreign aid and programmes on public service reforms in African countries is that it ignores context, and thus become ill-fitted.[105] Such delink is antithetical to the ambitions of continental harmonisation of standards, detracts from important democratic ideals, and undercuts the ideational quest of understanding local issues before offering prescriptions. Understanding the different contexts not only helps in developing appropriate strategies but also assists in shaping the legitimacy of intervention strategies. In this respect, the AU will be in tandem with the different local dynamics and be able to ensure that intervention by external actors respond to these dynamics.

Lastly, is the design of incentives for compliance with AU objectives on public administrations. This could take the form of the establishment of a compliance fund, through which member states that have shown the satisfactory levels of adherence to

[103] Article 2 of the African Charter on Values and Principles of Public Service and Administration (2011).

[104] According to Shivji (2007), the involvement of member states with considerable talent pool in terms of human resources and skills development in other member states could serve as a practical way of cooperation and prevent manipulation by big powers.

[105] Ayee (2005) p. 45; Mkandawire (2002), pp. 17–18.

AU norms on public administration can have access to financial and human assistance.[106] Such fund should be managed by the AU, RECs, AfDB and representatives of civil society. Contributions to the fund could come from member states, international partners and the private sector.[107]

The four pillars outlined above (broader institutional realignment and reforms, self-restraining measures, bottom-up supranational regionalism, and enhanced state capacity) are further impacted by two key variables. One is the extent to which the AU can manage and eventually harmonise the structures of the eight recognised RECs under a continental umbrella. As discussed in the previous chapter, this point has been a key issue since the establishment of the AU. In 2019, the AU adopted a new protocol to replace the 2008 protocol on relations with the RECs. The protocol has now become law. Furthermore, these RECs are at different stages of development, thereby making a definitive time-frame of harmonisation almost impossible.[108] According to an assessment done by AUDA-NEPAD, the capacity of RECs remain hindered by issues such lack of citizen participation, limited financial resources, over-reliance on development partners, and fragmented and incoherent planning mechanisms.[109] Similarly, the Africa Capacity Report of 2014 highlighted that the capacities of RECs are hampered by factors such as funding to recruit competent staff, lack of effective research units on economic and policy planning, and weak evaluation mechanisms.[110] In addition, there have been cases of rivalry and competition between AU and RECs regarding subsidiarity functions and access to substantial resources from donor organisations.[111] These issues have raised the question of whether RECs, having attained the requisite level of success and influence, would be willing to cede powers to the AU. The answer to this lies in a pragmatic understanding of what continental regionalism means. In other words, it speaks to accepting the diversity and different dynamics that continue to push and pull regional integration efforts at the RECs, and how these connect with AU objectives. This would require the acceptance of the strength of certain RECs regarding AU objectives on free trade, free movement and infrastructure development, and then proceeding to place such RECs at the heart of the continental implementation of those projects, with the AU managing the quality-control process.

The second variable is the North Africa/Sub-Saharan Africa divide that has been in existence since the creation of the Organisation of African Unity (OAU) in 1963. The politics of many North African countries (which looks towards the Arab world and Euro-America), and the treatment of black Africans in those countries, have enhanced the perceptions that North African states such as Morocco, Egypt, Tunisia

[106] Fagbayibo (2019b), pp. 462–463.

[107] Ibid.

[108] Byiers et al. (2019), pp. 2–3.

[109] NEPAD (2015), pp. 26–29.

[110] ACBF (2014), p. 58.

[111] ICG (2017), pp. 14–16.

and Libya do not consider themselves as part of the continent.[112] The discovery of "slave markets" in Libya, where black African refugees and migrants were sold at auctions by Libyans further highlighted the problematic issue of racism and discrimination in North Africa.[113] Although the limited participation of North African states in AU activities has in recent times changed, with Morocco's admission into the AU, and Egypt becoming the chair of the AU Assembly for 2019, there are still concerns about how these will change the perceptions of division. Another problematic issue is that a platform such as the Arab Maghreb Union (AMU), which is one of the eight recognised AU RECs and is composed of North African countries, is essentially inoperative due to internal wrangling and conflicts among member states. An effective AMU could have provided a platform through which North Africans are able to play a more meaningful role in continental regionalism.

This line of division is one that undermines the possibility of a strong continental unit. The way out of this quagmire is to utilise the increasing engagement of pivotal states, such as Morocco and Egypt, in continental integration activities as a platform for combatting the scourge of racism and discrimination. This will require policies that legislate against discrimination and racism in North African countries; promote people-to-people interaction and raise awareness around the idea of pan-Africanism; and place continental integration agenda at the heart of national programmes through the adoption and implementation of programmes on free movement and trade.

5.3.2 External Dynamics: Navigating the Shifting Global Geo-Political Landscape

AU's relationship with external actors remain an integral, albeit controversial, component of its institutional existence. Okumu and Makinda identify three key contexts through which Africa and its regional organisations engage with external parties.[114] The first is whether such partners view Africa as a source of problem or a source of opportunity.[115] The second speaks to the extent of the genuineness of respect shown by external partners towards African core values, equality and joint ownership of projects and policies.[116] The third relates to competition by external actors in pursuit of interests across Africa.[117] The issue is not so much about the need for external engagement as it is the quality of such interaction. In other words, the overriding question is whether such interaction enhances the legitimacy of the AU as Africa's preeminent regional organ.

---

[112] Lambert and Ramadan (2015); Sawahel (2019).

[113] Quackenbush (2017).

[114] Cited in Makinda et al. (2016), p. 141.

[115] Ibid.

[116] Ibid.

[117] Ibid.

To understand this point, the question starts from whether the AU has the mandate to negotiate on behalf of African states in the global arena. As things currently stand, the AU has no supranational mandate to ensure this, albeit its Constitutive Act endows it with an intergovernmental, non-binding mandate to pursue this objective.[118] What this implies is that member states are not legally compelled to participate in any AU arrangement on common position regarding negotiations with external parties. However, the AU has put in place measures to ensure that it has a common position on trade negotiations and has also appointed Carlos Lopes as its high representative to support member states in trade negotiations with the EU post-2020.[119] This appointment followed the adoption of the AU African common position on negotiating a post-Cotonou trade agreement with the EU by the AU Executive Council on 19 March 2018. This common position proposes that Africa should negotiate as a group, to be represented by the AU, separately from the African Caribbean and Pacific (ACP) group of states.[120] Carbone, however, noted that the common position was far from being consensual as member states were divided between removing Africa from the ACP or remaining within the group.[121] In addition, the "Africa+1" summits with external parties is increasingly becoming a platform through which some African governments position their countries as favourable destinations for foreign investments.[122] The implication of this is the preference for bilateral rather than multilateral trade negotiations. Such preference for bilateral arrangements is seen as obstructive to the objectives of collective negotiation.[123]

The AU programmes and projects are excessively funded by external partners, thereby bringing into question the credibility of its existence, and its claim to be the prime driver of regionalism in Africa. As things stand, the EU provides the bulk of the funding for the AU's peace and security budget, and also funds a number of governance, human rights and democracy building initiatives of the organisation.[124] Since the inception of the AU Peace and Security Architecture (APSA), the EU has remained its biggest funder by allocating EUR 50 million annually to APSA for the 2014–2020 programme phase.[125] Other partners such as China, Japan, India and individual EU member states also provide strategic financial support. Although China prioritises bilateral arrangements with individual African countries, it has in the past decade, funded continental integration projects such as the building of the

[118] Article 3(d) of the AU Constitutive Act provides that the AU shall "promote and defend African common positions on issues of interest to the continent and its peoples". Article 3(i) further enjoins the organisation to "establish the necessary conditions which enables the continent to play its rightful role in the global economy and international negotiations".

[119] AU (2018b); AU (2018d).

[120] AU (2018b).

[121] Carbone (2018), p. 487.

[122] Soulé (2020).

[123] Ogutu (2020).

[124] ICG (2017).

[125] Vanheukelom (2019), p. 7.

AU secretariat, the China-Africa Peace and Security Fund, the Pan-African Infrastructure Development Fund, and the development of information technology infrastructure.[126] These external funding remain the lifeline of many of AU activities, thereby putting the organisation in a vulnerable and compromising position in terms of the sustainability of projects, and also asserting itself as the primary driver of continental integration within and outside the continent. While this reality has spurred initiatives such as the 0.2% import tax levy, the readjustment of member state contribution, and the substantial decrease of AU budget, the tepid commitment of member states to decisions remains a key concern.

These increasing interest in African issues is seen by some as the new scramble for Africa. External actors are increasing their diplomatic presence on the continent in an unprecedented fashion. Between 2010 and 2016, more than 230 embassies and consulates were opened across the continent.[127] The "new scramble for Africa" description is not far off the mark considering how some of the global actors openly question each other's (mercantilist) motives. Such contestation is sometimes akin to parents (global actors) jostling over the custody of the children (Africa). Introducing the new White House strategy on Africa, the former U.S. national security adviser, John Bolton, described the Chinese and Russian involvement in Africa as predatory and exploitative, as it has only encouraged corruption, deepened debt crisis in many African states, and thus pose a threat to U.S. national security.[128] While the volume of Chinese investment has been a major source of concern to countries in the global north, its expanding military presence on the continent, particularly in Djibouti, remains a bigger nagging issue for the U.S. government.[129] Apart from viewing China's military presence as a rival to the US African Command (AFRICOM), it is seen as a way of entrenching China's political and economic interests in Africa to the exclusion of the U.S.[130]

While the top sources of foreign direct investment (FDI) in Africa are from companies in the U.S., Britain and France, China has recorded an impressive increase in its African investments by reaching a USD40 billion mark in 2016.[131] The EU has had to respond to China's growing presence in Africa by adopting the geostrategic option of cooperating rather than competition with China on African issues.[132] However, this has not prevented the EU from privately expressing reservations that despite its huge contributions to continental integration, the AU seems to always give preferential treatment to China.[133] Observers have raised questions on China's pursuit of its national geopolitical interests in Africa, the neo-colonial

---

[126]Monyae (2018), pp. 288–289.

[127]The Economist (2019).

[128]Pilling (2018); McMaster (2020).

[129]The Economist (2019).

[130]Osbourne (2020).

[131]The Economist (2019).

[132]Hooijmaaijers (2018), pp. 448–449.

[133]ICG (2017), p. 20.

elements of its relations with African countries, the lack of consideration of democratic governance and human rights in its dealings with AU member states, and the link between its loans and the growing debt crisis in some Africa states.[134] Between 2000 and 2017, the Chinese government, banks and companies have lent about USD 143 billion to Africa, with these debts making up a significant chunk of external debt services in some African countries (33% in Kenya, 17% in Ethiopia and 10% in Nigeria).[135] As Gandhi observed, African countries make up half of the top 50 nations that are most indebted to China as a percent of GDP.[136] According to the World Bank's 2020 debt statistics, African countries owe a total of USD 493.6 billion public, publicly guaranteed, and private nonguaranteed debt.[137] In 2019, African countries such as Angola, The Gambia, Republic of Congo, Ghana, Zambia and Cameroon spent over 20% of government revenue on external debt repayment.[138] This was more than the percentage of revenue that these countries spent on health.[139]

These external supports are not particularly altruistic as certain situations have shown how they have been used to undermine the legitimacy of the AU. For example, it was alleged that after handing over the AU secretariat building, China deliberately left open the AU computer network, a factor that allowed it to spy on the organisation from January 2012 to January 2017.[140] Through its extensive funding, the EU has also engaged in many activities calculated at undermining the legitimacy of the AU. These include channelling funds to regional security arrangements outside the purview of the AU security framework, choosing to negotiate its Economic Partnership Agreements (EPAs) with sub-regional groupings rather than an AU composed negotiating team, and the cherry-picking of projects to support regardless of compatibility with continental integration priorities.[141]

In addition to the factors noted above are uncertain global trends that will, in the medium-to-long term, vary continued relations with Africa. China currently faces a sluggish economic growth, ballooning debt problem, and growing domestic concerns in China regarding the spending of taxpayers' money abroad.[142] The rise of right wing, racist and xenophobic parties across Europe, with strong anti-immigration sentiments that is fuelled by the influx of African and Middle East refugees into Europe, are increasingly influencing EU's approach to security and

[134] Chutel (2018); Dahir (2019); Were (2019).

[135] Aljazeera (2020).

[136] Gandhi (2019).

[137] The World Bank (2020).

[138] Jubilee Debt Campaign (2020).

[139] Ibid.

[140] Tilouine and Kadiri (2018).

[141] Vanheukelom (2016), p. 11; ICG (2017), pp. 12–13; Sicurelli (2010), p. 183; Carbone (2018), p. 491.

[142] Dahir (2019).

migration policies on Africa.[143] In this respect, the EU has channelled more funds towards military operations, securitisation of borders and the offering of incentives for stemming migratory flow to repressive governments in Africa.[144] Similarly, the government of the then U.S. president, Donald Trump, was unabashedly opposed to migratory flows from Africa and the Middle East. As expressed in its African strategy, the U.S. is more concerned about funding security and anti-terrorist programmes and securing U.S. business interests in Africa.[145] What these point to is that global actors have intensified the paradigmatic lenses of security and business for engaging Africa and would not hesitate to remove any obstacles to achieving such objectives. The vacuum created by poor and compromised leadership at the national levels further aids the deepening of this skewed and non-beneficial relationship.[146] In addition, some scholars have observed that the demand for Africa's natural resources has not encouraged the push for industrialisation and export diversification, and furthermore exposes African economies to volatility due to fluctuations in commodity prices.[147]

As these global actors continue to extend and deepen their tentacles around the continent, with the AU compromised by its dependence on their funding, the pertinent issue is how to reset and re-centre the calculus of engagement. In its current state, the AU is even in a weaker position than some small member states to follow through on measures that border on power and autonomy.[148] This is further accentuated by the peripheral negotiating role played by the AU in forums such as the Forum of China-African Cooperation (FOCAC), Tokyo International Cooperation on African Development (TICAD), India-Africa Forum Summit (IAFS) and the EPAs. Navigating this fraught global geo-political landscape requires a refocused AU, one that is properly situated at the centre of integration matrix, with the powers to take binding strategic decisions in, and on behalf of, member states. This is the focus of the next subsection.

[143] ICG (2017), pp. 8–9.

[144] Ibid, p. 8.

[145] Pilling (2018).

[146] Murithi (2018), pp. 304–306.

[147] Mkandawire (2015), p. 240.

[148] Soulé (2020) highlighted the four ways in which African states are using the "Africa+1" summits to enhance their domestic and foreign policy goals. These are: to attract investments in a competitive environment; to diversify economic partners to reduce dependency; to tactically claim back their economic policy space; and to escape political isolation by getting more visibility.

5.3.3 *Syncretic Dynamics: Towards "Strategic Hybridisation"*

The last frame of analysing the feasibility of continental supranationalism is what this chapter terms "strategic hybridisation". Strategic hybridisation is premised on the logic that both the external and internal dynamics affecting feasibility are interlocking, and as such require a pragmatic approach that centres African peculiarities and issues in internal and external dealings. It also fits into the narrative of repurposing Africa's worldview in a way that enhances supranational regionalism. Questions around self-financing of regionalism, situating the design and implementation of transnational laws and policies with a pan-African ecosystem, enhancing civil society participation in the dynamics of supranational regionalism, and anchoring continental regionalism to properly planned and feasible ideological paradigm can only be realised through a functional and strategic worldview. As Moghalu rightly opined,

> Self-interest, often couched as "national interest", is the fundamental principle that should guide Africa in its relations with China and the rest of the world. It is up to African countries to define, articulate, and apply that interest.[149]

The reality is that many of the external factors that directly and indirectly negatively impact continental supranationalism have become entrenched, and thus require careful planning to address.[150] For example, issues such as the military presence of external powers; France's (paternalistic) hold over its former colonies; growing Chinese investment and loans, and how they diminish good governance; the debt crisis that has made some African governments beholden to external parties, and the AU's continued reliance on EU funding are some of the intricate variables. Similarly, the lack of willingness to endow AU with meaningful powers, bad governance and economic mismanagement in member states, undemocratic tendencies, the inability to devise an Afrocentric path to achieving regional integration, and political instability are some internal contradictions that continue to militate against the effective realisation of continental supranationalism in Africa.

It is against this background that this chapter proposes three broad objectives to guide the feasible implementation of "strategic hybridisation". These objectives weave together strands of engagement that seek to balance internal and external dynamics, out of which a beneficial strategic approach can be developed. It must be emphasised that these suggestions are not a one-size-fits-all idea considering the diversity of the continent and how this informs the dynamics of regionalism. Rather, the suggestions are a response to these dynamics, having at their essence adaptation and flexibility of implementation. Thus, while the central goal is continental supranationalism, the design and implementation of these suggestions should be flexible and based on the context of particular regions and member states. This then requires

---

[149] Moghalu (2013), p. 31.

[150] See Chap. 4 (Sect. 4.2) and Sect. 5.3.2 above.

member states and/or RECs that are already advanced in terms of the suggested measures to come on board and to share strategies and lessons with the rest. The central role of the AU in terms of assessing implementation and overseeing quality control is key.

The three objectives are investment in area studies, the prioritisation of an Afrocentric epistemic framework in the design and implementation of continental objectives, and a feasible guideline for the adaptation of best practises from elsewhere to move ahead with continental supranationalism. The importance of area studies should not be underemphasised in the matrix of building continental supranationalism. One of the ways in which external parties have been able to extend and entrench their national geopolitical interests is by carefully studying and gaining acute knowledge of the variables that shape the continent. This is especially done through governmental and non-government research institutes, funding of projects, and the funding of programmes that enable their citizens to explore the African continent. The EU, US, China, Japan and individual EU member states all aggressively invest in area studies programmes and have been able to use this to enhance their soft power status across the continent.[151] As Mkandawire observed, the weakness of research institution in Africa and the ignorance of the conditions underlining African research had led to writings on Africa that is based on anecdotes and "heavily-footnoted travelogues".[152] The task now is for Africa to move beyond being the object of study by sharpening its own tools to qualitatively explores the intentions and approaches of others. In this respect, the AU should be at the forefront of partnering with research and academic institutions across the continent on programmes that explore the intimate link between the (inter)national dynamics of external actors and how these impact on regional integration programmes.[153] Such partnership should cut across disciplines and be arranged in a way that it encourages coalitions and cooperation among the institutions on one hand, and with the AU on the other hand. This will also require the private sector to come on board in terms of financing research projects and endowing research chairs in African universities on issues that can enhance the ideational capacity of area studies.

Another key component of area studies is the need to take programmes that build the negotiating capacity of stakeholders across different sectors. Beyond corruption, one major impediment to managing external political and economic relations in Africa is that many African countries lack well-trained negotiating teams. It is a truism under international relations that the effectiveness of a state in the global arena largely depends on its capacity to negotiate.[154] Due to this, states that have insufficient administrative capacity to formulate coherent and strategic negotiation issues are likely to either be silent during crucial international negotiations or accede

[151]Tella (2016a, b).

[152]Mkandawire (2015), p. 234.

[153]For example, Ofodile suggests that for Africa to benefit from Sino-African trade, the knowledge of Chinese legal, political and social system is essential. One way of doing this is learning Mandarin. Ofodile (2008), pp. 582–583.

[154]Panke (2019), p. 7.

to measures that may be detrimental to their positions.[155] As states largely negotiate from the position of their strength and the vulnerability of the negotiating partner, states or entities with stronger capacity can easily coerce or manipulate the other party into submission. As already mentioned in the foregoing sub-section, the EU has in some cases used its strength to undermine and fragment AU common position on trade negotiations and security.

Addressing this requires a multidimensional understanding that encompasses the acquisition of technical negotiating skills as an integral element of knowing who and what the other party is/are. One way to address this could be AUDA-NEPAD's suggestion of the "establishment of the capacity development knowledge hub for African multilateralism".[156] Although the suggestion was directed at enhancing "the coordinative and knowledge integration capacities" of the RECs, it could also play a significant role in articulating and shaping the administrative capacity of Africa to negotiate as a unit. This could be done through initiatives such as sustained and well-coordinated knowledge sharing programmes; enhanced technocratic and academic capacity training; situating the concept of transnational policy development within Africa's socio-cultural, political and economic realities; and the commitment of pivotal states to provide financial and human resources support. The AU (through its AUDA-NEPAD), the AfDB, the UNECA, ACBF, RECs, designated member states, academic and policy research institutions, and the private sector should be tasked with providing financial and technical support for this important idea.[157]

The AU should also encourage its Pan African University (PAU), located in five existing universities situated in Africa's five geographical regions, to have in-built programmes that encourage area studies. This includes water and engineering sciences (including climate change) located in the University of Algeria; life and earth science in the University of Ibadan, Nigeria; space science for telecommunication (to be hosted in Southern Africa); governance, humanities and social sciences in the University of Yaounde II, Cameroon; and basic science, technology and innovation in the Jomo Kenyatta University, Kenya. The PAU has already started operations in West, East, Central and North Africa, and the process of establishing the Southern African wing is ongoing. The AU should, in the process of establishing and operating these institutions, be mindful of the risks associated with outsourcing the financing of these programmes to external parties.[158]

---

[155] Ibid.

[156] NEPAD (2015), p. 32.

[157] An example is the AUDA-NEPAD MSME Academy, in partnership with the ECOBANK group, which aims to support Micro, Small and Medium Enterprises (MSMEs) across the continent through initiatives such as practical training and resources on financing opportunities and building digital presence for business ventures. See AUDA-NEPAD website. Another example is the annual Ibrahim Leadership Fellowship, sponsored by Mo Ibrahim, aimed at mentoring future African leaders (men under the age of 40, and women under the age of 45) by giving them the opportunity to work in international organisations such as the AfDB, UNECA and the International Trade Centre (ITC) to enhance their technocratic and leadership skills. See the Mo Ibrahim website.

[158] The PAU is financed from three sources: the host country, AU and thematic partners, with each party expected to contribute a third of the total budget. Funders include the World Bank (which

The second objective speaks to the imperative of positioning Afrocentric initiatives and methods at the core of the idea of continental supranationalism. This should go beyond the oft-repeated platitudes in normative documents and political rhetoric. The first measure in this respect would be to build a broad-based movement of non-state actors that continue to scrutinise aspects of continental supranationalism, and ways in which grassroots ideas and strategies could help make a substantial contribution. Issues that require immediate concern include:

a) *Citizen funding of continental integration programmes*: The underlining elitist approach to the issue of self-financing of the AU is one that has excluded many African citizens from the discussion. The involvement of citizens is one that speaks to awareness, ownership and sustainability of the integration process. Through this kind of engagement, the AU will be able to explore innovative ways of raising funds such as crowdfunding, salary deductions, and the voluntary contributions from informal traders, and the private sector.[159] Furthermore, it presents an opportunity for wider civil society to know more about the AU and rigorously discuss policies that speak directly, and indirectly, to the autonomy of the AU. It will also add to the discussion on the need for accountability and transparent financial management in the AU as African citizens will consider themselves as stakeholders in the regional integration process.[160] The role of the diaspora (both African migrants and multigenerational *diasporans*) is also crucial in this respect. Through structures like the AU African Diaspora Investment Fund (ADIF) framework, which is charged with "mobiliz(ing) diaspora funds for structured profitable investment in socially responsible and impactful ventures and schemes",[161] the AU should come up with feasible modalities on how diaspora investments can be channelled into strategic projects. Beyond the financial benefits,[162] the AU should also see this as an important aspect of bringing together Africans on the continent and the diaspora, and further providing the diaspora a stake in the continental integration project.[163]

---

provided the USD 5 million seed funding), China, Germany, India, Japan and Sweden. See Woods et al. (n.d.), p. 8.

[159] Fagbayibo (2019a).

[160] In 2005, African civil society proposed a draft constitution of the "United States of Africa", which outlined the principles that should underline the supranational composition of such entity. Under Art. 9(1)(b) of the constitution, it was proposed that an Africa "shall contribute the value of a day's work per quarter for the development of his or her region". Art. 9(1)(c) further proposed that 6% of the revenue of African corporate bodies and companies working in Africa should be contributed to the development of the continent. ACSO (2005), p. 29.

[161] AU (2019).

[162] At the heart of the ADIF's resource mobilisation strategy are three key start-up financial products: Issuance and Management of Diaspora Bonds; Management of Diaspora Mutual Funds; Management of Diaspora Endowment Trust Fund (the Endowment Fund will be created through the innovative finance mechanism of Remittance Match Funding). These three products will be managed through a multilateral financial institution, the African Diaspora Finance Corporation (ADFC). See Faal (2019), pp. 3–4.

[163] The inter-regional effort by the AU and Caribbean Community (CARICOM) in strengthening Afro-Caribbean relations is a step in the right direction. The first CARICOM-Africa Summit was

The role of non-state business actors in capacity building and funding of regional integration initiatives is another crucial component of citizen funding. An example is the AfroChampions Initiative, a public-private partnership jointly chaired by former president Thabo Mbeki and Aliko Dangote, in raising funds for operationalisation of the AfCFTA. In 2019, it proposed a US$1 trillion investment framework for projects such as the Djibouti to Dakar railway and the Democratic Republic of Congo's Inga Dam.[164] Similarly, Nigerian businessman, Tony Elumelu, has launched the Tony Elumelu Entrepreneurship Programme (TEEP), with a seed capital of USD100 million. It aims to fund 10,000 African start-ups over 10 years, 1000 start-ups per year, with the intention of creating 1 million new jobs and USD10 billion in annual revenue for Africa's economy.[165] Although these initiatives are still at early stages, they point to the possibility of creating multi-purpose platforms for addressing the scarcity of resources for integration. More importantly, they also speak to the importance of mainstreaming private sector initiatives into the broader institutional pan-African integration drive.

b) *The Design of curriculum on the nexus between indigenous knowledge systems and the advancement of continental regionalism*: The imperative of a progressive and context related pedagogy within the matrix of achieving continental supranationalism cannot be understated. As Asante explained, the teaching of African integration from primary school to the university level has the potential to "infuse among the younger generations of Africans a tradition of integrative spirit and thinking".[166] This then begs the question: what kind of education can enhance "integrative spirit and thinking"? The answer lies in understanding that the quality of the pedagogy of regional integration lies in questioning the "copy-and-paste" Eurocentric analysis of regionalism. It speaks to situating the concepts and ideas of African regionalism within socio-cultural, legal, economic and political contexts of the African condition. Issues such as pre-colonial manifestations of trade, diplomacy and peace and security strategies; pan-African ideals that reflect the exigencies of unity; competing ideological principles underlining the praxis of regionalism; hegemonic underpinnings of trade and diplomatic negotiations; the relevance of Africa's intangible cultural heritage; and the role of African customary law in the jurisprudence of regional courts and harmonisation of laws must reflect in the curriculum on continental supranationalism. The idea is to create critical minds that depart from prescribing unfit Eurocentric ideas and policies to asking questions and proffering

hosted in Kenya on the 7th of September 2021, with a mandate to establish closer institutional cooperation between the CARICOM Secretariat and the AU Commission. See CARICOM (2021). See also, Bardouille (2021). In the same vein, the African Export-Import Bank (Afreximbank) and Barbados have signed a Memorandum of Understanding (MoU), with the former putting down a financial facility of USD250 million, to promote trade and investment initiatives between Africa and Barbados. Afreximbank (2021).

[164] African Business (2019).

[165] Edozie (2018), p. 784.

[166] Asante (1997), p. 175.

context-related theories and solutions to the challenges impeding the optimal realisation of regional integration in Africa.

c) *Investment in innovative technology ideas that enhance people-to-people interactions*: Continental supranationalism depends on reconfiguring the state-centric nature of African regionalism by transferring binding powers on issues such as trade, free movement and promotion of democratic governance to transnational institutions. The exercise of this competence thus requires innovative and effective means of carrying African populace along and providing platforms for extensive interactions among peoples. Envisaging an integrated Africa in the twenty-first century without adequate consideration and investment in innovate technologies simply amounts, at the very best, to a pipe dream. According to Cappellin, technology can further regional integration in two ways: improve cohesion and enhance economic development in less developed regions.[167] More than political rhetoric, technology has the capacity of creating a borderless African community. The availability of technology in the form of borderless network initiatives and cheap and fast communication will ease the process of collaboration on academic, leisure and business projects across the continent, and stimulate cross-border trade. Since integration also requires cooperation of interest and voluntary groups across frontiers, technology will help create a platform for enhancing such initiatives. The realisation of this objective will depend on partnership between the AU and technology companies on programmes that speak to regional integration and policies. Such collaboration should explore ways in which the private sector can invest in ICT start-ups that are working on pan-African issues (and placing emphasis on gender equality and empowerment) and putting an AU/Pan-African imprint on technologies that speak to bringing people closer. This partnership is not so much financial as it is a political statement which confirms technology as an indispensable driver of African integration.

d) The involvement of traditional authorities in the dissemination and implementation of integration values at community level: An important element of underlining continental supranationalism with African culture and values is the inclusion of traditional authorities in the process of regional integration. This point is stipulated in the Charter for African Cultural Renaissance. Article 14 of the Charter enjoins African states to officially recognise the role and importance of traditional leadership and integrate them into modern mechanisms of conflict resolution and inter-cultural dialogue system. Traditional authorities can play meaningful roles in explaining some of the measures around enhanced integration and situating them within relevant cultural contexts. Pan-African cultural expressions like *Ubuntu*,[168]

[167] Cappellin (2004) p. 207.

[168] *Ubuntu* is a South African cultural expression that emphasises that everyone's humanity ideally rests on his or her harmonious relationship with the larger community. The concept has been used to underline South Africa's transition from an apartheid state to a democratic society, and the imperative of reconciliation. It has also featured in South African jurisprudence, see for example *S v Makwanyane*. See also, Metz (2011).

Kagisano,[169] *Harambee*,[170] and *Omoluabi*[171] could become important vehicles for showing why ideals such as tolerance for foreigners, imperative of free movement, and free trade across African borders are necessary and central to cultural contexts. Sanni observed that the decolonisation of African boundaries must be located within the realm of the pan-African "right of humanism".[172] He described this as

> the intrinsic right to be treated as a human being. In other words, we are noumenal selves, we give value to things and must see value in every human being. Even if the 'stranger' deserved to be turn away, it must be done without posing a threat to strangers' lives ... I subscribe to a humanist position as a valid normative argument for the treatment of migrants within Africa. This is because it does not prioritise the right of one human being over the other. Humanism focuses on the moral obligation that is due to every human.[173]

Similarly, as customary law practitioners, traditional authorities are important elements in the matrix of ensuring that transnational norms and jurisprudence reflect pan-African cultural values, and central to the process of the harmonisation of laws. This kind of involvement is, however, predicated on their inclusion in many of the official and informal national and regional integration initiatives.

It is imperative that the AU develop an effective communication stream that collates and feeds these discussions into AU structures and processes. For example, the AU might adopt innovative communication channels to transmit its objectives, and then allow for a window period to allow citizens to present their views; next the AU can provide a final report to address concerns and issues raised. In this respect, the AU would have created an effective two-track interactive system that balances engagements with both state and non-state actors. These bottom-up processes could help provide continental regionalism with much needed legitimacy and momentum to address some of Africa's challenges. They also help bring into sharp focus the need to translate national policy priorities into transnational policy dialogues for the attainment of policy sovereignty at continental level.

The third objective provides that in order to turn continental integration into a truly transformative phenomenon, Africa, in the words of Mazrui, "must stand ready to selectively borrow, adapt, and creatively formulate its strategies for planned

---

[169] *Kagisano* is a Setswana word that means harmony and well-being. The first president of Botswana, Seretse Khama, emphasised the idea as the guiding principle of national development in the early years of independence. Parsons et al. (1995), p. 283.

[170] The first president of Kenya, Jomo Kenyatta, enthusiastically promoted the idea of *Harambee* (Ki Swahili for "pull together") to encourage self-help development projects. Meredith (2011), p. 265.

[171] The Yoruba concept of *Omoluabi* speaks to ethical and morally conscious behaviour. According to Olanipekun, it encompasses the following facets: "*Oro Siso* (Spoken word, the Yoruba accord great respect for intelligent and expert use of language); *Inu Rere* (Goodwill, Having a good mind towards others); *Otito* (Truth); *Iwa* (Character/behaviour); *Akinkanju* (Bravery); *Ise* (Hardwork); *Opolo Pipe* (Intelligence); and *Iwa Rere* (Good character/behaviour)". See Olanipekun (2017), p. 218.

[172] Sanni (2020), p. 22.

[173] Ibid, p. 22. See also Moyo (2020).

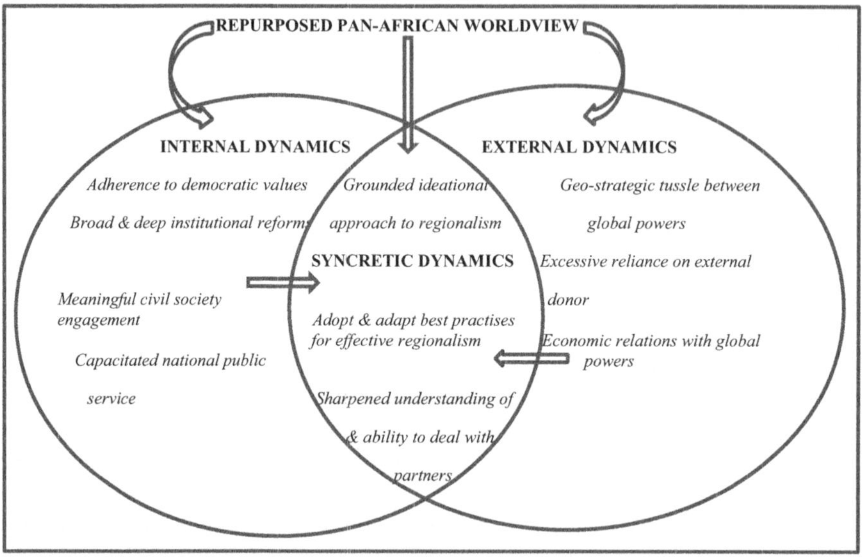

Fig. 5.1 Interlocking dynamics of continental supranationalism. Source: Author's construction

development".[174] Such "translative" process is one that recognises the centrality of Africa's cultural contexts and peculiarities, but is also mindful that external interactions and ideas could serve useful purposes. Infrastructure development and management, agriculture, energy, communication technology, citizen participation, and poverty alleviation strategies are some of the measures that for which one cannot ignore lessons from the rest, especially from other countries in the global South. As already indicated in the foregoing, continental supranationalism can also learn useful lessons from the practises of existing RECs in terms of the implementation of free movement, free trade and citizen involvement in the shaping of regional integration agenda.

The AU has thus far failed to properly situate some of its adopted policies and programmes within a cultural/contextual feasibility paradigm. The AU has adopted neoliberal, Eurocentric strategies on trade, socio-economic development, negotiations with external parties and its institutional set-up without systematically assessing these measures against its oft-stated pan-Africanism philosophy. In going forward, the organisation would benefit from being more introspective and critical by developing assessment mechanisms that include discursive platforms where ideas are rigorously debated before application (Fig. 5.1).

The figure above illustrates the interlocking nature of the dynamics discussed above. It shows how the syncretic dynamics intersects both the external and internal exigencies. Moderating the interactive flow between and among the three dynamics is an ideational pursuit that is grounded in a repurposed pan-African worldview. It is

[174] Mazrui (2008).

only through a repurposed pan-African worldview that state and non-state actors can fully understand and implement effective supranational policies.

5.4 Conclusion

In terms of its population size, diversity of cultures and landmass, Africa remains one of the biggest continents in the world. In addition, its peculiar geo-strategic advantage continues to attract the global light beam. The challenge of turning its geo-strategic placement to its advantage rather than providing the turf for traditional and emerging global players to whet their resource-seeking appetite is an issue of urgent concern. It is impossible to create a powerful continental union without a pragmatic understanding and control of the dynamics that shape how the African continent relates within itself, and then use this as a platform for strategically engaging others. The link between autonomy and power is one that essentially speaks to getting one's house in order before interacting with outsiders. As Kambudzi rightly asserted,

> the process of building towards an ultimate union should be pegged on incremental confidence-building among the AU, RECs and the member states, with sufficient safety nets being put in place as insurance against unforeseen situations, including incidental disruptions within or beyond Africa, that could have an impact on Africa, risking a slowdown or disintegration in the process of building a union.[175]

The inability to show unity and strength of purpose continues to expose the continent to incalculable exploitation and diminished stature in the global matrix of power relations.

It is against this backdrop that this chapter has shown the essential points that are necessary for a viable continental supranationalism. It is only through an effective and efficient continental integration process that Africa can build the capacity to drive sustainable socio-economic and political development. In advancing this framing, the chapter adopted a "triptych" notion of discourse. These are the internal, external and syncretic dynamics. Under the internal dynamics, variables such as technocratic context and competence of continental regionalism, strengthening self-restraining measures, and bottom-up approaches to continental integration were considered. External dynamics looked at the influence of global actors on processes that impact on continental sovereignty and autonomy. Syncretic dynamics viewed both external and internal dynamics as continuous and contiguous, and thus recommended a methodical approach that balances both to provide a feasible strategic path for realising meaningful continental supranationalism. It termed this approach "strategic hybridisation". It includes measures such as investment in area studies, prioritisation of an Afrocentric epistemic framework in the design and implementation of continental objectives, and feasible guidelines for the adaptation

[175] Kambudzi (2008), pp. 22–23.

of best practices. The implementation agenda of continental integration, especially the AU's Agenda 2063 and the African Continental Free Trade Area (AfCFTA), cannot afford to ignore these variables, and actors will have to be innovative in applying them.

References

Acharya A (2012) Comparative regionalism: a field whose time has come? *Int Spect* 47(1):3–15

Acharya A (2020) The myth of the "civilisational state": rising powers and the cultural challenge to world order. *Ethics Int Aff* 34(2):139–156

Achebe C (2011, January 16) Nigeria's promise, Africa's hope. New York Times. https://www.nytimes.com/2011/01/16/opinion/16achebe.html. Accessed 4 Oct 2021

Aerts D, Apostel L, de Moor B, Hellemans S, Maex E, van Belle H, van der Veken J (1994) World views: from fragmentation to integration. VUB Press, Brussels

Africa Renewal (2002) You must first set your house in order create the conditions for integration says Prof Adedeji. https://www.un.org/africarenewal/magazine/september-2002/you-must-first-set-your-house-order. Accessed 4 Oct 2021

Africa Youth Charter (2006). https://au.int/sites/default/files/treaties/7789-treaty-0033_-_african_youth_charter_e.pdf. Accessed 4 Oct 2021

African Business (2019) AfroChampions Initiative presents $1trn AfCFTA investment framework. https://africanbusinessmagazine.com/sectors/finance/afrochampions-initiative-presents-1trn-afcfta-investment-framework/. Accessed 4 Oct 2021

African Charter on Values and Principles of Public Service and Administration (2011). https://au.int/en/treaties/african-charter-values-and-principles-public-service-and-administration. Accessed 4 Oct 2021

African Civil Society Organisation (2005) Third draft of the constitution of the United Africa (UA) (The United States of Africa). African Civil Society Organisation, Yaounde

African Export-Import Bank (2021, October 9) Afreximbank and Government of Barbados Enter Milestone Understanding for Africa Diaspora Trade Ties. https://www.afreximbank.com/afreximbank-and-government-of-barbados-enter-milestone-understanding-for-africa-diaspora-trade-ties/. Accessed 4 Oct 2021

African Union, Strategic plan of the Commission of the African Union: Volume 2: 2004-2007 Strategic framework of the African Union Commission (2004). http://www.iri.edu.ar/publicaciones_iri/anuario/CD%20Anuario%202005/Africa/08-au_commision-strategic%20plan%2002.pdf. Accessed 4 Oct 2021

African Union (2007) Audit of the African Union. https://www.securitycouncilreport.org/atf/cf/%7B65BFCF9B-6D27-4E9C-8CD3-CF6E4FF96FF9%7D/RO%20Audit%20of%20the%20AU.pdf. Accessed 4 Oct 2021

African Union (2009) African Union Commission, Strategic plan 2009–2012. https://reliefweb.int/sites/reliefweb.int/files/resources/08D09FE21F9917E8492575F500211460-EX%20EnglishCL%20501_XV_%20%20-%20Strategic_Plan%20Rev%209%20_b2_.pdf. Accessed 4 Oct 2021

African Union (2011) African Union Assembly declaration on creating employment for accelerating youth development and empowerment, Assembly/AU/Decl.1(XVII) https://au.int/sites/default/files/decisions/9647-assembly_au_dec_363-390_xvii_e.pdf. Accessed 4 Oct 2021

African Union (2018a, November 27) African Union strengthens its sanction regime for non-payment of dues. https://au.int/en/pressreleases/20181127/african-union-strengthens-its-sanction-regime-non-payment-dues. Accessed 4 Oct 2021

African Union (2018b, 27 March) The African Union Executive Council adopts the African common position for negotiations of a new cooperation agreement with the European Union.

https://au.int/en/pressreleases/20180327/african-union-executive-council-adopts-african-common-position-negotiations. Accessed 4 Oct 2021

African Union (2018c) Assembly of the African Union eleventh ordinary session, Ext/Assembly/AU/Dec. 1-4 (XI). https://au.int/sites/default/files/decisions/36425-ext_assembly_dec._1-4xi_e.pdf. Accessed 4 Oct 2021

African Union (2018d, July 13) The Chairperson of the Commission of the African Union, Moussa Faki Mahamat, has appointed Professor Carlos Lopes as his High Representative to support member states in the negotiation of a new agreement with the European Union post-2020. https://au.int/en/pressreleases/20180713/chairperson-commission-african-union-moussa-faki-mahamat-has-appointed. Accessed 4 Oct 2021

African Union (2019, November 18) African Diaspora Investment Fund (ADIF) validation workshop. https://au.int/en/pressreleases/20191118/african-diaspora-investment-fund-adif-framework-validation-workshop. Accessed 4 Oct 2021

African Union (2020a) First continental report on the implementation of Agenda 2063. https://au.int/sites/default/files/documents/38060-doc-agenda_2063_implementation_report_en_web_version.pdf. Accessed 4 Oct 2021

African Union (2020b) Ten quick facts about the African Union gender parity project 2025. https://au.int/sites/default/files/documents/38583-doc-ten_quick_facts_on_au_gender_parity_project.pdf. Accessed 4 Oct 2021

African Union (n.d.-a) African Union Youth Volunteer Corps (AU-YVC) https://au.int/en/volunteer/african-union-youth-volunteer-corps. Accessed 4 Oct 2021

African Union (n.d.-b) Youth development. https://au.int/en/youth-development. Accessed 4 Oct 2021

African Union and the United Nations Economic Commission for Africa (2006) Assessing regional integration in Africa II: Rationalising regional economic communities. https://repository.uneca.org/bitstream/handle/10855/5611/bib-42496_I.pdf?sequence=1&isAllowed=y. Accessed 4 Oct 2021

African Union Commission (2019) African regional integration report: Towards an integrated and prosperous and peaceful Africa. https://au.int/sites/default/files/documents/38176-doc-african_integration_report-eng_final.pdf. Accessed 4 Oct 2021

African Union Development Agency (AUDA-NEPAD). MSME academy. https://msmeacademy.nepad.org. Accessed 4 Oct 2021

Aljazeera (2020, April 13) China is Africa's top creditor, but will it lead debt relief? Aljazeera. https://www.aljazeera.com/ajimpact/china-africa-top-creditor-lead-debt-relief-200413140129629.html. Accessed 4 Oct 2021

Allison S (2020, March 3) Exclusive: A 'mafia-style' cartel is running the African Union, claim staff. Mail & Guardian. https://mg.co.za/article/2020-03-12-exclusive-a-mafia-style-cartel-is-running-the-african-union-claim-staff/. Accessed 4 Oct 2021

Alter K, Gathii J, Helfer L (2016) Backlash against International Courts in West, East and Southern Africa: causes and consequences. Eur J Int Law 27(2):293–328

Asante S (1997) *Regionalism and Africa's development*. Macmillan, London

Ayee J (2005) Public sector management in Africa. https://www.afdb.org/fileadmin/uploads/afdb/Documents/Publications/00457499-EN-ERWP-82.PDF. Accessed 4 Oct 2021

Azikiwe N (1968) *Renascent Africa*. Frank Cass & Co, London

Bach D (2017) *Regionalism in Africa: genealogies, institutions and trans-state networks*. Routledge, London

Bardouille N (2021) CARICOM-AU Relations: Summitry in the Making. https://www.afronomicslaw.org/category/analysis/caricom-au-relations-summitry-making. Accessed 4 Oct 2021

Bretherton C, Volger J (1999) *The European Union as a global actor*. Psychology Press, London

Byiers B, Woolfrey S, Medinilla A, Vanheukelom J (2019) The political economy of Africa's regional 'spaghetti bowl'. Synthesis report. European Centre for Development Policy

Management (ECDPM). https://ecdpm.org/publications/political-economy-africas-regional-spaghetti-bowl-synthesis-report/. Accessed 4 Oct 2021
Cabral A (2007) *Unity & struggle: speeches and writings*. UNISA Press & Tsehai Publishers, Pretoria
Cappellin R (2004) International knowledge and integration networks for European integration, cohesion and enlargement'. *Int Soc Sci J* 56(180):207–225
Carbone M (2018) Caught between the ACP and the AU: Africa's relations with the European Union in a post-Cotonou Agreement context. *S Afr J Int Aff* 25(Special Issue):481–496
Caribbean Community (2021, September 9) CARICOM African leaders identify areas of co-operation at historic first summit. https://caricom.org/caricom-african-leaders-identify-areas-of-co-operation-at-historic-first-summit/. Accessed 4 Oct 2021
Chayes A, Chayes H (1993) On compliance. *Int Organ* 47(2):175–205
Cheeseman N (2019) A divided continent – BTI 2018 regional report Africa. https://www.bertelsmannstiftung.de/fileadmin/files/BSt/Bibliothek/Doi_Publikatio en/Regional-Report_NW_BTI-2018_Africa-A-Divided-Continent_2019.pdf. Accessed 4 Oct 2021
Chinweizu. (2011) Pan Africanism: rethinking key issues. In: Bankie F, Zimunya V (eds) Sustaining the new wave of Pan Africanism. National Youth Council of Namibia, Windhoek, pp 62–95
Chutel L (2018) No, China is not taking over Zambia's national electricity supplier. Not yet, anyway. https://qz.com/africa/1391111/zambia-china-debt-crisis-tests-china-in-africa-relationship/. Accessed 4 Oct 2021
Cini M (2002) The European Commission. In: Warleigh A (ed) *Understanding European Union institutions*. Routledge, London, pp 41–60
Constitutive Act of the African Union (2000). https://au.int/sites/default/files/pages/34873-file-constitutiveact_en.pdf. Accessed 4 Oct 2021
Dahir A (2019) The "debt-trap" narrative around Chinese loans shows Africa's weakness. https://qz.com/africa/1542644/china-debt-trap-talk-shows-africas-weak-economic-position/. Accessed 4 Oct 2021
Dawuni J (2018) Beyond the numbers: Gender parity on the African Court on Human and Peoples' Rights – A lesson for African regional courts? https://ilg2.org/2018/08/28/beyond-the-numbers-gender-parity-on-the-african-court-on-human-and-peoples-rights-a-lesson-for-african-regional-courts/. Accessed 4 Oct 2021
de Silva N (2019) Individual and NGO access to the African Court on Human and Peoples' Rights: The latest blow from Tanzania. https://www.ejiltalk.org/individual-and-ngo-access-to-the-african-court-on-human-and-peoples-rights-the-latest-blow-from-tanzania/. Accessed 4 Oct 2021
Diop C (1987) *Black Africa: The economic basis for a federated state*. Lawrence Hill Books & Africa World Press, Chicago IL & Trenton NJ
du Plessis C (2020, December 6) Silencing the guns': African Union to extend deadline for peace on continent by another 10 years. News24. https://www.news24.com/news24/southafrica/news/silencing-the-guns-african-union-to-extend-deadline-for-peace-on-continent-by-another-10-years-20201206. Accessed 4 Oct 2021
Economic Community for West African States (ECOWAS) Supplementary Protocol A/SP.1/01/05 (2005). http://www.courtecowas.org/wp-content/uploads/2018/11/Supplementary_Protocol_ASP.10105_ENG.pdf. Accessed 4 Oct 2021
Edozie R (2018) Pan-Africanism is Africa's third way: the cultural relevance of Africa's political economy. In: Oloruntoba S, Falola T (eds) *The Palgrave handbook of African politics, governance and development*. Palgrave Macmillan, New York, pp 783–799
Escola de Cultura de Pau (2021) Alert 2021! Report on conflicts, human rights and peacebuilding. https://reliefweb.int/sites/reliefweb.int/files/resources/alerta21i.pdf. Accessed 4 Oct 2021
Faal G (2019) Strategic, business and operational framework for an African Diaspora Finance Corporation: African Union legacy project on diaspora investment, innovative finance and social enterprise in Africa (Abridged version). https://au.int/sites/default/files/documents/37383-doc-adfc_business_framework_-_abridged_version.pdf. Accessed 4 Oct 2021

Fagbayibo B (2012) The (ir)relevance of the office of the Chair of the African Union Commission: analysing the prospects for change. *J Afr Law* 56(1):15–28

Fagbayibo B (2016) Flexibility arrangements in the African Union: A way out of the integration conundrum? *Afr Rev* 8(2):156–170

Fagbayibo B (2018a) *Nkrumahism*, Agenda 2063, and the role of intergovernmental institutions in fast-tracking continental unity. *J Asian Afr Stud* 53(4):629–642

Fagbayibo B (2018b) Why the Pan-African Parliament must clean up its act if it wants to survive. https://theconversation.com/why-the-pan-african-parliament-must-clean-up-its-act-if-it-wants-to-survive-97095. Accessed 4 Oct 2021

Fagbayibo B (2019a) The African Union's self-financing agenda: 3 ideational measures that should guide it. https://www.africaportal.org/features/african-unions-self-financing-agenda-3-ideational-measures-should-guide-it/. Accessed 4 Oct 2021

Fagbayibo B (2019b) The legal regime of compliance with regional norms in Africa: reframing the paradigms of engagement. Afr J Int Comp Law 27(3):446–465

Femi Falana v. African Union, Application no. 001/2011. https://www.african-court.org/en/images/Cases/Judgment/Judgment%20Application%20001-2011-%20Femi%20Falana%20v.%20The%20AU.%20Application%20no.%20001.2011.EN.pdf. Accessed 4 Oct 2021

Finizo G (2018) Civil society involvement and ownership in the African Union integration process. In: Adar K, Finizo G, Meyer A (eds) *Building regionalism from below: The role of parliaments and civil society in regional integration in Africa*. Peter Lang, Bruxelles, pp 289–321

Franck T (1988) Legitimacy in the international system. *Am J Int Law* 82(4):705–759

Freedom House (2021) Countries and territories. https://freedomhouse.org/countries/freedom-world/scores. Accessed 4 Oct 2021

Gandhi D (2019) Figure of the week: China's 'hidden' lending in Africa. https://www.brookings.edu/blog/africa-in-focus/2019/07/10/figure-of-the-week-chinas-hidden-lending-in-africa/. Accessed 4 Oct 2021

Halloran R (2011) China's worldview: Three timeless truths. https://www.huffpost.com/entry/chinas-worldview-three-ti_b_804496. Accessed 4 Oct 2021

Heisenberg H, Richmond A (2002) Supranational institution-building in the European Union: a comparison of the European Court of Justice and European Central Bank. *Eur Public Policy* 9(2):201–218

Hooijmaaijers B (2018) China's rise in Africa and the response of the EU: a theoretical analysis of the EU-China-Africa trilateral cooperation policy initiative. *J Eur Integr* 40(4):443–460

Igbokwe-Ibeto C (2019) African bureaucracy and public administration: analysing the normative impediments and prospect. *Afr Public Serv Deliv Perform Rev* 7(1):1–11

International Action Network on Small Arms (IANSA)., Oxfam International., & Saferworld (2007) Africa's missing billions. https://oxfamilibrary.openrepository.com/bitstream/handle/10546/123908/bp-africas-missing-billions-111007-en.pdf;jsessionid=D8C72F6F8530F2F46034F4BE87403314?sequence=1. Accessed 4 Oct 2021

International Crisis Group (2017) Time to reset African Union – European Union relations. https://www.crisisgroup.org/africa/255-time-reset-african-union-european-union-relations. Accessed 4 Oct 2021

International Labour Organisation (2019) Making decent work a reality for Africa's youth. https://www.ilo.org/global/meetings-and-events/regional-meetings/africa/arm-14/programme/WCMS_731215/lang%2D%2Den/index.htm. Accessed 4 Oct 2021

International Monetary Fund (2001) West Africa Economic and Monetary Union: Recent economic developments and regional policy issues in 2000. https://www.imf.org/external/pubs/ft/scr/2001/cr01193.pdf. Accessed 4 Oct 2021

Jubilee Debt Campaign (2020, April 12) Sixty-four countries spend more on debt payments than health. https://jubileedebt.org.uk/press-release/sixty-four-countries-spend-more-on-debt-payments-than-health. Accessed 4 Oct 2021

Kambudzi A (2008) Portrayal of a possible path to a single government for Africa. In: Murithi T (ed) *Towards a union government for Africa: challenges and opportunities*. Institute for Security Studies, Pretoria, pp 13–27

Kufuor K (1996) Securing compliance with the judgements of the ECOWAS Court of Justice. *Afr J Int Comp Law* 8:1–11

Lambert I, Ramadan N (2015) Being black in Egypt. https://www.alaraby.co.uk/english/features/2015/7/23/being-black-in-egypt. Accessed 4 Oct 2021

Makinda S, Okumu F, Mickler D (2016) *The African Union: addressing the challenges of peace, security and governance*. Routledge, London

Mazrui A (1967) *Towards a Pax Africana: a study of ideology and ambition*. University of Chicago Press, Chicago

Mazrui A (1994) Africa: in search of self-pacification. *Afr Aff* 93(370):39–42

Mazrui A (2008) Africa: Continent must not just remain a learner. https://allafrica.com/stories/200809200089.html. Accessed 4 Oct 2021

Mbeki T (1998) The African renaissance, South Africa and the world. http://archive.unu.edu/unupress/mbeki.html. Accessed 4 Oct 2021

McMaster H (2020) How China sees the world, and how we should see China. https://www.theatlantic.com/magazine/archive/2020/05/mcmaster-china-strategy/609088/. Accessed 4 Oct 2021

Meredith M (2011) *The state of Africa: a history of the continent since development*. Simon & Schuster, London

Metz T (2011) *Ubuntu* as a moral theory and human rights in South Africa. *Afr Human Rights Law J* 11(2):532–559

Mkandawire T (2002) Incentives, governance and capacity development in Africa. *Afr Iss* 30(1): 15–20

Mkandawire T (2015) Fifty years of African independence: a personal reflection. In: Soyinka W, Amin S, Selassie B, Mugo M, Mkandawire T (eds) *Reimagining pan-Africanism: Distinguished Mwalimu Nyerere lecture series 2009-2013*. Mkuki na Nyota Publishers Ltd, Tanzania, pp 199–258

Mo Ibrahim Foundation (2019) Africa's first challenge: the youth bulge stuck in 'waithood'. https://mo.ibrahim.foundation/news/2019/africas-first-challenge-youth-bulge-stuck-waithood. Accessed 4 Oct 2021

Mo Ibrahim Foundation (n.d.) The Ibrahim leadership fellowship. https://mo.ibrahim.foundation/fellowships. Accessed 4 Oct 2021

Moghalu K (2013) Emerging Africa: how the global economy's 'last frontier' can prosper and matter. Bookcraft, Ibadan

Monyae D (2018) The African Union – China partnership: prospects and challenges. In: Karbo T, Murithi T (eds) *The African Union: Autocracy, diplomacy and peacebuilding in Africa*. I.B. TAURIS, London, pp 283–302

Moyo I (2020) On decolonising borders and regional integration in the Southern African Development Community (SADC) region. *Soc Sci* 9(4):1–12

Mpanyane S (2009) Transformation of the Pan-African Parliament: a path to a legislative body? https://issafrica.s3.amazonaws.com/site/uploads/Paper181.pdf. Accessed 4 Oct 2021

Murithi T (2018) The African Union in transition: Sustaining the momentum. In: Karbo T, Murithi T (eds) *The African Union: autocracy, diplomacy and peacebuilding in Africa*. I.B. TAURIS, London, pp 303–310

Musila G (2007) United States of Africa: positioning the Pan-African Parliament and Court in the political union debate. https://issafrica.s3.amazonaws.com/site/uploads/Paper142h.pdf. Accessed 4 Oct 2021

Ndhlovu F (2017) Southern development discourse for Southern Africa: linguistic and cultural imperatives. *J Multicult Discour* 12(2):89–109

NEPAD Planning and Coordinating Agency (2015) Capacity development implementation plan for Africa's regional economic communities. https://www.nepad.org/publication/capacity-development-implementation-plan-africas-regional-economic-communities. Accessed 4 Oct 2021
Nkrumah K (2001) *Consciencism: philosophy and ideology for decolonization*. PANAF, London
Nyabola N (2016) Eulogy for pan-Africanism: long live man-Africanism. https://thenewinquiry.com/eulogy-for-pan-africanism-long-live-man-africanism/. Accessed 4 Oct 2021
Ofodile U (2008) Trade, empires, and subjects - China-Africa trade: a new fair trade arrangement, or the third scramble for Africa. *Vanderbilt J Transnatl Law* 41(2):505–584
Ogutu M (2020) Caught between Africa and the West: Kenya's proposed US free trade agreement. https://www.africaportal.org/features/caught-between-africa-and-the-west-kenyas-proposed-us-free-trade-agreement/. Accessed 4 Oct 2021
Olanipekun O (2017) Omoluabi: re-thinking the concept virtue in Yoruba culture and moral system. *Africol J Pan Afr Stud* 10(9):217–231
Oppong R (2011) *Legal aspects of economic integration in Africa*. Cambridge University Press
Oppong R (2014) Legitimacy of regional economic integration courts in Africa. *Afr J Legal Stud* 7: 61–85
Organisation of African Unity (1980) Lagos plan of action for economic development in Africa, 1980-2000. https://www.nepad.org/publication/lagos-plan-of-action. Accessed 4 Oct 2021
Osbourne K (2020) The U.S. military is worried about China's moves in Africa. https://nationalinterest.org/blog/buzz/us-military-worried-about-chinas-moves-africa-28872. Accessed 4 Oct 2021
Panke D (2019) African states in international organisations: a comparative analysis. *South Afr J Int Aff* 26(1):1–24
Parsons N, Henderson W, Tlou T (1995) *Serestse Khama 1921-1980*. Macmillan, Johannesburg
Pilling D (2018) Bolton accuses China and Russia of 'predatory practices' in Africa. https://www.ft.com/content/6645a26a-ff08-11e8-ac00-57a2a826423e. Accessed 4 Oct 2021
Protocol on the Statute of the African Court of Justice and Human Rights (2008). https://au.int/en/treaties/protocol-statute-african-court-justice-and-human-rights. Accessed 4 Oct 2021
Quackenbush C (2017, December 1) The Libyan slave trade has shocked the world: Here's what you should know. Time magazine. http://time.com/5042560/libya-slave-trade/. Accessed 4 Oct 2021
Rachman G (2019) China, India and the rise of the 'civilisation state'. https://www.ft.com/content/b6bc9ac2-3e5b-11e9-9bee-efab61506f44. Accessed 4 Oct 2021
Rules of Procedure of the Assembly of the Union, ASS/AU/2(I). https://www3.nd.edu/~ggoertz/rei/rei040/rei040.13tt1.pdf. Accessed 4 Oct 2021
S v Makwanyane 1995 6 BCLR 665 (CC). http://www.saflii.org/za/cases/ZACC/1995/3.html. Accessed 4 Oct 2021
Sanni J (2020) Decolonising borders: Re-imagining strangeness and spaces. *Theoria* 67(163):1–24
Sawahel W (2019) Tunisia: Violence against African students undermine HE plans. https://www.universityworldnews.com/post.php?story=20190122142157395. Accessed 4 Oct 2021
Shivji I (2007) The essential building blocks of the pan-African vision. https://www.pambazuka.org/pan-africanism/essential-building-blocks-pan-african-vision. Accessed 4 Oct 2021
Sicurelli D (2010) Regional partners? Perceptions and criticisms at the African Union. In: Lucarelli S, Fioramonti L (eds) *External perceptions of the European Union as a global actor*. Routledge, Abingdon and New York, pp 180–194
Sjöstedt G (1977) *The external role of the European Community*. Saxon House, Westmead England
Sommer L, Nshimbi C (2018) The African Continental Free Trade Area: An opportunity for informal cross-border trade. https://www.ictsd.org/sites/default/files/bridges_africa_june2018.pdf. Accessed 4 Oct 2021
Soulé F (2020) 'Africa+1' summit diplomacy and the 'new scramble' narrative: recentreing African agency. *Afr Aff* 119(477):633–646
Tella O (2016a) A declining or stable image? An assessment of the United States' soft power in Africa. *South Afr J Int Aff* 23(2):151–166

Tella O (2016b) Wielding soft power in strategic regions: an analysis of China's power of attraction in Africa and the Middle East. *Afr Rev* 8(2):133–144
Tella O (2021) *Africa's soft power: philosophies, political values, foreign policies and cultural exports*. Routledge, London
The African Capacity Building Foundation (2014) Africa Capacity Report 2014: Capacity imperatives for regional integration in Africa. https://www.acbf-pact.org/africa-capacity-report-2014-capacity-imperatives-regional-integration-africa. Accessed 4 Oct 2021
The Economist (2019, March 7) The new scramble for Africa. The Economist. https://www.economist.com/leaders/2019/03/07/the-new-scramble-for-africa. Accessed 4 Oct 2021
Tieku T (2017) Governing Africa: 3D analysis of the African Union's performance. Littlefield, Rowman and New York and London
Tieku T, Ganzle S, Trondal J (2020) People who run African affairs: staffing and recruitment in the African Union Commission. *J Mod Afr Stud* 58(3):461–481
Tilouine J, Kadiri G (2018) In Addis Ababa, the seat of the African Union spied by Beijing. https://www.lemonde.fr/afrique/article/2018/01/26/a-addis-abeba-le-siege-de-l-union-africaine-espionne-par-les-chinois_5247521_3212.html. Accessed 4 Oct 2021
Treaty Establishing the Common Market for Eastern and Southern Africa (1993). https://www.comesa.int/wp-content/uploads/2019/02/comesa-treaty-revised-20092012_with-zaire_final.pdf. Accessed 4 Oct 2021
Treaty for the Establishment of the East African Community (2006). https://www.eacj.org//wp-content/uploads/2012/08/EACJ-Treaty.pdf. Accessed 4 Oct 2021
United Nations Economic Commission for Africa, African Union & the African Development Bank (2012) Assessing regional integration in Africa V: Towards an African Continental Free Trade Area. https://www.uneca.org/sites/default/files/PublicationFiles/aria5_print_uneca_fin_20_july_1.pdf. Accessed 4 Oct 2021
Vanheukelom J (2016) The political economy of regional integration in Africa: The African Union. https://ecdpm.org/publications/political-economy-regional-integration-african-union/. Accessed 4 Oct 2022
Vanheukelom J (2019) Regional peace architectures in Africa: A reality check. https://ecdpm.org/wp-content/uploads/DP-249-Regional-peace-architectures-in-Africa-A-reality-check.pdf. Accessed 4 Oct 2021
Vennesson P (2007) European worldviews: ideas and the European Union in world politics Working paper. European University Institute (EUI). https://cadmus.eui.eu/bitstream/handle/1814/6749/RSCAS-2007-07.pdf?sequence=1&isAllowed=y. Accessed 4 Oct 2021
Viljoen F, Louw L (2007) State compliance with recommendations of the African Commission on Human and Peoples' Rights, 1994–2004. *Am J Int Law* 101(1):1–34
Were A (2019) Debt Trap? Chinese loans and Africa's development options. https://saiia.org.za/wp-content/uploads/2018/09/sai_spi_66_were_20190910.pdf. Accessed 4 Oct 2021
Windridge O (2020) Under attack? Under the radar? Under-appreciated? All of the above? A time of reckoning for the African Court on Human and Peoples' Rights. https://opiniojuris.org/2020/05/07/under-attack-under-the-radar-under-appreciated-all-of-the-above-a-time-of-reckoning-for-the-african-court-on-human-and-peoples-rights/. Accessed 4 Oct 2021
Woods D, Padayachee A, Chanie P, Olsson A (n.d.) Case study: Pan-African University. https://www.oecd.org/sti/Pan%20African%20University%20final.pdf. Accessed 4 Oct 2021
World Bank (2020) International debt statistics. https://datatopics.worldbank.org/debt/ids/region/SSA. Accessed 4 Oct 2021
Yahya M (2017) Africa's defining challenge. https://www.africa.undp.org/content/rba/en/home/blog/2017/8/7/africa_defining_challenge.html. Accessed 4 Oct 2021

Chapter 6
Conclusion

Summary and the Way Forward

6.1 Summary of Findings

This book has assessed the politico-legal contours of achieving effective continental supranationalism in Africa. At the heart of this analysis is the understanding that for the African Union (AU) to efficiently drive the quest for deepened regionalism in Africa, there must be a deliberate strategic approach that understands the interplay of law and politics in the continental integration process. As shown in the preceding chapters, politics can, for good or bad, shape the dynamics of legal integration at the implementation level. The continued inability of African integration to respond the exigencies of supranationalism is fundamentally shaped by member states' attitude to the politics of regionalism. To change this "mental model", this book has argued that some fundamental politico-legal issues must be addressed. The prescriptive aspect of this book, Chap. 5, discussed the imperative of understanding how internal and external dynamics shape the supranational ambitions of the African Union (AU), and the need to craft a strategic outlook for achieving this. Before arriving at these policy prescriptions, the book engaged in some theoretical and situational analysis of the regionalism in Africa.

In situating the theoretical basis of the book, Chap. 2 engaged in a discourse of the idea of continental supranationalism. This discussion started with placing the idea of supranationalism within its Eurocentric foundation by showing how the components that make up the concept of supranationalism came from the study of the political and legal development of regionalism in post-second World War Europe. This was then followed by an analysis of integrative pan-Africanism as the source of the aspiration for continental supranationalism in Africa. Lastly, the ideational paradigms through which continental supranationalism in Africa is conceptualised was analysed. These are pace or speed (which speaks to immediacy of approach versus the gradual implementation of the idea); nature (intergovernmental versus supranationalism; leftist ideology versus neo-liberal, market-based integration approach; federalism versus confederal set-up of the intended supranational arrangement)

B. Fagbayibo, *Transcending Member States*,
https://doi.org/10.1007/978-3-031-12451-8_6

and context (which prioritises an integration approach that is centred around pan-African traditional norms and values).

The focus of Chap. 3 was the analysis of how the AU continues to navigate the intergovernmental/supranational politico-legal terrain of achieving continental supranationalism in Africa. This chapter argued that the discussion of the extent to which the AU conforms or diverges from supranationalism must be much broader than the archetypical Eurocentric assessment. There is no doubt that the AU still has a lot of work to do in terms of attaining its supranational ambitions; however, a contextual assessment allows for a proper understanding and dissection of the situation. In this regard, the chapter adopted three contextual assessment paradigms: intention, action and outcomes. Under intention, the question was whether through its normative frameworks, there exists allusions to the intention on the part of the drafters to create an organisation that transcends the politico-legal structures of member states. In terms of action, the question was whether the AU has been endowed with the requisite powers to exercise binding powers over its member states. The answer to this lies in the complex interplay between hard and soft law activities in the AU, and the mixed results in terms of the adoption of decisive protocols and policy documents, the active role of the epistemic community in the shaping of AU policies, refusal of member states to transfer meaningful powers to AU institutions and comply with normative directives. The chapter observed that outcomes denotes the way in which the AU has been able to acquire and exercise legitimacy. While it enjoys a significant amount of symbolic legitimacy, there is a significant deficiency of actual legitimacy especially as it relates to compliance with its norms and regulations. This point remains a key focus of reform efforts at the AU.

Chapter 4 looked at the interplay of law and politics in the operational milieu of continental supranationalism in Africa. Law and politics have always played both conflictive and cooperative roles in the dynamics of Africa's regionalism. The lacuna between adoption and implementation of norms often provides the material for assessing such interplay. In the context of this chapter, three broad examples of such interaction were discussed. The first was the extent to which the AU has "copied and pasted" the European Union (EU) integration process, and the implications of such imitation. The way in which the EU regards itself as the financial and ideological "mentor" of the AU is one such implication. In this regard, the EU remains the biggest funder of AU activities, and ensures that the latter remains committed to a neo-liberal integrative agenda. This imitative exercise also limits the AU from pursuing a more contextual integration path, one that links its policy objectives to the fundamental realities on the ground. The second prism was the complex intra-African relational dynamics, particularly the AU – RECs, AU – Member states, and AU – Civil society. The chapter showed how the lack of a definitive relational framework between the AU and the RECs, multiple membership of RECs by member states, the problem of non-compliance with AU norms, and the restrictive space that limits the participation of civil society in the implementation of regional integration programmes are factors that continue to hinder the attainment of continental supranationalism. Lastly, the chapter considered how the politics of reforms in the AU provides a turf for contestations between ideological parties, and the way in which reform efforts remain hampered by non-commitment by member states, the inability to anchor reform priorities to durable institutions and the limited participation of African citizens in the ideational articulation and implementation of reform objectives.

The prescriptive dimension of the book was addressed in Chap. 5. The chapter started with a discussion of the idea of worldview, and how this is central to Africa's pursuit of continental supranationalism. The understanding of the interlocking dynamics that will shape continental supranationalism has to start from the position of a repurposed worldview, one in which Africa is in full grasp and control of how it should relate with itself and external parties. The chapter then moved to discuss the three important interrelated dynamics that are central to the realisation of continental supranationalism. These are internal dynamics (broader institutional realignment and reforms; self-restraining measures; bottom-up supranational regionalism and enhanced state capacity), external dynamics (the influence of external actors in shaping the trajectory of continental supranationalism in Africa), and the syncretic dynamics or "strategic hybridisation" (investment in area studies, prioritisation of an Afrocentric epistemic framework in the design and implementation of continental objectives, and feasible guidelines for the adaptation of best practices). Through this discussion, the chapter was able to highlight nuance politico-legal policy issues that should inform the pragmatic enhancement of the powers of AU institutions (particularly the AU Commission, ACJ&HR, and PAP) and the involvement of civil society in process of continental supranationalism.

6.2 Issues for Further Research and Policy Approaches

The question on how we should imagine, or even re-imagine, the nature and context of continental supranationalism is one that has been at the heart of political and scholarly endeavours for decades. In line with this objective, this book has provided three key insights into the ideational dynamics of continental supranationalism in Africa. The first of such is the indivisibility of law and politics in the broader context of realising the goals of continental supranationalism in Africa. In all the chapters of the book, this point is either explicitly or implicitly made by showing the interplay of law and politics at both the conceptual and practical planes of the continental integration process. In other words, the overriding point of the book is that serious attention should be paid to how law and politics intersect, and often conflict, in the policies and processes of continental integration in Africa, and then use this understanding to develop context-driven strategies for advancing regionalism. This was the primary engagement of Chap. 4, which then paved the way for the recommendations in Chap. 5.

Secondly, the book's discussion of the imperative of a contextual assessment of continental supranationalism in Africa provided some useful theoretical insights. Beyond making a general argument, Chap. 3 developed three conceptual framings through which a more holistic and context-driven assessment of the AU can be better made. As the chapter emphasised, the idea is not to present the AU as a supranational organisation but more importantly, to understand that the different institutional activities that lean towards supranationality are worth considering in the assessment matrix. These activities encompass a broad range of state and non-state actors' engagements that directly and indirectly impact the objectives of continental supranationalism. As such, this kind of consideration is critical for a nuanced understanding of the AU.

The third insight is the book's consideration of internal and external dynamics as interlocking variables that shape the process of continental supranationalism in Africa. Chapter 4 showed how the imitation of the European integration process not only enhances interference of the EU in the AU but also the inability of policy makers to be more innovative and contextual in the design of regional integration ideas. Chapter 5 further highlighted how global powers are increasingly using Africa as a pawn in their geo-strategic tussles. In navigating these dynamics, the book proposed a "strategic hybridisation" strategic approach that balances internal and external dynamics. This programmatic approach speaks to the studied understanding of external partners and their motives, centring Afrocentric issues in the design and implementation of continental integration measures, and the careful borrowing and adaptation of best practises elsewhere.

The idea of this book is not to present a foreclosed argument on how to pursue meaningful and beneficial continental supranationalism in Africa. Rather, it seeks to stimulate further research and discourse around this important topic. Furthermore, the current initiatives on strengthening the powers of the AU is one that opens more multidisciplinary avenues for critical scholarship and policy direction. The assessment paradigms discussed in Chap. 3 can serve as both a theoretical and practical tool for taking a rigorous look at the current Eurocentric standard of assessment. Scholars interested in the AU, either from a comparative and/or situational perspective, can use these paradigms to develop more nuanced methodological tools for dissecting the complexities of regional integration. Furthermore, this kind of research engagement can further enhance the development of ideas around the decolonisation of regional integration, in its legal, political, economic and socio-cultural manifestations.

The dearth of measurable studies on the perceptions of the African populace on the politico-legal developments in African integration is another area that demands further research and policy initiatives. As discussed in this book, regional integration in Africa remains an elitist project, with little attention paid to how African citizens respond to critical issues of free movement, free trade, adherence to transnational democratic norms, and the pace of regional efforts. The availability of data on these issues can help provide researchers and policy makers with a more empirically nuanced understanding of how transnational policies should be developed and implemented.

As shown in this book, in its different iterations, the underpinning idea of continental supranationalism is to establish transnational arrangements that can enhance Africa's position as a global actor. In addressing this, Chap. 5 of this book discussed the necessary ingredients for achieving this. This discussion provides the opportunity for further critical engagements on situational and prognostic analysis of how a supranational AU fits into the global governance architecture and factors that may shape its actorness. Furthermore, research on the future of EU-AU relations, and relations with China and other emerging powers on core issues of AU's negotiation capacity, management of the sovereign right of member states to interact with these powers, and how the political will of member states are shaped by such external interactions, are of critical importance.

In conclusion, Africa's long walk towards closer cooperation and integration has by no means reached a definitive phase. The plethora of initiatives and attempts at forging a supranational framework to address many of Africa's problems continues to falter due to multiple factors which have been identified in this book. It is expected that this book may contribute to the design of policy frameworks aimed at strengthening of African regional institutions and processes. The African populace deserve qualitative and transformative regionalism, one which enhances their socio-economic status and general well-being. To paraphrase Julius Nyerere, the continent has no choice but to "run while others walk" towards creating the necessary conditions for an enhanced, truly beneficial and transformative regionalism.

List of Treaties

African Charter on Human and Peoples' Rights. (1981).
African Charter on Values and Principles of Public Service and Administration (2011).
Africa Youth Charter (2006).
Charter for African Cultural Renaissance (2006).
Constitutive Act of the African Union (2000)
Draft Protocol Amending the 2008 Protocol on Relations Between the African Union and the Regional Economic Communities, MYCM/AU/5(I) (2019).
Economic Community for West African States (ECOWAS) Supplementary Protocol A/SP.1/01/05 (2005).
Memorandum of Understanding on Cooperation in the Area of Peace and Security Between the African Union, the Regional Economic Communities (2008).
Organisation of African Unity Charter (1963).
Protocol on Amendments to the Protocol on the Statute of the African Court of Justice and Human Rights (2004).
Protocol on Relations between the African Union (AU) and the Regional Economic Communities (RECs) (2008).
Protocol on the Statute of the African Court of Justice and Human Rights. (2008).
Protocol relating to the establishment of the Peace and Security Council of the African Union. (2002).
Protocol to the Constitutive Act of the African Union relating to the Pan-African Parliament (2014).
Statutes of the Commission of the African Union, ASS/AU/2(1). (2002).
Statutes of the Economic, Social and Cultural Council of the African Union. (2004).
Treaty establishing the African Economic Community Treaty (1991).
Treaty establishing the Common Market for Eastern and Southern Africa. (1993).
Treaty for the establishment of the East African Community. (2006).
Treaty on the Harmonisation of the Business Law in Africa (OHADA) (1993).

B. Fagbayibo, *Transcending Member States*,
https://doi.org/10.1007/978-3-031-12451-8

List of Cases

Actions Pour La Protection Des Droits De L'homme (APDH) v. Republic of Cote d'Ivoire App. No. 001/2014.

Alex Thomas v. United Republic of Tanzania, App. No. 005/2013.

Ally Rajabu and Others v United Republic of Tanzania. Application No. 007/2015

Centre for Minority Rights Development (Kenya) and Minority Rights Group International on behalf of Endorois Welfare Council v Kenya (2009) AHRLR 75

Chief Ebrimah Manneh v The Republic of The Gambia. Community Court of Justice of the Economic Community of West African States (ECOWAS) Ruling No. ECW/CCJ/JUD/03/08

Commission v. Council. (Case 22/70) [1971] ECR 263

Democratic Republic of the Congo v Burundi, Rwanda and Uganda (2004) AHRLR 19

Ernest Francis Mtingwi v. Republic of Malawi App. No. 001/2013.

Femi Falana v. African Union, Application no. 001/2011

Guillaume Kigbafori Soro and Others v Republic of Cote d'Ivoire App. 012/2020

Institute for Human Rights and Development in Africa v Angola (2008) AHRLR 43

Interights & Ditshwanelo v Botswana [Communication 319/06 (2015).

International PEN, Constitutional Rights Project, Civil Liberties Organisation and Interights on behalf of Ken Saro-Wiwa v. Nigeria, Communications 137/94, 139/94, 154/96 and 161/97.

Media Rights Agenda and Others v Nigeria (2000) AHRLR 200.

Mike Campbell (Pvt) Ltd and Others v Republic of Zimbabwe (2/2007) [2008] SADCT 2

Musa Saidykhan v. Republic of The Gambia. Community Court of Justice of the Economic Community of West African States (ECOWAS) Ruling No. ECW/CCJ/RUL/05/09

Prof Anyang' Nyong'o & 10 others v. The Attorney General of the Republic of Kenya & 5 Others. Application No. 1 of 2006 (Arising from Reference No. 1 of 2006)

B. Fagbayibo, *Transcending Member States*,
https://doi.org/10.1007/978-3-031-12451-8

Recontre Africaine pour la Défense des Droits de l'Homme v Zambia [(2000) AHRLR 321

Sébastien Germain Ajavon v Republic of Benin. Application No. 013/2017

S v Makwanyane and Another (CCT3/94) [1995] ZACC 3.

Tangayika Law Society, The legal and Human Rights Centre v The United Republic of Tanzania App. 009/2011 and Rev. Christopher R. Mtikila v. United Republic of Tanzania App. No. 011/2011

The Nubian Community in Kenya v. The Republic of Kenya, Communication 317/2006

The manufacturer's authorised representative in the EU is Springer Nature Customer Service Centre GmbH, Europaplatz 3, 69115 Heidelberg, Germany. If you have any concerns regarding our products, please contact ProductSafety@springernature.com

Printed and bound by CPI Group (UK) Ltd, Croydon, CR0 4YY
30/09/2026
02225470-0019